A Practitioner's Guide to Mental Health Law

A Practitioner's Guide to Mental Health Law

Michael Butler

WS
&H

Wildy, Simmonds & Hill Publishing

Contains public sector information licensed under the Open Government Licence v1.0

ISBN: 9780854901142

British Library Cataloguing in Publication Data

A catalogue record for this book is available from the British Library

First published in 2014 by

Wildy, Simmonds & Hill Publishing
58 Carey Street
London WC2A 2JF
England
www.wildy.com

Typeset by Cornubia Press Ltd, Bristol.
Printed in Great Britain by CPI Antony Rowe, Chippenham, Wiltshire.

Contents

Table of Cases

Table of Statutes

References are to page numbers

Table of Statutory Instruments

References are to page numbers

Table of Conventions

Acknowledgements

Thanks are due to my colleagues at Butler and Co, Catrin Blake, Katherine Gifford and Chris Heery, for their enormously useful comments on the structure and content of the book. Thanks also to Claire Roney and John Smith for their contributions, and to Andrew Riddoch from Wildy & Sons for his invaluable advice. And thanks to Dinah, Joe and Sadie.

Chapter 1

Introduction

1.1   SCOPE OF THE BOOK

This book aims to provide an introduction to mental health law in England and Wales. Intended for use by lawyers and other mental health professionals alike, it is hoped that it is a useful source of information for those starting out in this area of law, and for those who specialise in other areas and require a working knowledge of the subject.

No one is discouraged from sitting down and reading the book from cover to cover, but the more realistic expectation is that it is used as and when required for a summary of a particular aspect of the law. The subject matter is divided up in an easily identifiable and logical way in order to render the law understandable, and considerable effort has been made to keep things as simple as possible and to clarify the key principles.

The book takes as its focus two particular pieces of legislation, the Mental Health Act 1983 (MHA 1983) and the Mental Capacity Act 2005 (MCA 2005). It looks at each Act separately, but also considers the ways in which the two Acts interact, and the impact that each has on the operation of the other.

The MHA 1983 is the principal source of mental health law in England and Wales, and is therefore the subject matter of the major part of the book. The Act's concern is mental disorder, and, in particular, the risks that an individual may cause to himself or others as a result of his mental disorder. The Act exists to manage these risks. It provides a comprehensive system for authorising and regulating compulsory detention and treatment in hospital, and for managing mental disorder in the community. The system is considered in detail in Chapters 2–21.

The MCA 2005 is quite different. It is concerned with mental capacity, not mental disorder. Moreover, its purpose is not to manage risk, but to regulate all aspects of decision-making on behalf of those who lack capacity. This may cover decisions concerning medical treatment, but also any other matter affecting a person's welfare or finances. In regulating decision-making, the Act aims to preserve the personal autonomy of the individual concerned as much as possible and to ensure that all decisions taken on his behalf are in his best interests. Chapter 22 provides an overview of the Act and considers, among other things, the role of the Court of Protection, the specialist court which oversees decision-making in this rapidly developing area of law. Chapter 23 then considers the Deprivation of Liberty Safeguards (DOLS) provisions contained in Schedule A1, which supply an alternative statutory framework to the MHA 1983 for the compulsory admission to hospital or care homes of patients who lack capacity. This new framework is, most would agree, one of the most significant developments in mental health law within the last few years.

Towards the end of the book, the focus moves away from the MHA 1983 and the MCA 2005. Chapter 24 considers a variety of legal issues which arise in relation to the care and treatment of children and young people with mental disorder. Chapter 25 provides a review of the way in which criminal law and procedure accommodates the needs of those with mental disorder. The book then concludes with a number of appendices, the purpose of which is to provide information which may be of practical assistance to lawyers and other professionals.

The aim is to set out the law as it applies to England and Wales. However, while the overall legal framework is the same for each country, there are significant areas of difference with which the reader requires at least a basic familiarity. It is not feasible in a book such as this to deal comprehensively with all areas of difference, and the solution therefore adopted is to set out law and procedure as it applies to England in the main body of the book, and to summarise in an appendix the key areas where the position in Wales differs.

For brevity throughout the book, masculine pronouns are used to represent both male and female.

Lastly, the law is set out as it applies on 10 April 2014, apart only from Appendix 12, which summarises certain proposed changes in the law due to come into effect in 2015.

1.2   GLOSSARY

Approved clinician	A clinician approved to act as such for the purposes of the MHA 1983 (section 145(1)). Power to approve clinicians rests with strategic health authorities (England) and local health boards (Wales). An approved clinician can come from one of the following professional groups: registered medical

practitioners (doctors), chartered psychologists, nurses (qualified in mental health or learning disability), registered occupational therapists, registered social workers. The significance of being an approved clinician is that the professional can then act as a patient's responsible clinician (see below).

Approved mental health professional	The mental health professional (usually a social worker) responsible for certain key decisions made under the MHA 1983. Responsibilities include applying for the patient's admission to hospital under section 2, 3 or 4, informing/consulting the nearest relative, agreeing to the imposition of a community treatment order, applying for guardianship, applying for a warrant to enter premises under section 135.
Attorney	A person appointed under the authority of a lasting power of attorney (section 9 of the MCA 2005) to make decisions on behalf of the donor of the power.
Care Quality Commission	The body responsible for regulating the provision of health and social care in England and monitoring the use of the MHA 1983. It appoints second opinion doctors, carries out visits, issues guidance on the law, and provides a system of registration. The equivalent body in Wales is the Healthcare Inspectorate Wales.
Clinical commissioning group	Set up by the Health and Social Care Act 2012, these groups, which replace primary care trusts, organise the delivery of NHS services in England at a local level. The equivalent in Wales are the local health boards.
Community patient	A patient who is subject to a community treatment order (see below).
Community treatment order	An order made when a patient is discharged from hospital following detention for treatment. It allows for conditions to be attached to the patient's discharge, and for the patient to be liable to recall to hospital (see Chapter 20).
Court of Protection	The specialist court set up by the MCA 2005 to oversee decision-making on behalf of those who lack capacity (see Chapter 22).

Deputy	A person appointed by the Court of Protection to make decisions on behalf of someone who lacks capacity (section 16 of the MCA 2005).
First-tier Tribunal	The judicial body which considers applications for discharge from, and references relating to, patients detained under the MHA 1983, patients subject to guardianship and patients subject to community treatment orders. It is commonly referred to as the mental health tribunal. The Welsh equivalent is the mental health review tribunal.
Hospital managers	The management body, identified for the purposes of each hospital by section 145 of the MHA 1983, which is legally responsible for a patient's detention under the Act. Hospital managers are allocated certain powers and responsibilities by the Act, including the power to transfer a patient from one hospital to another, the power to discharge a patient, the duty to provide the patient and his nearest relative with information regarding rights following detention and the duty to refer the patient's case to the First-tier Tribunal in certain circumstances.
Local social services authority	The local authority responsible for the provision of social services, which has certain responsibilities under the MHA 1983, including the duty to arrange an assessment of a patient's case by an approved mental health professional where there is reason to think the patient may need to be admitted to hospital or guardianship. The local social services authority will normally be the guardian when an application is made under section 7 of the MHA 1983.
Mental health casework section	The department within the Ministry of Justice which undertakes the Secretary of State for Justice's decision-making in relation to restricted patients.
Nearest relative	Most patients who are detained under the MHA 1983, or are subject to a community treatment order or guardianship, will have a nearest relative for the purposes of the Act. The only patients who will not

have a nearest relative are restricted patients and those unrestricted patients detained under section 35, 36 or 38. The nearest relative's identity is determined by the operation of section 26. Whoever is the patient's nearest relative according to section 26 has various powers, including: to apply for the patient's admission to hospital or guardianship, to object to, and therefore prevent, a patient's admission to hospital for treatment under section 3, and to discharge a patient from hospital, a community treatment order or guardianship.

P | The person who lacks, or may lack, capacity for the purposes of the MCA 2005.

Registered medical practitioner | A doctor registered with the General Medical Council, who has several responsibilities under the MHA 1983, including providing the medical recommendation upon which any application for admission is based, providing the medical opinion on which a court order or prison transfer is based, and acting as responsible clinician. Where an application or court order is based on two recommendations (as is usually required), at least one will normally be required to come from a registered medical practitioner who is approved under section 12 as having special experience in the diagnosis or treatment of mental disorder.

Responsible clinician | The approved clinician with overall responsibility for a patient's case (section 34 of the MHA 1983).

Restricted patient | A patient who is detained in hospital as a result of a court order or a prison transfer and is subject to special restrictions as a consequence. A patient to whom section 41, 49 or 45A of the MHA 1983 applies.

Second opinion appointed doctor | A registered medical practitioner appointed by the Care Quality Commission who is responsible for providing a second opinion as a safeguard in respect of certain treatment under the MHA 1983.

Upper Tribunal | The appellate tribunal to which appeals against First-tier Tribunal decisions are referred.

1.3   ABBREVIATIONS

AMHP	approved mental health professional
ASW	approved social worker
AWOL	absent without leave
BIA	best interests assessor
CAMHS	Child and Adolescent Mental Health Services
CCG	clinical commissioning group
CTO	community treatment order
DOLS	Deprivation of Liberty Safeguards
DOLS Code	Code of Practice of the Mental Capacity Act 2005, specific to Deprivation of Liberty Safeguards provisions
DSM-5	*Diagnostic and Statistical Manual of Mental Disorders*, 5th edition
DVCVA 2004	Domestic Violence, Crime and Victims Act 2004
DVLA	Driver and Vehicle Licensing Agency
ECT	electroconvulsive therapy
ECHR	European Convention for the Protection of Human Rights and Fundamental Freedoms 1950 (European Convention on Human Rights)
ECtHR	European Court of Human Rights
FACS	*Fair access to care services – guidance on eligibility criteria for adult social care* (Department of Health, 2003)
HMCTS	Her Majesty's Courts & Tribunals Service
HRA 1998	Human Rights Act 1998
ICD-10	*International Classification of Diseases*, Version 2010
IMHA	independent mental health advocate
LPA	lasting power of attorney
LSSA	local social services authority
MCA 2005	Mental Capacity Act 2005
Mental Health Regulations 2008	Mental Health (Hospital, Guardianship and Treatment) (England) Regulations 2008 (SI 2008/1184)
MHA 1983	Mental Health Act 1983
MHA 2007	Mental Health Act 2007
MHCS	mental health casework section, Ministry of Justice
MHT	mental health tribunal
MOJ	Ministry of Justice
NHSCCA 1990	National Health Service and Community Care Act 1990

PACE 1984	Police and Criminal Evidence Act 1984
PACE Code C	Code of Practice C of the Police and Criminal Evidence Act 1984
RC	responsible clinician
RMP	registered medical practitioner
RTA 1988	Road Traffic Act 1988
SCT	supervised community treatment
SOAD	second opinion appointed doctor
SSH	Secretary of State for Health
SSJ	Secretary of State for Justice
SST	Secretary of State for Transport
Tribunal Procedure Rules 1998	Tribunal Procedure (First-tier Tribunal) (Health, Education and Social Care Chamber) Rules 2008 (SI 2008/2699)
1983 Code	Code of Practice of the Mental Health Act 1983
2005 Code	Code of Practice of the Mental Capacity Act 2005

Part One

Overview of the Mental Health Act 1983

Chapter 2

Mental Health Act 1983 – Overview

2.1   INTRODUCTION

The MHA 1983 remains by far the most important piece of mental health legislation in England and Wales. Its stated purpose upon enactment was to 'consolidate the law relating to mentally disordered persons', and it is in large part based on the principles set out in its immediate predecessor, the Mental Health Act 1959, which is generally regarded as having provided the framework for modern mental health law. Like its predecessor, the main feature of the MHA 1983 is the framework that it provides for the compulsory admission to hospital and treatment of those with mental disorder.

The MHA 1983's starting point is that detention may only be contemplated where a person has a mental disorder. Where that is established, an individual may be detained, but only when it is necessary, because of risks either to the individual himself or to members of the public at large. The Act therefore requires a threshold of risk to be crossed before interference with an individual's liberty may be justified.

The MHA 1983 authorises compulsory admission to hospital under a civil procedure, that is, on the authority of clinicians, without the need for a court order; or, alternatively, under a criminal procedure, that is, on the authority of a criminal court or the Secretary of State for Justice (SSJ).

The prevailing philosophy behind the MHA 1983 is that detention may not be justified for its own sake, and when therefore someone is detained because of a mental disorder, then, apart from in the short term for assessment, that detention must be for the purpose of treatment. Equally importantly, the Act provides safeguards for those detained under its provisions, notable examples being the requirement that, in the absence of the patient's consent, a second medical opinion is required in respect of certain types of treatment, and the right that is given to the patient to apply to an independent tribunal for discharge from detention.

As well as providing a framework for compulsory admission to hospital and treatment, the MHA 1983 also provides a framework for the delivery of community-based care and treatment involving a degree of compulsion.

2.2   STRUCTURE OF THE MENTAL HEALTH ACT 1983

The MHA 1983 is divided into 11 parts, one of which, Part VII, was repealed by the MCA 2005.

Part I (section 1) is the shortest part of the MHA 1983. It confirms that the Act is only of application to the mentally disordered, and provides a definition of the term.

Part II (sections 2–34) contains the provisions for compulsory civil admissions to hospital. It contains the criteria for admission (sections 2 and 3) and the procedure which must be followed (sections 11–13). It also contains the provisions for emergency admissions and holding powers (sections 4 and 5). It contains the rules governing the length of admission and the circumstances in which detention for treatment may be extended (section 20). It contains rules governing the granting of leave (section 17) and transfer to another hospital (section 19). It sets out the circumstances in which a patient may be discharged, by his responsible clinician (RC), by hospital managers or by his nearest relative (section 23). It contains provisions for compulsory care and treatment in the community (sections 7 and 17A). It also contains provisions concerning the identification of a patient's nearest relative (section 26).

Part III (sections 35–55) contains the provisions governing the compulsory admission to hospital of mentally disordered offenders. It provides criminal courts with the power to direct the admission of a defendant to hospital for assessment or treatment, either before or at the point of sentence, and provides the SSJ with the power to direct the transfer of a remand or sentenced prisoner to hospital for assessment or treatment.

Part IV (sections 56–64) contains the provisions governing the clinical treatment of patients detained under the MHA 1983 and provides the authority for the treatment of a patient without consent. In exceptional circumstances, some of its provisions will also apply to patients who are not detained under the Act. There are some detained patients (those detained under the Act's short-term provisions, sections 4, 5, 135 and 136) to whom this Part's provisions do not apply at all.

Part 4A (sections 64A–64K) contains the provisions governing clinical treatment of patients subject to community treatment orders (CTOs).

Part V (sections 65–79) contains the provisions concerning the role of mental health tribunals (MHTs). It contains the rules setting out when a detained patient may apply to the MHT, when an automatic reference of a patient's case to the MHT must take place, and the powers available to the MHT.

Part VI (sections 80–92) contains the powers available to remove and return patients within the UK and elsewhere.

Part VII (sections 93–113) is repealed.

Part VIII (sections 114–125) sets out miscellaneous functions of local authorities and the Secretary of State for Health (SSH).

Part IX (sections 126–130) sets out various criminal offences that may be committed under the MHA 1983.

Part X (sections 130A–149) contains various miscellaneous and supplementary provisions.

2.3   MENTAL HEALTH ACT 2007

Although the MHA 1983 might generally have been regarded as providing a sound legal framework for compulsory admission to hospital and treatment, it was made subject to significant amendments as a result of the Mental Health Act 2007 (MHA 2007). Broadly speaking, the changes reflected a political desire to use mental health legislation to provide greater public protection from acts committed by those with mental disorder. More specifically, the changes reflected concerns that mental disorder was too narrowly defined by the MHA 1983, that the Act did not take account of the increasing emphasis on community-based care and treatment, that it did not provide any credible means of enforcing compulsory community-based treatment, and that the Act's 'treatability test' (long-term detention could only be justified if treatment was 'likely to alleviate or prevent a deterioration') meant that dangerous patients not susceptible to treatment, particularly psychopaths, were being discharged while still posing a significant risk to the public.

The MHA 2007 was an amending Act. Apart from some changes to the MCA 2005 in respect of DOLS (see Chapter 23), the MHA 2007's main purpose was to amend the MHA 1983. The most significant amendments were as follows.

2.3.1 Definition of mental disorder

The definition of mental disorder was broadened and simplified and the need to classify mental disorder was removed (see Chapter 3).

2.3.2 Appropriate treatment test

The 'treatability test' for those detained for treatment was removed and replaced with an 'appropriate treatment' test, considered in Chapter 4. No longer does treatment have to be 'likely to alleviate or prevent a deterioration' in a patient's condition.

2.3.3 Broadening of professional roles

Until 2007, key functions under the MHA 1983 were performed by the approved social worker (ASW) and responsible medical officer (RMO). These two roles were removed and replaced by, respectively, the approved mental health professional (AMHP) and the RC. The AMHP need not now be a social worker, and the responsible clinician (RC) need not be a registered medical practitioner (RMP). Subject to meeting the appropriate regulations, an AMHP may be a nurse, an occupational therapist or a psychologist, and the RC may be a nurse, an occupational therapist or a social worker.

2.3.4 Nearest relative

As a result of the 2007 changes, the patient has joined the ranks of those eligible to apply to the county court under section 29 of the MHA 1983 for his nearest relative to be displaced (see para 5.3). The grounds for displacement have also been extended and now include the nearest relative being 'unsuitable' to act as such. For the purposes of determining the identity of a patient's nearest relative, civil partnerships have equal footing with marriages.

2.3.5 Independent mental health advocates

Section 130A of the MHA 1983 now places a duty on the SSH and the Welsh Minister to make arrangements for independent mental health advocates (IMHAs) to be available to provide help and support to all 'qualifying patients' (essentially, all those detained or subject to compulsory powers in the community; see para 8.3.3).

2.3.6   Community treatment orders

Sections 17A–17G of the MHA 1983 contain new provisions allowing for certain patients to be made subject to a CTO at the point of discharge from hospital. These powers are considered in Chapter 20.

2.4   CODE OF PRACTICE (SEE ALSO APPENDIX 12)

The MHA 1983 is accompanied by its own Code of Practice (1983 Code), last amended in 2008 to reflect the changes brought about by the MHA 2007. The requirement on the SSH to produce the 1983 Code comes from section 118 of the MHA 1983.

According to section 118(1) of the MHA 1983, the 1983 Code's purpose is to provide guidance to mental health professionals on the operation of the Act. The Act creates no legal duty on the part of professionals to comply with the 1983 Code, but in *R v Ashworth Hospital Authority (now Mersey Care NHS Trust) ex parte Munjaz* [2005] UKHL 58, the House of Lords concluded that (at [21]):

> the guidance should be given great weight. It is not instruction, but it is much more than mere advice which an addressee is free to follow or not as it chooses. It is guidance which any hospital should consider with great care, and from which it should depart only if it has cogent reasons for doing so.

In *Munjaz v UK* (Application No 2913/06) [2012] ECHR 1704, the European Court of Human Rights (ECtHR) supported this view, although holding on the facts that a seclusion policy could be in accordance with the law even though it departed from the 1983 Code.

2.5   MENTAL HEALTH HOSPITAL, GUARDIANSHIP AND TREATMENT (ENGLAND) REGULATIONS 2008

Sections 9, 17F(2), 19(1) and (4), 19A(1), 32(1), (2) and (3), 57(1)(b), 58A(1)(b), 64(2), 64H(2), 134(3A)(a) and 134(8) of the MHA 1983 give the SSH the power to make regulations governing the operation of various aspects of the Act, including, for example, hospital admission, guardianship, CTOs, hospital transfer and patient correspondence. All of these regulations are brought together in the Mental Health (Hospital, Guardianship and Treatment) (England) Regulations 2008 (SI 2008/1184) (Mental Health Regulations 2008). The Regulations prescribe the various forms that hospital managers, mental health professionals and clinicians must use when performing their statutory functions.

2.6   REFERENCE GUIDE TO THE MENTAL HEALTH ACT 1983

Following the implementation of the changes arising from the MHA 2007, the Department of Health's *Reference guide to the Mental Health Act 1983* (TSO, 2008) sits alongside the 1983 Code as a further resource for those who wish to understand the operation of the Act.

2.7   THE MENTAL HEALTH ACT 1983 AND THE EUROPEAN CONVENTION ON HUMAN RIGHTS

The European Convention on Human Rights (ECHR) was incorporated into UK domestic law by the Human Rights Act 1998 (HRA 1998), with effect from October 2000. The Act rendered enforceable for the first time in the UK certain Convention rights, that is, rights established by the Articles of the ECHR. Various rulings from the ECtHR, and from UK courts applying the ECHR, have since had a significant effect on the operation of the MHA 1983. The main Convention rights are contained within Articles 2–18. Of these, Articles 3, 5, 6 and 8 are of most relevance to mental health law.

2.7.1   Article 3 – prohibition of torture

Article 3 of the ECHR provides that, 'no one shall be subjected to torture or to inhuman or degrading treatment or punishment'.

In *Herczegfalvy v Austria* (Application No 10533/83) [1992] ECHR 83, the ECtHR held that mentally ill patients detained and treated against their will are subject to the protection of Article 3 of the ECHR, but that it will usually be for the medical authorities to decide 'on the basis of recognised rules of medical science' what treatment should be used. The court noted that, as a general rule, 'a measure which is a therapeutic necessity cannot be regarded as inhuman or degrading', but suggested that any court required to rule on the point must 'satisfy itself that the medical necessity has been convincingly shown to exist'.

MS v UK (Application No 24527/08) [2012] ECHR 804, was a case where there were delays in arranging the transfer of a man with severe mental health problems from a police station to hospital following his arrest under section 136 of the MHA 1983. The man's claim that his treatment was in breach of Article 3 of the ECHR was upheld by the ECtHR, which noted his state of 'great vulnerability throughout the entire time at the police station, as manifested by the abject condition to which he quickly descended inside his cell'. The persistence of this state of affairs 'diminished excessively his fundamental human dignity'. The absence of any intention to humiliate or debase did not prevent a finding of a breach of his right under Article 3.

2.7.2   Article 5 – right to liberty and security

Article 5(1) of the ECHR provides that, 'everyone has the right to liberty and security of person'. It goes on to state, therefore, that no one shall be deprived of his liberty save in certain specified cases. The detention of 'persons of unsound mind' is such a specified case (Article 5(1)(e)), but only if the detention is 'in accordance with a procedure prescribed by law'.

Article 5(4) of the ECHR provides that, 'everyone who is deprived of his liberty by arrest or detention shall be entitled to take proceedings by which the lawfulness of his detention shall be decided speedily by a court and his release ordered if the detention is not lawful'.

In *Winterwerp v The Netherlands* (Application No 6301/73) [1979] ECHR 4, the ECtHR ruled that no one may be detained as a person of unsound mind (Article 5(1)(e) of the ECHR) unless the detaining authority can show, 'using objective medical expertise, a true mental disorder of a kind or degree warranting compulsory treatment'. The court also noted that, 'continued confinement depends upon the persistence of a true mental disorder'.

In *HL v UK* (Application No 45508/99) [2004] ECHR 471, the ECtHR held that the detention of a severely autistic man in a care home on the basis of the common law doctrine of necessity meant an absence of procedural safeguards to protect against arbitrary detention and was therefore in violation of Article 5(1) of the ECHR. It also meant a violation of Article 5(4) since the patient had no procedure available to him which allowed the lawfulness of his detention to be challenged speedily by a court.

In *R (on the application of H) v MHRT, North and East London Region and Another* [2001] EWCA Civ 415, the Court of Appeal reviewed the statutory discharge criteria to be considered at tribunal hearings. It declared sections 72 and 73 of the MHA 1983, as then drafted, to be incompatible with Articles 5(1) and 5(4) of the ECHR. The burden of proof at the time being on the patient to show why he should be discharged meant that a tribunal was not required, as it should be, to discharge a patient unless it could be shown that the patient was suffering from a mental disorder warranting detention. The incompatibility was remedied by the Mental Health Act 1983 (Remedial) Order 2001 (SI 2001/ 3712), which reversed the burden.

In *MH v Secretary of State for Health and others* [2005] UKHL 60, the House of Lords was asked to consider whether the MHA 1983 was compatible with Article 5(4) of the ECHR in that it failed to provide an effective right of access to a tribunal for patients detained under section 2 who lacked the capacity to make an application themselves. Finding that there was no incompatibility, Baroness Hale distinguished between a right to take proceedings, which is covered by Article 5(4), and a right to be brought before a court, which is not. Although acknowledging that the right to take proceedings may be 'theoretical and illusory' in the case of a patient without capacity, she suggested that the answer was that, 'every sensible effort should be made to enable the patient to exercise the right to apply'.

Dealing with the same case 8 years later, however, the ECtHR, in *MH v UK* (Application No 11577/06) [2013] ECHR 1008, disagreed. It found that the right to take proceedings under Article 5(4) of the ECHR is guaranteed to everyone, which therefore means that, 'special safeguards are called for in the case of detained mental patients who lack legal capacity to institute proceedings before judicial bodies', and the absence of such safeguards in relation to patients detained under section 2 meant a breach of Article 5(4). Quite what those safeguards should now be, however, remains to be seen.

2.7.3   Article 6 – right to a fair trial

Article 6(1) of the ECHR provides that, 'in the determination of his civil rights and obligations or of any criminal charge against him, everyone is entitled to a fair and public hearing within a reasonable time by an independent and impartial tribunal established by law'.

Arguments regarding the right to a hearing from an independent and impartial tribunal have been aired regularly in the context of MHT hearings. A lack of impartiality, or bias, has been argued where:

- the MHT medical member has been employed by the health authority responsible for detaining the patient (*R (on the application of PD) v West Midlands and North West MHRT* [2004] EWCA Civ 311);
- the MHT contains a member who has been a member of a tribunal which has previously considered the applicant's case (*R (on the application of M) v MHRT* [2005] EWHC 2791 (Admin));
- an MHT member has expressed a firm view on a hearing's outcome before the close of the evidence (*MB v BEH MH NHS Trust* [2011] UKUT 328 (AAC));
- the medical member has formed an opinion on the patient's mental disorder and detainability as a consequence of a preliminary examination

conducted under rule 34 of the Tribunal Procedure (First-tier Tribunal) (Health, Education and Social Care Chamber) Rules 2008 (SI 2008/ 2699) (Tribunal Procedure Rules 2008) (*R (on the application of S) v MHRT* [2002] EWHC 2522 (Admin) and *R (on the application of RD) v MHRT* [2007] EWHC 781 (Admin)).

These cases are considered further in Chapter 15.

The right to an independent and impartial tribunal under Article 6 of the ECHR is indistinguishable from the common law right to an impartial and unbiased hearing, and cases have been argued on the basis of either or both principles.

In *MA v SSH and Others* [2012] UKUT 474 (AAC), the Upper Tribunal ruled that the rights available to the patient's nearest relative under the MHA 1983 constitute civil rights protected by Article 6 of the ECHR.

2.7.4   Article 8 – right to respect for private and family life

Article 8 of the ECHR protects an individual's right to privacy and to family life.

Article 8(1) of the ECHR provides that, 'everyone has the right to respect for his private and family life, his home and his correspondence'.

Article 8(2) of the ECHR provides that:

> there shall be no interference by a public authority with the exercise of his right except such as is in accordance with the law and is necessary in a democratic society in the interests of national security, public safety or the economic well-being of the country, for the prevention of disorder or crime, for the protection of health or morals, or for the protection of the rights and freedoms of others.

In *Glass v UK* (Application No 61827/00) [2004] ECHR 103, a case involving medical treatment of a severely mentally and physically disabled child, the ECtHR held that treatment of the child by hospital staff against the wishes of his mother, his 'legal proxy', constituted an interference with the child's right to respect for a private life under Article 8 of the ECHR, in particular his 'right to physical integrity'. It was further held that the interference could not be justified under Article 8(2). For it to be so, the treatment would have had to be 'necessary', a finding the ECtHR did not feel itself able to make, taking into account the unjustified failure by the hospital to refer the dispute to the High Court for resolution before the treatment was started.

In *X v Finland* (Application No 34806/04) [2012] ECHR 1371, the ECtHR reiterated the principle that a 'medical intervention in defiance of the subject's will' constitutes an interference with the right to respect for a private life under Article 8 of the ECHR. Finding that the interference in question, in this case the forcible administration of medication following detention, could not be regarded as 'in accordance with the law' for Article 8(2) purposes, the court said that:

> forced administration of medication represents a serious interference with a person's physical integrity and must accordingly be based on a 'law' that guarantees proper safeguards against arbitrariness. In the present case such safeguards were missing. The decision to confine the applicant to involuntary treatment included an automatic authorisation to proceed to forced administration of medication when the applicant refused the treatment. The decision-making was solely in the hands of the treating doctors who could take even quite radical measures regardless of the applicant's will. Moreover, their decision-making was free from any kind of immediate judicial scrutiny: the applicant did not have any remedy available whereby she could require a court to rule on the lawfulness, including proportionality, of the forced administration of medication and to have it discontinued.

In *JT v UK* (Application No 26494/95) [2000] ECHR 133, JT applied to the ECtHR for a declaration that the absence of any right under section 29 of the MHA 1983 for a patient to apply to the county court to displace the nearest relative was a violation of the right to a private and family life under Article 8 of the ECHR. The proceedings concluded following a settlement between JT and the UK government, in which the government agreed to amend section 29 so that a patient would be given the power to make an application to displace where the patient reasonably objected to the existing nearest relative. The MHA 2007 subsequently amended section 29(2) and (4) of the MHA 1983 so that a patient may now make an application to displace his nearest relative on the ground, among others, that the nearest relative is 'not a suitable person to act as such'.

2.7.5   Convention rights and the Code of Practice of the Mental Health Act 1983

The 1983 Code, drafted to accompany the MHA 1983, contains a number of references to the importance of Convention rights to the operation of the Act.

Guiding principles

Firstly, and most generally, when setting out the MHA 1983's guiding principles, the 1983 Code states (para 1.7) that all decisions under the Act must be lawful, which 'necessarily involves compliance with the Human Rights Act 1998'.

Privacy and safety

In order to reflect the right to a private life under Article 8 of the ECHR, the 1983 Code advises (para 16.2) that hospital staff 'should make conscious efforts to respect the privacy of patients while maintaining safety'.

Treatment

The 1983 Code notes (para 23.39) that the administration of medical treatment without consent may involve an infringement of a patient's right to a private life under Article 8 of the ECHR and the right to freedom from inhuman or degrading treatment under Article 3. In relation to the latter, the 1983 Code identifies the key principles from *Herczegfalvy v Austria* (Application No 10533/83) [1992] ECHR 83.

Transfer

The 1983 Code notes (para 30.15) that the transfer of a patient from one hospital to another under section 19 of the MHA 1983 may interfere with his right to a family life under Article 8 of the ECHR. Therefore, among factors which need to be considered when a decision is made is 'whether the transfer would give the patient greater access to family or friends, or have the opposite effect' (para 30.18).

Zone of parental control

Chapter 36 of the 1983 Code looks at decision-making concerning children and young people. For those children or young people who lack competence or capacity, the 1983 Code introduces the notion of the zone of parental control as an attempt to define the area within which parents may lawfully make decisions. As the 1983 Code notes (para 36.9), the concept 'derives largely from case law from the European Court of Human Rights'.

Chapter 3

Mental Disorder

3.1 INTRODUCTION

Mental disorder is the cornerstone of the MHA 1983. At the Act's very beginning, section 1(1) makes clear that its provisions only apply 'to the reception, care and treatment of mentally disordered patients, the management of their property and other related matters'. It is only to patients with mental disorder that the Act applies, and no other patient may be admitted or treated under its provisions.

In legal terms, what constitutes a mental disorder is rarely a source of dispute since the MHA 1983 defines the term broadly and there is a large amount of consensus on the types of condition that will fall within the definition, the law generally tending to fall in line with what the medical profession regards as a mental disorder. The Act's definition of mental disorder is, however, drafted so that special provisions apply in the case of certain conditions (learning disability, and drug and alcohol dependency) which would otherwise be regarded as mental disorder.

3.2 STATUTORY DEFINITION OF MENTAL DISORDER

3.2.1 Section 1(2) of the Mental Health Act 1983

The MHA 1983 defines mental disorder as 'any disorder or disability of the mind' (section 1(2)). This is a simple, flexible definition designed to provide clinicians with significant discretion when deciding whether to admit someone to hospital under the Act. It applies without variation throughout the Act, whether the proposal is to admit someone for a short period for assessment or for a longer period for treatment. There is no requirement to classify the type of mental disorder before a person is admitted under the Act's provisions.

3.2.2   Removal of classifications of mental disorder

The flexibility of the definition is best illustrated by a comparison with the definition which existed before the MHA 1983 was amended by the MHA 2007. Before then, the definition of mental disorder necessarily involved classification since a person had to be suffering from a certain type of disorder before detention in the longer term for treatment could be authorised. The MHA 1983 defined mental disorder as 'mental illness, arrested or incomplete development of the mind, psychopathic disorder and any other disorder or disability of the mind', and went on to state that only those with one of the main classifications within that definition (mental illness, arrested or incomplete development of the mind, psychopathic disorder) could be detained for *treatment*. Those with 'any other disorder or disability of the mind' could only be detained for *assessment*.

That someone could only, therefore, be detained for treatment if shoe-horned into one of those particular types of mental disorder, meant an unhelpful focus on classification at the outset of any admission, and also, inevitably, that many who ought to have been eligible for detention for treatment were not because they fell into the 'any other disorder or disability of the mind' category. A person diagnosed with personality disorder, for example, could only be detained for treatment if he fell within the classification of 'psychopathic disorder', defined by the MHA 1983 as 'a persistent disorder or disability of the mind (whether or not including significant impairment of intelligence) resulting in abnormally aggressive or seriously irresponsible conduct'.

Faced with what many regarded as an unsatisfactory situation, the MHA 2007 amended the MHA 1983 and did away with the notion that only certain types of mental disorder should merit detention for treatment. As had always been the case for assessment, any disorder might now also justify detention for treatment, and so the need to classify was removed. There was no longer any need to incorporate classification within the definition itself and the new, more flexible definition was created.

3.3   MEANING OF THE TERM 'MENTAL DISORDER'

3.3.1   Reliance on good clinical practice and accepted standards

Having a flexible definition of mental disorder is one thing, finding a precise meaning for the words within that definition is another. Rather than look for one, however, it is better to assume that there can be no precise definition of 'disorder or disability of the mind' and to rely instead on the fact that there is, generally, agreement as to the types of condition that are covered by the term.

The MHA 1983 itself provides no assistance on the meaning of the term and the expectation is that reliance will be placed on generally accepted standards within the medical profession. The 1983 Code, therefore, advises (para 3.2) that, 'relevant professionals should determine whether a patient has a disorder or disability of the mind in accordance with good clinical practice and accepted standards of what constitutes such a disorder or disability'. The 1983 Code also provides (para 3.3) examples of the most common clinically recognised conditions which could fall within the definition:

- affective disorders, such as depression and bipolar disorder
- schizophrenia and delusional disorders
- neurotic, stress-related and somatoform disorders, such as anxiety, phobic disorders, obsessive compulsive disorders, post-traumatic stress disorder and hypochondriacal disorders
- organic mental disorders such as dementia and delirium (however caused)
- personality and behavioural changes caused by brain injury or damage (however acquired)
- personality disorders
- mental and behavioural disorders caused by psychoactive substance use ...
- eating disorders, non-organic sleep disorders and non-organic sexual disorders
- learning disabilities ...
- autistic spectrum disorders (including Asperger's syndrome) ...
- behavioural and emotional disorders of children and adolescents

3.3.2   Diagnostic manuals

The 1983 Code's list is for illustrative purposes only, and most psychiatrists will diagnose by reference to one or other of two widely-used diagnostic manuals, the World Health Organisation's *International Classification of Diseases* (ICD-10) and the American Psychiatric Association's *Diagnostic and Statistical Manual of Mental Disorders*, the 5th edition of which, DSM-5, was published in May 2013. Each is an authoritative diagnostic tool and breaks down mental disorder into hundreds of different classifications according to common characteristics. Guidance is provided in the manuals on the number and inter-relation of symptoms required for a diagnosis according to a certain classification to be made. In the UK, diagnosis tends to be made by reference to ICD-10.

In most cases, therefore, although diagnosis by reference to the manuals is for clinical purposes, a patient diagnosed as having a condition identified in either of these manuals is regarded as having a mental disorder for legal purposes. This is not a definitive rule, however, and the fact that a condition is referred to in either manual does not mean that it must be regarded as a mental disorder as a matter of law. There are significant differences in classification between the two manuals, there are controversial diagnoses in each, and neither purports to be a definitive diagnostic manual for legal purposes. However helpful these manuals may be, the law must reserve to itself the final judgement on the question of whether a condition is, in fact, a mental disorder (see *DL-H v Devon Partnership NHS Trust and SSJ* [2010] UKUT 102 (AAC)).

Similarly, just as a condition's inclusion in either manual does not mean that as a matter of law it must be a mental disorder, so the fact that a condition does not appear in either diagnostic manual does not mean that it cannot constitute a mental disorder for the purposes of the MHA 1983.

Assessment for mental disorder normally involves a review of the patient's psychiatric history (present and past) and a mental state examination.

Areas covered by the examination are:

- appearance and behaviour;
- speech;
- mood (objective and subjective);
- affect (current emotional state as manifested);
- thought content;
- perception;
- cognition;
- insight.

3.3.3   The odd and the deviant

Legal and clinical practice are agreed that, 'disorder or disability of the mind' may not be defined so as to include the merely odd or socially deviant. The 1983 Code is keen to emphasise (para 3.6) that a diagnosis of mental disorder may not be made solely on either a person's 'political, religious or cultural beliefs, values or opinions', or his 'involvement, or likely involvement, in illegal, anti-social or "immoral" behaviour', and the ICD-10 (*Clinical descriptions and diagnostic guidelines*, page 11) emphasises that mental disorder is associated in most cases 'with distress and with interference with personal functions', also therefore warning that, '[s]ocial deviance or conflict alone, without personal dysfunction, should not be included in mental disorder as defined here'.

3.4 LEARNING DISABILITY

While the law generally chooses to take its lead from clinical practice on what constitutes mental disorder, learning disability (referred to as 'intellectual disability' in DSM-5 and 'mental retardation' in ICD-10) is a rare example of a situation where the law and clinical practice part company. For clinicians, the issue is straightforward, and someone with a learning disability has a mental disorder; for the purposes of classification, it is treated no differently than any other mental disorder. For the MHA 1983, on the other hand, the issue is more complicated, and a person with a learning disability is not regarded as having a mental disorder unless certain additional criteria are met.

3.4.1 Mental Health Act 1983 definition of 'learning disability'

The MHA 1983 provides its own definition of the term. Section 1(4) defines it as 'a state of arrested or incomplete development of the mind which includes significant impairment of intelligence and social functioning'. There are therefore two requirements which must be met for there to be a learning disability:

- a state of arrested or incomplete development of the mind; and
- a significant impairment of intelligence and social functioning.

Care must be taken to distinguish those for whom the significant impairment of intelligence and social functioning is a result of arrested or incomplete development of the mind, which would constitute a learning disability, from those for whom it is a result of accident, injury or illness, which would not.

3.4.2 Exclusion from the definition of mental disorder

The definition of learning disability in the MHA 1983 does not set it apart from the diagnostic manuals. According to section 1(2A), however, a person with a learning disability 'shall not be considered by reason of that disability to be suffering from a mental disorder ... unless that mental disorder is associated with abnormally aggressive or seriously irresponsible conduct'. In other words, whether or not a clinician forms the view that a patient is suffering from learning disability, that patient may not be regarded as having a mental disorder as a matter of law and will not, therefore, be detainable under the Act, unless the clinician is also able to conclude that the learning disability is associated with abnormally aggressive or seriously irresponsible conduct.

3.4.3 Abnormally aggressive or seriously irresponsible conduct

Neither 'abnormally aggressive' nor 'seriously irresponsible' conduct is defined by the MHA 1983, but guidance on interpretation is provided by the 1983 Code.

For deciding whether behaviour is abnormally aggressive, the 1983 Code suggests (para 34.8) that the following factors may be relevant:

- when such aggressive behaviour has been observed, and how persistent and severe it has been;
- whether it has occurred without a specific trigger or seems out of proportion to the circumstances that triggered it;
- whether, and to what degree, it has in fact resulted in harm or distress to other people, or actual damage to property;
- how likely, if it has not been observed recently, it is to recur; and
- how common similar behaviour is in the population generally.

For deciding whether behaviour is seriously irresponsible, the 1983 Code suggests (para 34.9) that the following factors may be relevant:

- whether behaviour has been observed that suggests a disregard or an inadequate regard for its serious or dangerous consequences;
- how recently such behaviour has been observed and, when it has been observed, how persistent it has been;
- how seriously detrimental to the patient, or to other people, the consequences of the behaviour were or might have been;
- whether, and to what degree, the behaviour has actually resulted in harm to the patient or the patient's interests, or in harm to other people or ... damage to property; and
- if it has not been observed recently, how likely it is to recur.

3.4.4 Exceptions to this rule

Sections 2, 4, 5, 135 and 136 of the MHA 1983 do not fall within this rule (section 1(2B)). A patient may, therefore, be regarded as having a mental disorder and detained under one of these short-term detaining provisions on the basis of learning disability alone, without the need for abnormally aggressive or seriously irresponsible conduct.

3.5 DRUG AND ALCOHOL DEPENDENCY

Drug and alcohol dependency is a further example of a different approach taken by lawyers and clinicians to the definition of mental disorder. As with learning disability, while clinicians would generally regard drug or alcohol dependency as a type of mental disorder, section 1(3) of the MHA 1983 specifically provides that, as a matter of law, it is not. This is a longstanding exclusion from the legal definition of mental disorder, and was deliberately preserved in spite of changes to the definition brought about by the MHA 2007. It continues to be the case, therefore, that a person may not be detained under the Act on the basis of drug or alcohol dependency alone 'even though in other contexts, their dependence would be considered clinically to be a mental disorder' (Explanatory Notes to the MHA 2007).

It should be noted that the exclusion is specific to disorders relating to *dependency* on alcohol or drugs, and there are other drug- or alcohol-related mental disorders which are not covered by the exclusion. Acute intoxication, withdrawal state, withdrawal state with delirium, alcohol- or drug-induced psychosis, amnesic (e.g. Korsakoff's) syndrome would all still, therefore, constitute a mental disorder for the purposes of the MHA 1983.

In any event, a person suffering from a drug or alcohol dependency may also have a co-existing mental disorder which might form the basis of detention. In these circumstances, a person may be treated for alcohol or drug dependency under section 63 of the MHA 1983 if such treatment falls within treatment for the mental disorder for which he is detained (see para 9.5).

3.6 PROMISCUITY, OTHER IMMORAL CONDUCT AND SEXUAL DEVIANCY

Until the 2007 amendments to the MHA 1983, 'promiscuity or other immoral conduct' and 'sexual deviancy' were also specifically excluded from the definition of mental disorder. As with drug or alcohol dependency, no one could be detained under the Act on the basis of any of those conditions alone. Unlike drug and alcohol dependency, however, these exclusions from the definition were removed.

3.6.1 Promiscuity or other immoral conduct

The decision to remove the exclusion in relation to 'promiscuity or other immoral conduct' was taken on the basis that it was simply redundant. It was thought inconceivable that any clinician would any longer ever seek to detain on the basis that either promiscuity or other immoral conduct was a mental disorder, and so there was no longer any need for it to be specifically excluded.

3.6.2   Sexual deviancy

The decision to remove sexual deviancy's exclusion from the definition of mental disorder was taken for a radically different reason, the aim being to bring one specific group, paedophiles, within the ambit of the MHA 1983.

Whatever the legal definition of mental disorder, clinicians have always been clear that paedophilia is a form of mental disorder. Prior to 2007, however, the exclusion of sexual deviancy from the legal definition of mental disorder meant that paedophilia, alongside other disorders or sexual preference, could not by itself provide the basis of detention under the MHA 1983. As a result of the 2007 amendments, however, the law and clinicians now take the same approach and regard sexual deviancy as a mental disorder capable on its own of justifying detention.

In its report on the Mental Health Bill (the Bill which later became the MHA 2007), the Joint Committee on Human Rights (*Legislative Scrutiny: Mental Health Bill*, Fourth Report of Session 2006–07, HC 288, The Stationery Office, 2007) observed (at page 8):

> The Government's intention is to ensure that paedophiles can be subject to indeterminate detention under the Mental Health Act 1983, without the need for any other accompanying mental disorder. Persons who pose a risk of sexual offences will be open to detention on grounds of personality disorder, but the Government is concerned that the sexual deviancy exclusion might give clinicians discretion not to detain such persons, and wishes to remove that possibility.

Concerns were expressed, however, that removing the sexual deviancy exclusion in order to allow for the detention of paedophiles would also bring within the scope of the MHA 1983 a large number of other, less harmful types of perceived sexual deviancy (e.g. transexualism, masochism, gender identity dysphoria, transvestic fetishism) on the basis that they also appear in the diagnostic manuals as mental disorders. The suggestion was, therefore, made by the Joint Committee that the exclusion for sexual deviancy should be retained, subject to a specific exception for paedophiles. However, this proposal was rejected by the government on the basis that, paedophilia aside, there are, conceivably, other abnormalities of sexual preference which may reach a level of clinical significance so as to justify the definition of mental disorder.

Part Two

Civil Admissions under the Mental Health Act 1983

Chapter 4

Civil Admissions under the Mental Health Act 1983 – Legal Criteria

4.1 INTRODUCTION

Although anyone with a mental disorder may be liable to detention under the MHA 1983, it cannot be right, plainly, that he is detained on the basis of that mental disorder alone. Detention under the Act carries with it a loss of liberty and, potentially, highly invasive treatment without consent, and there must therefore be a mechanism for deciding that the consequences of the disorder are serious enough to justify such an outcome. In other words, for deciding, as was found to be required in *Winterwerp v The Netherlands* (Application No 6301/73) [1979] ECHR 4 (see para 2.7.2), that the mental disorder is 'of a kind or degree warranting compulsory treatment'.

The mechanism is provided by sections 2 and 3 of the MHA 1983, the main civil detaining provisions of the Act, each of which establishes a seriousness threshold which must be crossed in order to justify either detention in the short term for assessment (section 2) or detention in the longer term for treatment (section 3). According to each, certain criteria must be met before detention can be considered. These criteria are considered in this chapter.

4.2 DETENTION FOR ASSESSMENT

4.2.1 Section 2 of the Mental Health Act 1983

A person with mental disorder may be detained in the short term for assessment under section 2 of the MHA 1983. Detention will be for a period of up to 28 days and the consequences are considered in more detail in Chapter 8. Detention for assessment may only be authorised, however, if the person meets the relevant criteria, which are set out in section 2(2). Accordingly, a person may only be detained for assessment where:

(a)   he is suffering from mental disorder of a nature or degree which warrants the detention of the patient in a hospital for assessment (or for assessment followed by medical treatment) for at least a limited period; and

(b)   he ought to be so detained in the interests of his own health or safety or with a view to the protection of other persons.

In other words:

- Is there a mental disorder?
- If so, is it of a nature or degree which warrants detention in hospital for assessment or assessment followed by treatment?
- If so, ought the person to be detained in the interests of his own health or safety, or with a view to the protection of others?

If the answer to any of these questions is 'no', the person may not be detained.

4.2.2   Applying the criteria under section 2 of the Mental Health Act 1983

To begin with, the patient must be 'suffering from mental disorder'. The meaning of the term 'mental disorder' is considered in Chapter 3. The requirement that the patient is 'suffering' from mental disorder means no more than that the patient has a mental disorder, and should not be interpreted to mean that the patient must be symptomatic.

Next, the mental disorder must be 'of a nature or degree which warrants detention in hospital'. A patient may be detained on the basis of the nature of the disorder or the degree, or both. Neither term is defined by the MHA 1983. 'Nature' is a reference to the fundamental characteristics of the disorder. Is it chronic? Is it relapsing? Is it responsive to medication? What are the symptoms associated with relapse? Is the disorder characterised by a lack of insight? A reference to a disorder's nature calls for a survey of its pattern. 'Degree' is a reference to the 'current manifestation' of the disorder (1983 Code, para 4.3). A reference to a disorder's degree calls for a snapshot of how it currently is. With a chronic, relapsing disorder, for example, is the patient in remission or is he symptomatic? Invariably, it will be the degree of the mental disorder that prompts the MHA assessment, and it will be unusual for an asymptomatic patient to be admitted to hospital on the basis of nature alone. Once in hospital, however, and assuming the degree of the disorder has been brought under control, it is more likely to be the nature of the disorder (e.g. liability to relapse) that is relied on to prolong detention.

The nature or degree must mean that detention should be 'warranted'. In *AM v South London and Maudsley NHS Foundation Trust and SSH* [2013] UKUT 365 (AAC), it was held that, 'for detention to be "warranted", it has to be "necessary" in the sense that the objective set out in the relevant statutory test cannot be achieved by less restrictive measures'.

Does the prospect of relapse of mental disorder through non-compliance with medication justify detention on the grounds of the nature of the disorder? It depends how likely there is to be a relapse and, if so, when it will occur. In *CM v Derbyshire Healthcare NHS Foundation Trust and SSJ* [2011] UKUT 129 (AAC), HHJ Levenson held that there needs to be a probability of relapse in the near future. In that case, a scenario of release followed by a period of 6 months before the resumption of a chaotic lifestyle, eventually leading to non-compliance, with a risk of relapse after at least 2 months of non-compliance, was adjudged not to create a risk of relapse in the near future.

Detention must be warranted for 'assessment (or for assessment followed by medical treatment)'. Although detention under section 2 is primarily for assessment, a patient can also be treated for his mental disorder while detained. 'Assessment' should be given its ordinary meaning. Medical treatment is defined in section 145 of the MHA 1983 and is considered further in Chapter 9.

The final judgement that must then be made is that the patient 'ought to be so detained in the interests of his own health or safety or with a view to the protection of other persons'. The obvious difficulty in applying this aspect of the test is deciding how it is meant to be applied alongside the 'warranted' test, but, presumably, if it is felt that the nature or degree 'warrants' detention, then it will be easy to conclude that the patient 'ought to be so detained in the interests of his own health or safety or with a view to the protection of other persons'.

Somewhat surprisingly, 'health', 'safety' and 'the protection of other persons' are not defined by the MHA 1983, and there is little in the way of assistance from case law. Each term tends to be interpreted broadly, however. 'Health' is generally accepted as being a reference to mental and physical health. 'Safety' refers to the danger to which a person may expose himself, and will typically cover reckless decisions regarding personal safety or provocative behaviour towards others. 'Protection of other persons' is a reference to harm that the patient may cause to others, harm including 'psychological as well as physical harm' (1983 Code, para 4.8).

4.3   DETENTION FOR TREATMENT

4.3.1   Section 3 of the Mental Health Act 1983

A person with mental disorder may, alternatively, be detained in hospital in the longer term for treatment under section 3 of the MHA 1983. With many cases, the question of whether to use section 2 or section 3 is a difficult one. This is considered further at para 4.4. If it is to be section 3, however, it will initially be for a period of up to 6 months, although this may be extended. The consequences of detention under section 3 and the provisions concerning renewal are considered further in Chapter 8.

Detention under section 3 of the MHA 1983 may only be contemplated if the person meets the relevant criteria. These are set out in section 3(2). Accordingly, a person may only be detained for treatment where:

> (a)   he is suffering from mental disorder of a nature or degree which makes it appropriate for him to receive medical treatment in a hospital; and
>
> (b)   ...
>
> (c)   it is necessary for the health or safety of the patient or for the protection of other persons that he should receive such treatment and it cannot be provided unless he is detained under this section; and
>
> (d)   appropriate medical treatment is available for him.

In other words:

- Is there a mental disorder?
- If so, is it of a nature or degree which makes hospital treatment appropriate?
- If so, is it necessary for the health or safety of the patient or for the protection of others that he should receive such treatment, which cannot be provided unless he is detained under this section?
- If so, is appropriate treatment available?

Again, if the answer to any of these questions is 'no', the person may not be detained.

4.3.2   Applying the criteria under section 3 of the Mental Health Act 1983

Many of the terms used in section 3 of the MHA 1983 (mental disorder, nature, degree, health, safety, protection of other persons, etc) are the same as those used in section 2, and have the same meaning (see para 4.2.2). Areas of difference are considered below.

Section 3 of the MHA 1983 requires the mental disorder to be 'of a nature or degree which makes it appropriate for him to receive medical treatment in a hospital'. This does not require an assessment of whether detention in a hospital is appropriate, simply whether treatment is.

The view must also be taken that it is 'necessary for the health or safety of the patient or for the protection of other persons that he should receive such treatment'. Assuming in-patient treatment is found to be appropriate, the question then is whether it can also be said to be necessary. This must be established by reference to the patient's health or safety or to the protection of others.

It must then be concluded that treatment 'cannot be provided unless he is detained', and in-patient treatment on a voluntary basis must have, therefore, been ruled out as a viable option.

Lastly, an application for admission for treatment may only be made on grounds that, 'appropriate medical treatment is available for him' (section 3(2)(d)). For these purposes, section 3(4) defines appropriate medical treatment as 'medical treatment which is appropriate in his case, taking into account the nature and degree of the mental disorder and all other circumstances of his case'. In the majority of cases, the 'appropriate treatment test' is relatively easy to satisfy, and it should be noted that the test simply requires *appropriate* treatment, not *the most appropriate* treatment.

4.3.3   Appropriate treatment test

The appropriate treatment test is an embodiment of the principle that detention under the MHA 1983 for treatment must be for a therapeutic purpose; clinicians and hospital staff should not be mere custodians. For some patients, treatment can, however, mean relatively little intervention, and the 1983 Code notes (para 6.16) that there may be:

> patients whose particular circumstances mean that treatment may be appropriate even though it consists only of nursing and specialist day-to-day care under the clinical supervision of an approved clinician, in a safe and secure therapeutic environment with a structured regime.

Given the broad definition of treatment and the concession in the 1983 Code that treatment for some may mean relatively little intervention, there may be some for whom the difference between detention for treatment and detention for public safety alone is hard to discern. In *D L-H v Devon Partnership NHS Trust and SSJ* [2010] UKUT 102 (AAC), HHJ Jacobs therefore highlighted the need for MHTs to 'investigate behind assertions, generalisations and standard phrases to make sure that there is in fact a regime with therapeutic benefits'.

In some cases, appropriate treatment may mean little more than preventing a condition or its symptoms getting worse, and there may be some patients for whom 'management of the undesirable effects of their disorder may be all that can be reasonably hoped for' (1983 Code, para 6.15). However, simply preventing a deterioration in a condition is unlikely to satisfy the appropriate treatment test in cases 'where normal treatment approaches would aim (and be expected) to alleviate the patient's condition significantly' (1983 Code, para 6.15).

Another feature of the test is that appropriate treatment need only be available and need not actually be accepted by the patient. The 1983 Code suggests (para 6.18) that, 'an indication of unwillingness to cooperate with treatment generally, or with a specific aspect of treatment, does not make such treatment inappropriate'. It was noted in *D L-H v Partnerships in Care and SSJ* [2013] UKUT 500 (AAC), however, that, 'the patient's attitude is one of the circumstances of the case that the tribunal must take into account 'when considering whether treatment is appropriate'.

4.4   CHOICE BETWEEN SECTION 2 AND SECTION 3 OF THE MENTAL HEALTH ACT 1983

Both section 2 and section 3 of the MHA 1983 provide the means by which a patient with a mental disorder may be admitted to hospital against his will. Whereas section 2 is designed for use when the primary purpose of the admission is assessment, section 3 is for use when the primary purpose is treatment. There is, therefore, an essential difference between the two. Each section is, nevertheless, available as an option in any case. Although many patients are first detained under section 2 for assessment and then detained under section 3 for treatment, there is no requirement that this should be the case, and there is nothing wrong in principle with a patient being detained under section 3 without use being made of section 2 at all.

The choice of which section to use will fall to the person making the application, usually the AMHP. Decision-making in this regard is not necessarily straightforward, and the choice of which section to use may not be a clear-cut one. There will be many cases where, on any reasonable view, the patient meets the criteria for detention under either section.

There is a commonly held perception that section 3 of the MHA 1983 should be used where the patient is well known to mental health services and where there is a well-established diagnosis and treatment plan. Many AMHPs may, therefore, forgo the opportunity to apply for detention under section 2 because it is felt that little in the way of in-patient assessment is required. Guidance from the 1983 Code certainly seems to provide some support for this perception. It provides (para 4.27) that section 3 should be used if 'the nature and current degree of the patient's mental disorder, the essential elements of the treatment plan to be followed and the likelihood of the patient accepting treatment on a voluntary basis are already established'.

AMHPs should, however, exercise caution before assuming that they can dispense with the need for detention under section 2. The 1983 Code advises (para 4.26) that section 2 of the MHA 1983 should be used if:

- the full extent of the nature and degree of a patient's condition is unclear;
- there is a need to carry out an initial in-patient assessment in order to formulate a treatment plan, or to reach a judgement about whether the patient will accept treatment on a voluntary basis following admission; or
- there is a need to carry out a new in-patient assessment in order to re-formulate a treatment plan, or to reach a judgement about whether the patient will accept treatment on a voluntary basis.

It is clearly envisaged, therefore, that there are various reasons why an initial period of in-patient assessment may be required, even in the case of a patient who is well known to the mental health services.

While the choice for AMHPs between section 2 and section 3 of the MHA 1983 may not always be a straightforward one, there is one circumstance in which use of section 2 would be impermissible. As explained in Chapter 5, the AMHP is merely required to inform the nearest relative of the application when applying for detention under section 2, whereas he is required to consult the nearest relative in cases under section 3 and may not proceed with the application if the nearest relative objects. The AMHP may not, however, use section 2 simply as a way of by-passing the need to consult the nearest relative and of getting the patient into hospital against the wishes of a reluctant nearest relative (see para 5.3.5).

Chapter 5

Civil Admissions under the Mental Health Act 1983 – Procedure

5.1 INTRODUCTION

Whatever the circumstances behind it, any decision to admit a person to hospital under the MHA 1983 requires a formal assessment involving three key sets of participants: an AMHP, a nearest relative and (usually) two RMPs. The AMHP's role is to organise the assessment of the patient, to make the decision whether to apply for admission to hospital and, where appropriate, to make the application itself. The nearest relative's role is to be informed of the application in cases under section 2, or to be consulted in cases under section 3. The role of the RMP is to conduct the medical examination and to recommend to the AMHP whether or not the person meets the criteria for admission. This chapter considers each role in turn.

5.2 ROLE OF THE APPROVED MENTAL HEALTH PROFESSIONAL

5.2.1 Who is the approved mental health professional?

There is little in the way of any statutory duty to assess an individual who may be in need of admission to hospital in respect of a mental disorder. What little duty there is, however, falls on the local social services authority (LSSA) (see para 5.2.2), which will, generally, delegate its responsibility in this regard to an AMHP.

The AMHP is the mental health professional approved to act as such by the LSSA under section 114 of the MHA 1983. The AMHP must have 'appropriate competence' in dealing with persons with mental disorder, which requires, inter alia, completion of an approved course. The AMHP must also fulfil the 'professional requirement', which means being a first level nurse practising in mental health or learning disabilities nursing, an occupational therapist, a social worker or a chartered psychologist (regulation 3 of the Mental Health (Approved Mental Health Professionals) (Approval) (England) Regulations 2008 (SI 2008/1206)). Invariably, the AMHP will, in fact, be a social worker.

5.2.2 Arrangements to assess the patient

Section 13(1) of the MHA 1983 requires an LSSA to make arrangements for an AMHP to consider a patient's case where there is 'reason to think that an application for admission to hospital or a guardianship application may need to be made in respect of a patient within their area'. More specifically, section 13(4) places a duty on the LSSA, 'if so required by the nearest relative of a patient residing in their area, to make arrangements ... for an approved mental health professional to consider the patient's case with a view to making an application for his admission to hospital'. Whether or not prompted by the nearest relative, therefore, the duty is no more than to 'consider' the patient's case.

5.2.3 Duty to interview the patient

If an application for detention under the MHA 1983 is to be made, however, the AMHP must have interviewed the patient concerned.

Section 13(2) of the MHA 1983 requires the AMHP to 'interview the patient in a suitable manner and satisfy himself that detention in a hospital is in all the circumstances of the case the most appropriate way of providing the care and medical treatment of which the patient stands in need'.

An AMHP cannot insist that a patient responds to any questions put, but he must ensure that an interview has taken place. The interview need not, however, be a particularly long one, and, in *Re GM: Patient Consultation* [2000] 1 MHLR 41, Burton J noted that there might be circumstances in which 'the approved social worker can arrive at a sufficient conclusion for the purposes of the relevant interview under section 13(2) within seconds if, for example, extreme violence is used'.

While the patient should normally be given the opportunity to speak to the AMHP alone during any assessment, the AMHP should insist that another professional is present if he is concerned for his safety (1983 Code, para 4.53). If the AMHP is unable to access premises in order to conduct an interview, he should consider applying for a warrant under section 135(1) of the MHA 1983 (see para 6.2.3). The 1983 Code provides (para 4.52) that the patient is entitled to have someone present for moral support during the course of an assessment, if that is possible to arrange.

5.2.4 Duty to inform/consult the nearest relative

There is a duty on the AMHP to make contact with the nearest relative during the assessment process, although the nature of the duty varies according to whether an application under section 2 or section 3 of the MHA 1983 is being contemplated. In the former case, the AMHP need only *inform* the nearest relative of the application; in the latter, he must *consult*, and may not proceed if the nearest relative objects (see paras 5.3.3 and 5.3.4).

In either case, however, the AMHP is required to identify the nearest relative, and, where it appears that the patient has no nearest relative, the AMHP should advise the patient of his right to apply to the county court to have someone appointed as such.

The nearest relative should also be advised of his rights and duties. Section 11(3) of the MHA 1983 requires the AMHP when informing the nearest relative of a proposed section 2 application to inform him of his power to discharge the patient. There is no such duty on the AMHP in cases under section 3 (presumably because the AMHP may not proceed if the nearest relative objects), but the 1983 Code confirms (para 4.64) that when *consulting* the nearest relative, the AMHP should 'inform the nearest relative of their role and rights under the Act'.

The duty to inform under section 2 or to consult under section 3 of the MHA 1983 is subject to the patient's right under Article 8 of the ECHR to privacy, and an AMHP is entitled to conclude that he need not contact the nearest relative if that would contravene the wishes of the patient (see *R (on the application of E) v Bristol City Council* [2005] EWHC 74 (Admin)). The role of the nearest relative is, however, a significant safeguard for the patient and, in the words of Bennett J, 'should not lightly be removed'.

5.2.5 Arranging the medical recommendation

No application for admission may be made unless it is founded on the appropriate medical recommendations. A person may not be admitted unless he meets the criteria in section 2 or section 3 of the MHA 1983, and confirmation that he does must come from two RMPs. It is for the AMHP to arrange medical assessments by the RMPs, 'unless different arrangements have been agreed locally between the relevant authorities' (1983 Code, para 4.40).

The RMPs and the AMHP must reach decisions on the need for detention independently of each other, but a patient should be seen jointly by the AMHP and at least one of the RMPs (1983 Code, para 4.44).

5.2.6   Deciding on admission

Having interviewed the patient, informed or consulted the nearest relative and obtained the recommendations from the RMPs, the AMHP must then decide whether an application is called for. Responsibility for making the decision is his alone. Section 13(1A) of the MHA 1983 provides that the AMHP should make the application if:

> (a)   satisfied that such an application ought to be made in respect of the patient; and
>
> (b)   of the opinion, having regard to any wishes expressed by relatives of the patient or any other relevant circumstances, that it is necessary or proper for the application to be made by him.

The fact that a person meets the criteria for detention does not decide the issue, and the MHA 1983 requires the AMHP to reach his own judgment on the need for the application, taking account of 'whether or not there are alternatives to detention under the Act' and 'bringing a social perspective to bear on the decision' (1983 Code, para 4.51).

The first question is whether hospital admission is required at all. The 1983 Code is clear (para 4.32). A proper assessment 'cannot be carried out without considering alternative means of providing care and treatment'. AMHPs and doctors should therefore, as far as possible, 'identify and liaise with services which may potentially be able to provide alternatives to admission in hospital'.

The second question will then be whether hospital admission can be achieved without the need to use the MHA 1983. Section 131(1) confirms what common sense would otherwise dictate, that a patient may agree to admit himself to hospital for psychiatric in-patient treatment, and in most cases, voluntary admission will be the better option for all concerned, and should always be considered before use is made of the Act's compulsory powers. This is subject however to the following considerations:

•   there may be cases where the patient requires detention even though he is consenting to admission, for example, where the patient 'presents a clear danger to themselves or others because of their mental disorder' (1983 Code, para 4.10) or where as a result of their current mental state or as a result of past experience, there is a 'strong likelihood that they will have a change of mind about informal admission' (1983 Code, para 4.11);

- the patient's agreement to admission to hospital should not be obtained as a result of the threat of detention otherwise (1983 Code, para 4.12).

If the AMHP decides not to apply for admission, he should record his decision in writing. He should also notify the nearest relative and advise him of his own right to apply for the patient's admission.

5.2.7   Arranging admission

Although it is for the AMHP to organise and coordinate all aspects of the assessment process, the 1983 Code advises (para 4.75) that it is the responsibility of the RMPs to take the necessary steps to secure the hospital bed, unless there is a local agreement to the contrary.

A hospital is under no duty to accept a patient referred to in an application. While patients should be moved as soon as possible, this should not therefore be until the AMHP is satisfied that the hospital named in the application is willing to take the patient (1983 Code, para 4.92).

The AMHP should provide the detaining hospital with a report at the time of admission setting out the details of the application and of any practical matters about the patient's circumstances (1983 Code, para 4.94).

5.3   ROLE OF THE NEAREST RELATIVE

5.3.1   Who is the patient's nearest relative?

The identity of the patient's nearest relative is not a matter of choice but is decided by rules set out in section 26 of the MHA 1983. A list of relatives is provided in section 26(1), arranged in a hierarchy (husband, wife or civil partner; son or daughter; father or mother; brother or sister; grandparent; grandchild; uncle or aunt; nephew or niece). According to section 26(3), the relative highest up the list will be the patient's nearest relative for the purposes of the Act. The application of the list is subject to the following rules:

- if two or more relatives appear in the same category (e.g. children, parents, siblings), the eldest will be preferred (section 26(3));
- if two or more relatives appear in the same category, a relative of 'the whole blood' will be preferred to one of 'half-blood' (section 26(3));

- where the patient ordinarily resides with or is cared for by one or more of his relatives, that relative or those relatives will be preferred over any other, and as between themselves, the eldest relative will be preferred, and any relative of the whole blood will be preferred over one of half-blood (section 26(4));
- where a patient is ordinarily resident in the UK, a relative who is not ordinarily resident in the UK will be discounted (section 26(5));
- a husband or wife or civil partner who is 'permanently separated' from the patient will be discounted (section 26(5));
- a relative under the age of 18 will be discounted except where the relative is a husband, wife, civil partner, father or mother of the patient (section 26(5));
- the terms 'husband', 'wife' and 'civil partner' are defined to include any partner who has been living with the patient as such for a minimum of 6 months (section 26(6)).
- a person who is not a relative but who has been ordinarily residing with the patient for a period of 5 years will be treated as a relative of the patient (section 26(7)). Although such a person will then be treated as appearing last in the hierarchy of relatives for the purposes of identifying the nearest relative, he will qualify as nearest relative on the basis that he ordinarily resides with the patient (section 26(4)) unless there is a closer relative who ordinarily resides or cares for the patient. However, a person who has resided with the patient for 5 years, and who would therefore otherwise qualify as nearest relative, will not supplant the husband, wife or civil partner as nearest relative unless the patient is permanently separated from, has deserted or has been deserted by the husband, wife or civil partner (section 26(7)(b)).

Delegation of nearest relative's powers

Regulation 24 of the Mental Health Regulations 2008 authorises a nearest relative to delegate his powers to any person apart from: the patient, a person disqualified from acting as nearest relative under section 26(5) of the MHA 1983, or any person who has been displaced as nearest relative under section 29(3)(b)–(e).

Displacement of nearest relative

Under section 29 of the MHA 1983, an application can be made to the county court to displace a nearest relative, and appoint an alternative, on one of the following grounds:

- the patient has no nearest relative or it is not reasonably practicable to ascertain whether he has one or, if so, who it is (section 29(3)(a));
- the nearest relative is incapable of acting as such by reason of mental disorder or other illness (section 29(3)(b));
- the nearest relative unreasonably objects to a section 3 or guardianship application (section 29(3)(c));
- the nearest relative has exercised his power of discharge, or is likely to, without due regard to the welfare of the patient or the interests of the public (section 29(3)(d));
- the nearest relative is otherwise not a suitable person to act as such (section 29(3)(e)).

5.3.2   Right of the nearest relative to make the application for admission

Section 11(1) of the MHA 1983 provides that an application for a person's admission to hospital under either section 2 or section 3 may in fact be made by his nearest relative, although, in practice, this option is rarely taken up and the overwhelming majority of applications are made by the AMHP.

5.3.3   Right of the nearest relative to be informed in cases under section 2 of the Mental Health Act 1983

Assuming the application is made by the AMHP, the role of the nearest relative in cases under section 2 of the MHA 1983 is limited. Although the nearest relative may be able to provide information which assists the AMHP in making a decision, he may not expect to be consulted and merely has the right to be informed if an application is made. As section 11(3) puts it:

> Before or within a reasonable time after an application for the admission of a patient for assessment is made by an approved mental health professional, that professional shall take such steps as are practicable to inform the person (if any) appearing to be the nearest relative of the patient that the application is to be or has been made.

Within a reasonable time

If the nearest relative is not informed before the application, he should be informed within a reasonable time after it is made. The MHA 1983 does not stipulate what is meant by reasonable time, and nor does the 1983 Code provide any guidance, but it is likely that the term will be interpreted restrictively given that the patient is detained for a limited period and for all the time that the nearest relative is not informed of the application, the patient is denied a potential avenue of discharge.

Such steps as are practicable

The MHA 1983 acknowledges that there may be circumstances in which the nearest relative is unable to be contacted, and requires only that he is informed if it is 'practicable'.

5.3.4   Right of the nearest relative to be consulted in cases under section 3 of the Mental Health Act 1983

In contrast, the nearest relative's role in cases under section 3 of the MHA 1983 is much more significant. Section 11(4) provides that an AMHP may not make an application for admission for treatment if either:

- the nearest relative has notified the AMHP or the LSSA that he objects to the application being made; or
- the AMHP has not consulted the nearest relative (or the person appearing to be the nearest relative) unless it appears to the AMHP that to consult the nearest relative would not be reasonably practicable or would involve unreasonable delay.

Generally speaking, therefore, the nearest relative must be consulted and the application may not proceed if he objects.

The potential for disagreement between the AMHP and the nearest relative cannot be side-stepped and is, in a sense, the whole point of the consultation. The consultation must put the nearest relative in the position to object if he wishes to and must be a real, not a token exercise (*Re Whitbread (Mental Patient: Habeas Corpus)* (1998) 39 BMLR 94 and *GD v Edgware Community Hospital and London Borough of Barnet* [2008] EWHC 3572 (Admin), [2008] 1 MHLR 282).

The AMHP does not, however, need to ask the nearest relative in terms whether he does in fact object, and need only provide him with the opportunity to object should he wish to do so. This merely requires therefore that, 'the social worker explains to the nearest relative that he or she is considering making an application and why' (*Re Whitbread (Mental Patient: Habeas Corpus)* (1998) 39 BMLR 94).

To prevent an application under section 3 of the MHA 1983, the nearest relative needs to positively object. A simple failure to consent would not render an application unlawful. The test for whether a nearest relative has actually objected, as opposed to, for example, simply expressing some reservations, is an objective one: Has the objection from the nearest relative been put forward in a way which it is reasonable to expect the AMHP to have understood as being an objection (see *M v East London NHS Foundation Trust and London Borough of Hackney* [2009] MHLR 154)?

Failure to consult

An application may also be rendered invalid by a failure to consult the nearest relative at all, unless the AMHP is able to show that a consultation was not reasonably practicable or would have involved unreasonable delay.

The question of unreasonable delay was considered in *R (on the application of GP) v Derby City Council* [2012] EWHC 1451 (Admin), where a patient detained in hospital under section 2 of the MHA 1983 which was due to expire at midnight was assessed for detention under section 3 at about 4.30 that afternoon. The assessment led to a decision to detain, but was concluded without consultation with the nearest relative. The AMHP had tried to contact the nearest relative by mobile telephone several times without success. The decision to detain was unlawful. An argument that the consultation with the nearest relative was not required because it would have involved unreasonable delay was rejected by the court. There was 'no obvious pressing need to certify (and) there was a substantial period from about 4.30 in the afternoon through until midnight in which the consultation process could have been undertaken before the section 3 admission request was signed'.

5.3.5   Consequences of an objection by a nearest relative in cases under section 3 of the Mental Health Act 1983

No application for detention for treatment may proceed where the nearest relative objects, no matter how ill-judged the AMHP believes the objection to be. What then are the options available to the AMHP in such circumstances?

While an AMHP might be tempted to apply for detention for assessment under section 2 of the MHA 1983 as an alternative (on the basis that the nearest relative does not then have the right to object), using section 2 simply as a way of side-stepping the views of an objecting nearest relative would be unlawful (*R v Wilson ex parte Williamson* (1996) COD 42).

Section 29 of the MHA 1983 allows an AMHP to make an application to the county court to displace an existing nearest relative (replacing him with someone more 'suitable') on the grounds 'that the nearest relative of the patient unreasonably objects to the making of an application for admission for treatment' (section 29(4)(c)). This may therefore provide a solution for the AMHP who is faced with an unreasonable nearest relative, but the difficulty for the AMHP is that the patient remains in the community whilst the displacement proceedings take their course. Section 38 of the County Courts Act 1984 does, however, allow the county court to make an interim displacement order, possibly even on a without notice basis (*R (on the application of Holloway) v Oxfordshire City Council* [2007] 1 MHLR 225). If the patient is already detained in hospital under section 2 of the MHA 1983 when the nearest relative objects to detention under section 3 and when the AMHP decides to instigate displacement proceedings as a consequence, section 29(4) of the Act provides that the patient's detention under section 2 will be extended beyond the normal 28-day period until the conclusion of the county court proceedings.

5.4   ROLE OF THE REGISTERED MEDICAL PRACTITIONER

5.4.1   The need for medical recommendations

An application for admission may not proceed without medical recommendations. Except in emergency cases (see para 5.6), there must be two. Both an application for admission for assessment and an application for admission for treatment must be 'founded on the written recommendations in the prescribed form of two registered medical practitioners' (section 2(3) and section 3(3) of the MHA 1983), and in each case the written recommendations must contain a statement to the effect that the relevant admission criteria are met.

5.4.2   Who should be the two registered medical practitioners?

Rules concerning the identity of the two RMPs are set out in section 12 of the MHA 1983. Unsurprisingly, one of the RMPs needs to be approved by the SSH as having special experience in the diagnosis or treatment of a mental disorder (section 12(2)), and if the approved RMP does not have 'previous acquaintance' with the patient, then the other recommendation should 'if practicable' come from an RMP who does (section 12(2)). 'Previous acquaintance' is not defined, but it is 'preferable' (1983 Code, para 4.73) if it is someone who has previously treated the patient.

In *TTM v London Borough of Hackney, East London NHS Foundation Trust and SSH* [2011] EWCA Civ 4, the Court of Appeal declined to offer a definition for the phrase 'if practicable', but noted that it should be interpreted with 'sufficient elasticity' to reflect the fact that applications may have to be made urgently and that professionals can be expected to discharge their responsibilities in a proper way. In that case, the court also noted that where an AMHP is in the invidious position of being faced with two conflicting medical opinions on whether a patient meets the criteria for detention, there is nothing wrong in principle with seeking out a third opinion and relying on that as one of the two recommendations upon which detention is then based.

5.4.3   Duty of the approved mental health professionals

Section 12(1) of the MHA 1983 requires the RMPs to have 'personally examined' the patient, either together or separately. In fact, the 1983 Code suggests (para 4.71) that this medical examination should include:

- direct personal examination of the patient and their mental state; and
- consideration of all available relevant clinical information, including that in the possession of others, professional or non-professional.

The 1983 Code also recommends (para 4.72) that if direct physical access to the patient is not immediately possible and if a postponement of the examination is not desirable, the RMP should consider asking an AMHP to apply for a warrant to enter premises under section 135(1) of the MHA 1983.

5.4.4   Nature of the recommendation

The RMP's recommendation will be in the prescribed form (Form A3 or Form A4 for cases under section 2 of the MHA 1983, Form A7 or Form A8 for cases under section 3), which must include a statement from the RMP that the relevant admission criteria are met.

The RMP should also set out:

- the reasons for reaching that conclusion;
- a description of the patient's symptoms and behaviour;
- an explanation of how the symptoms and behaviour have led to the opinion arrived at;
- (in cases under section 2) an explanation of why the patient ought to be admitted to hospital;
- (in cases under section 3) an explanation of whether other methods of treatment or care (e.g. out-patient treatment or social services) are available and, if so, why they are not appropriate;
- an explanation of why informal admission is not appropriate.

> A medical recommendation in cases under section 3 of the MHA 1983 must involve a certification by the RMP that appropriate treatment is available, and must therefore specify the hospital to which the patient should go. The RMP could certify that appropriate treatment is available if the patient goes to one of a number of specified hospitals (1983 Code, para 4.77). A patient may find himself detained under section 2, not section 3, where there is doubt as to which hospital he will be going to at the time the RMP provides the medical recommendation, and where the RMP is unable to certify therefore that appropriate treatment is available.

5.5   ADDITIONAL PROCEDURAL POINTS

The following additional procedural points apply:

- In cases under section 2 of the MHA 1983, the AMHP's application should be on Form A2 (regulation 4 of the Mental Health Regulations 2008) (or Form A1 if the application is made by the nearest relative). In cases under section 3, the application should be on Form A6 (or Form A5 if the application is made by the nearest relative).
- The medical recommendations must be signed on or before the date of the application (section 12(1)).
- If the RMPs see the patient separately, they must have seen him within 5 clear days of each other (section 12(1)).
- The application must be made within 14 days of the applicant last having seen the patient (section 11(5)). This does not necessarily mean 14 days from the date the AMHP interviewed the patient for the purposes of section 13(2).
- The application for admission should be addressed to the managers of the hospital concerned (section 11(2)) and delivered to an officer of the managers of the hospital, who is authorised by them to receive it (regulation 3(2) of the Mental Health Regulations 2008).
- An application duly completed provides the legal authority for the applicant or someone authorised by him to take and convey the patient to hospital (section 6(1)).
- The patient must be taken to hospital within 14 days of the date upon which the patient was last examined by an RMP providing one of the recommendations (section 6(1)(a)).
- Once admitted to hospital, the application provides a legal authority for the patient to be detained (section 6(2)).

5.6   URGENT ADMISSIONS FOR ASSESSMENT UNDER SECTION 4 OF THE MENTAL HEALTH ACT 1983

5.6.1   Introduction

One of the defining features of applications under section 2 and section 3 of the MHA 1983 is that they are based on two medical recommendations. In urgent cases however, where detention for *assessment* is being contemplated, the Act allows for an expedited procedure, the main effect of which is that an application for admission may be based on one medical recommendation.

This expedited procedure is provided for in section 4 of the MHA 1983. It is a direct alternative to detention under section 2, not section 3, and may only be adopted in the case of applications for admission for assessment. As with any expedited procedure, there is a danger that it may be used more frequently than is appropriate, but section 4 is clear that it is for 'emergency applications' only and the 1983 Code notes (para 5.2) that use of the procedure should be made 'in very limited circumstances'.

5.6.2   Criteria for use

The procedure under section 4 of the MHA 1983 may only be used where the person concerned is deemed to meet the section 2 admission criteria. Assuming that to be the case, section 4 may then be used when the applicant is able to certify that:

- it is of 'urgent necessity' that the patient is admitted under section 2; and
- compliance with the ordinary procedure under section 2 (namely the obtaining of two recommendations) will involve 'undesirable delay' (section 4(2)).

5.6.3   Procedure

If an applicant is able to certify 'urgent necessity' and 'undesirable delay', then the main procedural effect is that the application will be valid if founded on only one medical recommendation (section 4(3) of the MHA 1983). Otherwise, the procedure is essentially the same, albeit with the following modifications to reflect the urgency of the situation:

- the applicant (AMHP or nearest relative) must have personally seen the patient within the previous 24 hours, as opposed to the 14 days normally required (section 4(5));

- an application will be on Form A9 or Form A10, as opposed to Form A1 or Form A2 used in cases under section 2 (regulation 4(1)(e) of the Mental Health Regulations 2008);
- the single doctor making the recommendation (and using Form A11, not Form A3 or Form A4) need not be approved under section 12(2) as 'having special experience in the diagnosis or treatment of mental disorder,' but should 'if practicable' be a doctor who 'has previous acquaintance with the patient' (section 4(3)). Form A11 requires the doctor to estimate how long it would take for a second doctor to arrive and 'what risk such a delay would pose to the patient or other people';
- once completed, the application provides authority to take the patient and convey him to hospital at any time within the 24-hour period beginning with the time when the patient was examined by the doctor or the time when the application was made, whichever is the earlier (section 6(1)(b)).

5.6.4 Effect of detention under section 4 of the Mental Health Act 1983

Detention is authorised for a period of 72 hours from the time when the patient is admitted to the hospital (section 4(4) of the MHA 1983), during which (unless detention is converted to section 2), the patient is not subject to Part IV of the Act and may not be treated under its provisions without his consent (section 56).

Once admitted under section 4 of the MHA 1983, the patient should be examined by an appropriate second doctor as soon as possible, to decide whether he should continue to be detained (1983 Code, para 5.11). If the second medical recommendation required by section 2 is given within 72 hours, and if that second recommendation, together with the initial recommendation relied on for the admission, complies with all the requirements of section 12 (second recommendation should therefore be from a section 12 approved doctor, if the first was not), then section 4 is automatically converted to section 2 from the point at which the second recommendation is received by the hospital managers (section 4(4)). Where section 4 is converted to section 2, the 28-day period runs from the date of admission to hospital under section 4 (section 2(4)).

If the second doctor does not recommend detention under section 2 of the MHA 1983, however, the detention under section 4 continues to run for the 72-hour period, although the patient may be discharged by his nearest relative, by hospital managers or by his RC (section 23).

The patient is entitled to apply to the MHT for discharge (section 66(1)(a) of the MHA 1983), although this will be of little comfort as it is almost inconceivable that a tribunal hearing would be convened within the 72 hours.

The detention under section 4 of the MHA 1983 may not be 'converted' into detention under section 3, but there is nothing to prevent an AMHP making an application under section 3 within the 72-hour period supported by two fresh medical recommendations.

Chapter 6

Police Powers

6.1 INTRODUCTION

Even though no crime may have been committed, the police will often be involved in the process which leads to the admission to hospital of a person with mental disorder. Commonly, their involvement will be to facilitate access to private premises for an assessment under the MHA 1983, or to remove a person with a suspected mental disorder from a public place to a place of safety, again, usually, for an assessment under the Act. The powers created by the Act to cover such situations are considered in this chapter. Also considered are other common law and statutory powers which may be relevant in such circumstances, and the powers available to both the police and mental health professionals to deal with patients who have absconded.

6.2 GAINING ACCESS TO PREMISES FOR ASSESSMENT

6.2.1 Need to gain access

There are requirements on AMHPs and RMPs to have personal contact with a patient before applying for his admission to hospital. For example, the AMHP's interview with the patient before making an application (see para 5.2.3) should be conducted face to face, section 11(5) of the MHA 1983 provides that no application may be made unless the AMHP has 'personally seen' the patient, and section 12(2) requires that the RMPs supplying the medical recommendations must have 'personally examined' the patient.

These obligations carry with them no automatic right to access the premises of the individual concerned and the appropriate legal authority must, therefore, be obtained. Authority may, of course, come from the consent of the patient himself or, failing that, from another occupier of the premises who is entitled to grant access to visitors. Otherwise, the AMHP will need to look elsewhere.

6.2.2   Section 115 of the Mental Health Act 1983

Section 115 of the MHA 1983 provides one potential source of authority in that it allows an AMHP to 'enter and inspect any premises (other than a hospital) in which a mentally disordered patient is living, if he has reasonable cause to believe that the patient is not under proper care' (section 115(1)). This is not a particularly potent weapon in the AMHP's armoury, however. It does not allow access against the wishes of the occupier of the premises (even though by denying access without reasonable cause the occupier is committing an offence under section 129), it does not authorise the AMHP to remove the patient from the premises, and the AMHP cannot use it to insist on a doctor being present to facilitate an MHA assessment.

6.2.3   Section 135(1) of the Mental Health Act 1983

A more productive alternative is likely to be an application to a magistrates' court for a warrant under section 135(1) of the MHA 1983 allowing access to the premises without the consent of the patient.

Under section 135(1) of the MHA 1983, an AMHP may apply to magistrates for a warrant which, if granted, authorises:

> (1)   ...
> any constable to enter, if need be by force, any premises specified in the warrant in which that person is believed to be, and, if thought fit, to remove him to a place of safety with a view to the making of an application in respect of him under Part II of this Act, or of other arrangements for his treatment or care.

Need for a police officer

The *AMHP* is applying for a warrant to allow a *police officer* to gain access to the premises, but section 135(4) of the MHA 1983 requires that the police constable executing the warrant 'shall be accompanied by an approved mental health professional and by a registered medical practitioner', and the 1983 Code advises (para 10.3) that the doctor who accompanies the constable should be approved for the purposes of section 12(2).

Criteria

To obtain the warrant, section 135(1) of the MHA 1983 requires the AMHP to satisfy magistrates that there is reasonable cause to suspect that a person believed to be suffering from mental disorder:

(a)   has been, or is being, ill-treated, neglected or kept otherwise than under proper control, in any place within the jurisdiction of the justice, or

(b)   being unable to care for himself, is living alone in any such place.

In other words, the AMHP will need to satisfy magistrates that the patient may be suffering from a mental disorder and is either not being looked after properly by someone else or is living alone and not looking after himself properly.

Removal to a place of safety

The warrant authorises the constable 'if thought fit, to remove him to a place of safety with a view to the making of an application in respect of him under Part II of this Act, or of other arrangements for his treatment or care' (section 135(1) of the MHA 1983). Once access to the premises is obtained, therefore, the constable must decide in consultation with the mental health professionals whether the patient should be removed to a place of safety. The 1983 Code suggests (para 10.4) that, 'the AMHP and doctor between them, should, if feasible, carry out a preliminary assessment of the person to determine whether they need to be assessed further for an application under the Act or for other arrangements for care or treatment'.

The assumption is that any assessment under the MHA 1983 will be undertaken once the patient has been removed to a place of safety. The 1983 Code notes (para 10.4) that, 'it may be possible to carry out any such further assessment in the premises themselves', but the warrant provides no authority for this and it may only be done, therefore, with the permission of the patient.

Once removed, and taken to a place of safety, a person may be detained there for up to 72 hours (section 135(3) of the MHA 1983). What constitutes a place of safety and what happens during those 72 hours is considered at para 6.4.

6.2.4   Section 17(1)(e) of the Police and Criminal Evidence Act 1984

As a further alternative, perhaps in more urgent situations, the police might use section 17(1)(e) of the Police and Criminal Evidence Act 1984 (PACE 1984), which authorises a constable to enter premises without a warrant for the purpose of 'saving life or limb or preventing serious damage to property'. This authorises no more than entry to the premises, however, and carries with it no power to arrest or detain for an assessment under the MHA 1983 to take place. A person may, however, be arrested for any criminal offence he is suspected to have committed, and the assessment may then take place at a police station following arrest.

6.2.5   Common law power

Police also have the common law power to enter private premises without warrant in order to prevent a breach of the peace. A breach of the peace is committed 'whenever harm is actually done or is likely to be done to a person or in his presence to his property; or a person is in fear of being harmed through an assault, an affray, a riot, unlawful assembly or other disturbance' (*R v Howell* [1981] 3 WLR 501 (CA)). Not only does the common law afford the police the right to enter premises in anticipation of a breach of the peace, it also affords them the power to arrest someone who has committed or is about to commit a breach of the peace.

6.3   REMOVING A PERSON FROM A PUBLIC PLACE

6.3.1   Section 136(1) of the Mental Health Act 1983

Where there are concerns for the mental health of a person who is in a public place, the police may rely on their power under section 136(1) of the MHA 1983. It authorises a constable to remove a person from 'a place to which the public have access' to a 'place of safety' if:

- the person appears to be suffering from a mental disorder;
- the person appears to be in immediate need of care or control;
- the constable thinks it necessary to do so in the interests of that person or for the protection of other persons.

The power may not be used to remove a person from private premises. The *Reference guide to the Mental Health Act 1983* clarifies (para 30.17) that the power may be used in 'any place (whether indoors or outdoors) to which the public have access, whether by right, by explicit or implied permission, on payment or otherwise'.

The power to remove under section 136(1) of the MHA 1983 is a preserved power of arrest (section 26 of and Schedule 2 to the PACE 1984). Subsequent to arrest, therefore, the PACE 1984 provisions will apply.

6.3.2   Subsequent assessment

In contrast to section 135(1) of the MHA 1983, which specifically authorises removal to a place of safety so that an assessment can take place, the power of arrest under section 136(1) has the simple purpose of getting the person to a place of safety. Once there, however, section 136(2) provides that he may be:

(2)   … detained there for a period not exceeding 72 hours for the purpose of enabling him to be examined by a registered medical practitioner and to be interviewed by an approved mental health professional and of making any necessary arrangements for his treatment or care.

6.4   ASSESSMENT AT A PLACE OF SAFETY

6.4.1   Place of safety

For the purposes of sections 135(1) and 136(1) of the MHA 1983, the definition of the 'place of safety' is the same and is defined by section 135(6) as being:

(6)   … residential accommodation provided by a local social services authority under Part III of the National Assistance Act 1948, a hospital as defined by this Act, a police station, an independent hospital or care home for mentally disordered persons or any other suitable place the occupier of which is willing temporarily to receive that patient.

As part of their acute in-patient service, most NHS trusts will have an admission suite to be used for assessments under section 135(1) and section 136(1) of the MHA 1983, and a police station should be the place of safety only in 'exceptional' circumstances (1983 Code, para 10.21) or as a 'last resort' (PACE Code C, para 3.16).

6.4.2   Transfer between places of safety

Sections 135(3)(A) and 136(3) of the MHA 1983 expressly provide that a police officer, an AMHP or a person authorised by either of them may take a patient detained under section 135(1) or section 136(1) from one place of safety to another during the 72-hour period.

6.4.3   Seventy-two hours

Under both sections 135 and 136 of the MHA 1983, the power is to detain for up to 72 hours from the point at which the person arrives at the place of safety. There is a need to get things moving quickly. The 1983 Code notes (para 10.28) that the assessment should begin 'as soon as possible after the arrival of the individual at the place of safety', and PACE Code C notes (para 3.16) that it is 'imperative' the assessment should begin 'as soon as possible'.

Authority for detention lasts only as long as it takes for the assessment to be carried out and will come to an end before the end of the 72 hours if 'it has been decided to make no application in respect of (the patient) under Part 2 of the Act or other arrangements for their treatment or care' (1983 Code, para 10.31).

6.4.4   Rights while detained

Whatever the location of the place of safety, Part IV of the MHA 1983 does not apply and the patient may not be treated under its provisions during the 72-hour period. If the place of safety is a police station, PACE Code C applies. Among other things, this means that the patient has the right to legal advice, to have someone informed of his arrest and to have the assistance of an appropriate adult. If the place of safety is a hospital, the patient must be notified of the basis of his detention and his legal rights (section 132).

6.5   RETURNING PATIENTS WHO ARE ABSENT WITHOUT LEAVE

The MHA 1983 also contains certain powers which allow access to be gained to patients who are absent without leave (AWOL) so that they might be returned to hospital. The 1983 Code contains (para 22.2) a useful summary of the categories of patient who will be deemed AWOL for these purposes. AWOL patients are those who:

- have left the hospital in which they are detained without their absence being agreed (under section 17 of the Act) by their responsible clinician;
- have failed to return to the hospital at the time required to do so by the conditions of leave under section 17;
- are absent without permission from a place where they are required to reside as a condition of leave under section 17;
- have failed to return to the hospital when their leave under section 17 has been revoked;
- are supervised community treatment (SCT) patients who have failed to attend hospital when recalled;
- are SCT patients who have absconded from hospital after being recalled there;
- are conditionally discharged restricted patients whom the Secretary of State for Justice has recalled to hospital; or
- are guardianship patients who are absent without permission from the place where they are required to live by their guardian.

6.5.1   Section 18 of the Mental Health Act 1983

Section 18 of the MHA 1983 provides authority for any such AWOL patient to be taken into custody. In the case of patients on leave under section 17, patients recalled from a CTO and patients recalled from a conditional discharge, section 18 also authorises that they may then be returned to hospital. In the case of guardianship patients, section 18 authorises that they may be returned to the place where they are required to live by their guardian.

The patient on leave under section 17 of the MHA 1983 or recalled from a conditional discharge may be retaken by 'any AMHP, by any officer on the staff of the hospital, by any constable, or by any other person authorised in writing by the managers of the hospital' (section 18(1)). The recalled CTO patient may also be retaken by any of these individuals, and, additionally, by any person authorised in writing by the RC (section 18(2A)). The guardianship patient may be retaken by any officer on the 'staff of a LSSA, by any constable, or by any other person authorised in writing by the guardian or a LSSA' (section 18(3)).

6.5.2   Section 135(2) of the Mental Health Act 1983

Section 18 of the MHA 1983 does not authorise access to private premises in order to retake a patient. When, therefore, an AWOL patient is on private premises and refusing to allow access, separate authority to enter must be obtained. Applying to a magistrates' court for a warrant under section 135(2) is likely to be the most productive option.

Upon application from a constable or any other person who is authorised under the MHA 1983 to re-take the patient, magistrates may issue a warrant under section 135(2) if satisfied:

(a)   that there is reasonable cause to believe that the patient is to be found on premises within the jurisdiction of the justice; and

(b)   that admission to the premises has been refused or that a refusal of such admission is apprehended.

If issued, the warrant will authorise any constable to enter the premises, if need be by force, and remove the patient (section 135(2) of the MHA 1983).

Unlike a warrant under section 135(1) of the MHA 1983, there is no requirement for the constable to be accompanied by an AMHP and RMP, but the 1983 Code advises (para 10.6) that, 'it is good practice for the police officer to be accompanied by a person with authority from the managers of the relevant hospital to take the patient into custody'.

Once the warrant is executed and the patient is taken from the premises, the constable may rely upon his power under section 18 of the MHA 1983 to return him to the hospital or to the place where he must reside.

A patient under section 2 of the MHA 1983 who goes AWOL may not be returned to hospital using powers under section 18 once the 28-day period of detention has expired (section 18(5)).

A patient under section 3 of the MHA 1983 who goes AWOL may not be returned to hospital using powers under section 18 once 6 months have passed since the day he went AWOL, or the end of his detention period has been reached, whichever of these is the later date (section 18(4)).

In either case, if a patient is AWOL on the day that his detention would normally end, or in the week beforehand, then, as long as he arrives back in hospital before the end of the period in which the powers under section 18 of the MHA 1983 can be used to return him, his detention may be extended for a period of up to one week (section 21).

6.5.3   Section 17(1)(d) of the Police and Criminal Evidence Act 1984

As an alternative to a warrant under section 135(2) of the MHA 1983, a constable may enter premises under section 17(1)(d) of the PACE 1984 for the purpose of 'recapturing a person who is unlawfully at large and whom he is pursuing'. However, while there is no doubt that a patient liable to be retaken under section 18 would be a person unlawfully at large for these purposes, section 17(1)(d) only provides authority to enter the premises when the constable is in the act of 'pursuing'. In *D'Souza v DPP* [1992] 1 WLR 1073, a case where a patient, having absconded from hospital, was home by 3.55 pm, but where the police did not reach her house until 7 pm, it was held that the police could not rely on section 17(1)(d) because there was no sense in which they were actively pursuing the woman.

Chapter 7

Holding Powers

7.1 INTRODUCTION

The need to detain someone under the MHA 1983 may emerge after he has agreed to informal hospital admission. For example, a patient who has been admitted informally may then decide to leave hospital against medical advice, or disputes may emerge about treatment. To deal with such situations, section 5(1) allows an application to be made for detention under section 2 or section 3 in respect of a patient who is already receiving in-patient treatment.

Section 5 of the MHA 1983 goes further, however, and provides doctors and nurses with interim holding powers to prevent informal patients from leaving hospital when it is clear that detention under section 2 or section 3 may have become necessary and where an assessment therefore needs to be carried out as a matter of urgency. A doctor's holding power comes from section 5(2) and is for up to 72 hours. A nurse's comes from section 5(4) and is for up to 6 hours. This chapter considers each one.

7.2 DEFINITION OF 'IN-PATIENT'

Both types of holding power exist in relation to an 'in-patient', a term for which the MHA 1983 provides no definition, but which is said by the 1983 Code (para 12.6) to cover 'any person who is receiving in-patient treatment in hospital'. Whatever that means, section 5(4) states that the nurse's holding power only exists in relation to an in-patient 'who is receiving treatment for mental disorder'. For doctors, however, there is no such qualification and the holding power is therefore exercisable in respect of any in-patient receiving treatment in hospital, whether or not of a psychiatric nature.

No definition of the term 'in-patient' is provided either by the MHA 1983 or the 1983 Code. What then is one? According to Wilson J in *R (on the application of DR) v Mersey Care NHS Trust* [2002] EWHC 1810 (Admin), the term 'suggests the allocation and use, albeit not at all times, of a hospital bed'. If allocation of a bed is to be the determining factor, patients admitted electively for treatment completed within a day and not involving the use of a bed will not fall within the definition. A patient treated in an A & E department would also, presumably, fall outside the definition and could not, therefore, be subject to these holding powers.

7.2.1 Exclusions

As far as either power is concerned, someone who is already receiving in-patient treatment as *a detained patient* is specifically excluded from the definition (section 5(6) of the MHA 1983), the effect of which is to prevent section 5 being used to detain someone whose section is about to expire.

A *community patient* (subject to a CTO) who is temporarily in hospital receiving informal in-patient treatment is also specifically excluded from the definition (section 5(6) of the MHA 1983), and holding powers may not, therefore, be used to prevent a community patient from leaving hospital where a formal recall from the CTO is being contemplated.

7.3 DOCTOR'S HOLDING POWER

Section 5(2) of the MHA 1983 provides that a patient may be detained for up to 72 hours for the purpose of carrying out an assessment for admission under section 2 or section 3. The power is exercisable by the 'registered medical practitioner or approved clinician in charge of the patient's treatment', and it is therefore misleading to refer to it, as the 1983 Code does, as being a 'doctor's' holding power. It is exercisable by any professional who would qualify as an approved clinician under the Act (psychologists, nurses, occupational therapists and social workers).

Whoever exercises the power must be the person in charge of the patient's treatment at that time, and if the patient is receiving treatment for a physical condition, it will be the clinician in charge of that treatment. If so, that clinician should 'if possible' consult a psychiatrist or approved clinician before using the power (1983 Code, para 12.10).

The RMP or approved clinician in charge of the treatment may nominate one person to act for him under section 5(2) of the MHA 1983 in his absence. Anyone so nominated as a deputy must be on the staff at the same hospital (section 5(3A)), and should be 'competent to perform the role' (1983 Code, para 12.13).

7.3.1   When may the power be used?

There are no particular criteria that need be satisfied and the power may simply be relied upon to detain a patient where it appears to the RMP or the approved clinician in charge of that patient's treatment 'that an application ought to be made under this Part of this Act for the admission of the patient to hospital' (section 5(2) of the MHA 1983). In completing the necessary Form H1 (regulation 4(1)(g) of the Mental Health Regulations 2008), however, the RMP/approved clinician must state the reasons why he believes that detention is required and should give 'full reasons why informal treatment is no longer appropriate'.

7.3.2   Effect of detention under section 5(2) of the Mental Health Act 1983

Detention is authorised for 72 hours so that an assessment can take place. The 72 hours will run from the point at which the managers have Form H1 handed to them or, alternatively, the point at which the report is placed in the internal mail system (regulation 3(5) of the Mental Health Regulations 2008).

The MHA 1983 contains no mechanism to extend detention under section 5(2) and nor is it easy to imagine how more than 72 hours might be needed to arrange for an assessment. Authority to detain will lapse automatically at the conclusion of the 72-hour period if no detention under section 2 or section 3 has been authorised in the meantime.

Once detention begins, arrangements for an assessment should be put into place immediately (1983 Code, para 12.18). If the outcome of any assessment is that the patient ought to be detained, then detention under section 2 or section 3, as appropriate, will be effective from the point at which the application and supporting medical recommendations are submitted to and accepted by the hospital managers. If the outcome of the assessment is that the patient ought not to be detained then, although detention under section 5(2) lasts for 72 hours, the 1983 Code advises (para 12.20) that patients should 'be informed immediately that they are no longer detained … and are free to leave hospital'. Similarly, if the clinician decides on reflection that no assessment need be carried out, the patient should be told that he is free to leave.

During the 72 hours, the treatment provisions under Part IV of the MHA 1983 do not apply (section 56) and the patient may not, therefore, be treated under the Act without consent.

7.4   NURSE'S HOLDING POWER

Section 5(4) of the MHA 1983 provides a further stop-gap power to detain, this time for a period of 6 hours. The power is exercisable by nurses. Its purpose is to prevent informal patients from leaving hospital before an RMP or approved clinician arrives in order to consider furnishing a report under section 5(2). The power is only exercisable by nurses of the prescribed class, which effectively means those whose area of expertise is either mental health or learning disability nursing (regulation 2 of the Mental Health (Nurses) (England) Order 2008 (SI 2008/1207)).

7.4.1   Relevant criteria

Unlike the power under section 5(2) of the MHA 1983, there are specific criteria which must be met. Section 5(4) requires the nurse to be satisfied:

  (a)   that the patient is suffering from a mental disorder to such a degree that it is necessary for his health or safety or for the protection of others for him to be immediately restrained from leaving the hospital; and

  (b)   that it is not practicable to secure the immediate attendance of a practitioner or clinician for the purpose of furnishing a report under subsection (2) above.

The nurse is therefore required to carry out an assessment before exercising this power. Not only must the nurse consider whether the patient can, in fact, be persuaded to stay long enough to be seen by the RMP or clinician, he must also consider the harm that might occur to the patient or others if the patient does leave immediately. Are the risks to the patient's health or safety or to others so significant that immediate restraint from leaving is required?

Circumstances will determine whether or not it is possible to conduct a full assessment before exercising the power, but there must be an assessment of sorts, and any policy to use section 5(4) of the MHA 1983 as a matter of course in respect of any patient who attempted to leave the ward would be unlawful if it did not require an assessment to be carried out first.

7.4.2   Procedure

Assuming the criteria are met, a nurse must make a record in writing, Form H2 (regulation 4(1)(h) of the Mental Health Regulations 2008), which will then form the basis for the patient's detention (section 5(4) of the MHA 1983). The nurse must arrange for the delivery of that record to the hospital managers as soon as possible after it is made (section 5(5)). The 6 hours runs from the point at which Form H2 is completed (section 5(4)), not when it is received by the managers.

7.4.3   Effect of detention under section 5(4) of the Mental Health Act 1983

Once the record in writing is created, the patient may lawfully be detained for up to 6 hours or until the arrival of an RMP or clinician who is able to furnish a report under section 5(2) of the MHA 1983, if earlier. The 6-hour period is not renewable. It is questionable in fact whether the full 6-hour period would ever be required. As the 1983 Code points out (para 12.32):

> The use of section 5(4) is an emergency measure, and the doctor or approved clinician with the power to use section 5(2) in respect of the patient should treat it as such and arrive as soon as possible. The doctor or approved clinician should not wait six hours before attending simply because this is the maximum time allowed.

As soon as the RMP or approved clinician arrives, the authority to detain under section 5(4) of the MHA 1983 lapses, and, in theory at least, there is then no statutory basis to detain the patient while the RMP or approved clinician assesses whether to furnish a report under section 5(2). Assuming the report is furnished, detention will then run for 72 hours, but with the 72 hours beginning at the point at which the detention under section 5(4) began (section 5(5)). If the doctor decides not to furnish a report, the patient is free to choose whether or not to remain in hospital.

As with section 5(2) of the MHA 1983, the provisions in Part IV do not apply and the Act may not be used to treat the patient without his consent while he is detained under this section.

Part Three

**Detention and Treatment under the Mental
Health Act 1983**

Chapter 8

Consequences of Detention under Part II of the Mental Health Act 1983

8.1   INTRODUCTION

According to section 6(1) of the MHA 1983, a properly completed application will provide sufficient authority for the applicant, or any person authorised by him, to take and convey the patient to the hospital named in the application. Provided the patient is taken and conveyed to the hospital within the authorised timescale (14 days in cases under section 2 and section 3, and 24 hours in cases under section 4 (section 6(1)(a))), the application will then provide sufficient authority for the managers of that hospital to detain the patient in accordance with the provisions of the Act (section 6(2)). How long the patient then remains detained in hospital depends on the provisions of the section under which he is held, and the rules governing the duration of detention under section 2 and section 3 are reviewed in this chapter. Also considered are certain features of detention which are common to both section 2 and section 3.

8.2   RESPONSIBLE CLINICIAN

Once a patient is detained, generally speaking, decisions regarding his treatment will fall to the RC, who is 'the approved clinician with overall responsibility for the patient's case' (section 34 of the MHA 1983). While the range of clinicians who may perform this function is broad, overwhelmingly it will still tend to be psychiatrists. Hospitals should have local protocols in place to allocate RCs to patients, and the 'selection of the appropriate RC should be based on the individual needs of the patient concerned' (1983 Code, para 14.5).

8.3   RIGHTS WHILE DETAINED AND ASPECTS OF TREATMENT

8.3.1   Code of Practice of the Mental Health Act 1983 – statement of guiding principles

All those making decisions regarding patients detained under the MHA 1983 should be mindful of the 1983 Code's guiding principles (1983 Code, Chapter 1). These apply to all decision-making under the Act, but are of particular relevance to detained patients:

Purpose principle
1.2   Decisions under the Act must be taken with a view to minimising the undesirable effects of mental disorder, by maximising the safety and wellbeing (mental and physical) of patients, promoting their recovery and protecting other people from harm.

Least restriction principle
1.3   People taking action without a patient's consent must attempt to keep to a minimum the restrictions they impose on the patient's liberty, having regard to the purpose for which the restrictions are imposed.

Respect principle
1.4   People taking decisions under the Act must recognise and respect the diverse needs, values and circumstances of each patient, including their race, religion, culture, gender, age, sexual orientation and any disability. They must consider the patient's views, wishes and feelings (whether expressed at the time or in advance), so far as they are reasonably ascertainable, and follow those wishes wherever practicable and consistent with the purpose of the decision. There must be no unlawful discrimination.

Participation principle
1.5   Patients must be given the opportunity to be involved, as far as is practicable in the circumstances, in planning, developing and reviewing their own treatment and care to help ensure that it is delivered in a way that is as appropriate and effective for them as possible. The involvement of carers, family members and other people who have an interest in the patient's welfare should be encouraged (unless there are particular reasons to the contrary) and their views taken seriously.

Effectiveness, efficiency and equity principle
1.6   People taking decisions under the Act must seek to use the resources available to them and to patients in the most effective, efficient and equitable way, to meet the needs of patients and achieve the purpose for which the decision was taken.

8.3.2   Information as to legal status and rights

Section 132 of the MHA 1983 requires hospital managers to provide detained patients with information which explains their legal status and their rights, particularly the right to appeal to the MHT. The information should be given 'as soon as practicable after the commencement of the patient's detention' (section 132(1)).

8.3.3   Independent mental health advocates

Section 130A of the MHA 1983 places a duty on the LSSA to make arrangements for IMHAs to be available to provide support to qualifying patients, that is those who are detained under the MHA 1983 (apart from sections 4, 5, 135 and 136), those who are liable to detention under the Act and those subject to conditional discharges, guardianship and CTOs. According to section 130B, the role of the IMHA is to make sure that a patient understands:

(a)   the provisions of the Act by virtue of which he is a qualifying patient;
(b)   any conditions or restrictions to which he is subject by virtue of this Act;
(c)   what (if any) medical treatment is given to him or is proposed or discussed in his case;
(d)   why it is given, proposed or discussed;
(e)   the authority under which it is, or would be, given; and
(f)   the requirements of this Act which apply, or would apply, in connection with the giving of the treatment to him.

There is a duty on hospital managers (or the LSSA in the case of guardianship, or the RC in the case of conditionally discharged patients) to inform the patient of his right to an IMHA (section 130D of the MHA 1983).

8.3.4   Treatment

Patients detained under both section 2 and section 3 of the MHA 1983 are liable to be treated without consent under Part IV. The provisions in Part IV are considered in detail in Chapter 9. Where the RC is not a consultant psychiatrist, and is not therefore qualified to take decisions regarding treatment such as, for example, the administration of medicine, these decisions will be taken by the 'approved clinician in charge of treatment' rather than the RC (see section 58(3) by way of illustration).

8.3.5   Leave

The RC is authorised by section 17 of the MHA 1983 to grant a patient leave from the ward. A patient may not, in fact, leave the ward except with leave authorised by his RC. Section 17 covers leave to the hospital grounds, to the community and to the patient's home. The RC will normally provide the patient with graded leave over time, as a way of testing the patient's resilience to everyday life.

8.3.6   Transfer

A detained patient may be transferred to a different hospital under section 19 of the MHA 1983. Although responsibility for authorising the transfer falls to hospital managers, the responsibility is often, in fact, delegated to the RC (1983 Code, para 30.13).

8.3.7   Discharge

Section 23 of the MHA 1983 provides the RC with the discretionary power to discharge the patient at any time, and although there is no statutory guidance on how the discretion should be exercised, there is a clear duty on the RC to consider discharging as soon as he is satisfied that the criteria for admission are no longer satisfied. This is considered further in Chapter 18. Alternatively, the patient may be discharged by his nearest relative or hospital managers (also considered in Chapter 18), or may apply or have his case referred to the MHT (see Chapters 14–17).

8.4   DETENTION UNDER SECTION 2 OF THE MENTAL HEALTH ACT 1983

Detention under section 2 of the MHA 1983 may be for a period not exceeding 28 days, the period beginning on the day on which the patient is admitted to hospital (section 2(4)).

The 28-day period is not generally capable of extension (section 2(4) of the MHA 1983). The main purpose of detention under section 2 is assessment, and 28 days is regarded as sufficient time to decide, for example, whether longer-term in-patient treatment is required. Exceptionally, however, detention under section 2 may extend beyond 28 days in cases where an application is made under section 29(1) to the county court to displace the nearest relative on the grounds that he unreasonably objects to detention under section 3, or has exercised his power of discharge under section 23 without due regard to the welfare of the patient or the interests of the public. If such an application is made, section 29(4) provides that the patient's detention under section 2 will extend until the conclusion of the county court proceedings.

Detention under section 2 of the MHA 1983 often leads, of course, to detention under section 3. Where this is to occur, the same formal assessment procedure in respect of the proposed section 3 admission will need to be undertaken while the patient is detained under section 2. AMHPs need not wait until the conclusion of the 28 days before applying for detention under section 3. Where an application under section 3 is made during the currency of the detention under section 2, the detention under section 3 will begin on the date that the valid application is received by the hospital managers (section 5(1)). The detention under section 2 will then cease to have effect (section 6(4)).

There should be no back-to-back detentions under section 2 of the MHA 1983 (section 2(4)). If it becomes clear during the course of the 28 days that a patient requires detention for longer, the appropriate course is to apply for admission under section 3. It would be unlawful for there to be successive applications under section 2 simply as a way of extending detention beyond the initial 28-day period (*R v Wilson ex parte Williamson* (1996) COD 42).

Detention under section 2 of the MHA 1983 will almost always lead to one of the following outcomes:

- during the 28 days, the patient is discharged, either under section 23 or by the MHT, and either leaves hospital or remains in hospital voluntarily (section 131);
- before the expiry of the 28 days, the patient is assessed and detained under section 3;
- at the end of the 28 days, the section is allowed to lapse and the patient leaves hospital, or remains in hospital on a voluntary basis (section 131).

8.5   DETENTION UNDER SECTION 3 OF THE MENTAL HEALTH ACT 1983

The patient may be detained under section 3 of the MHA 1983 for treatment, initially for a period not exceeding 6 months, beginning on the date he was admitted to hospital (section 20(1)), or, if he was previously detained under section 2 or was an informal patient, beginning on the date the application under section 3 is received by the hospital managers (section 5(1)).

Unlike detention under section 2 of the MHA 1983, detention under section 3 is renewable. Following the initial 6-month period, detention may be renewed for a further period of 6 months and then for further periods of one year at a time (section 20(2)). If the detention is not renewed, authority to detain will lapse at the conclusion of the current period (section 20(1)).

8.5.1   Renewal of detention

Whether to renew detention under section 3 of the MHA 1983 is, in the first instance, a decision for the RC, who will examine the patient and, if satisfied that the criteria for detention remain in place, will furnish a report to the hospital managers. It is, in fact, the furnishing of the report which then forms the legal basis for renewal and for the patient's ongoing detention (section 20(3)).

Since the RC is defined as 'the approved clinician with overall responsibility for the patient's case' (section 34 of the MHA 1983) and might, therefore, be a consultant psychiatrist, a psychologist, an occupational therapist, a social worker or a nurse, it is possible, in theory at least, that the renewal of a patient's detention under section 20 may be on the basis of a report furnished by a clinician other than a psychiatrist. In *Winterwerp v The Netherlands* (Application No 6301/73) [1979] ECHR 4 (see para 2.7.2), the view expressed by the ECtHR was that for detention to be lawful, there must be evidence of mental disorder based on 'objective medical expertise'. The question arises, therefore, whether a renewal based on a report from, say, a social worker can be lawful. Is detention subsequent to that renewal based on 'objective medical expertise'? Arguably not. Even so, the problem may be remedied if the RC, when consulting another mental health professional as required (see para 8.5.2), ensures that the consultation is with someone who is able to demonstrate 'medical expertise'.

8.5.2   Responsible clinician's duty to consult

Although it is the RC's responsibility to furnish the report which forms the basis of renewal, he is required beforehand to 'consult one or more other persons who have been professionally concerned with a patient's medical treatment' (section 20(5) of the MHA 1983). In fact, the requirement goes further. The RC may not furnish his report authorising renewal unless a person who has been professionally concerned with the patient's medical treatment (and who is not a member of the same profession as the RC) states in writing that he agrees that the criteria for renewal are made out (section 20(5A)). The 1983 Code advises (para 29.6) that the second professional to be consulted by the RC should:

- have sufficient experience and expertise to decide whether the patient's continued detention is necessary and lawful, but need not be approved clinicians (nor be qualified to be one);
- have been actively involved in the planning, management or delivery of the patient's treatment; and
- have had sufficient recent contact with the patient to be able to make an informed judgement about the patient's case.

The 1983 Code also advises (para 29.9) that unless there are exceptional circumstances, the RC should accept the decision of the second professional even where he does not agree with it.

8.5.3   Criteria for renewal

In any event, the RC may only furnish a report renewing detention if satisfied that the renewal criteria set out in section 20(4) of the MHA 1983 are present. These are:

(a)   the patient is suffering from mental disorder of a nature or degree which makes it appropriate for him to receive medical treatment in a hospital; and

(b)   [....]

(c)   it is necessary for the health or safety of the patient or for the protection of other persons that he should receive such treatment and that it cannot be provided unless he continues to be detained; and

(d)   appropriate medical treatment is available for him.

8.5.4   Procedural requirements

Section 20(3) of the MHA 1983 requires the RC to examine the patient and, if appropriate, furnish the relevant report within the 2-month period ending on the day on which the patient would cease to be liable to be detained if his section were not renewed. The report must be in the prescribed form, Form H5 (regulation 13 of the Mental Health Regulations 2008). Section 20(3)(b) requires Form H5 to be furnished to the managers at the hospital where the patient is detained. It also requires managers to notify the patient of the renewal. It is not for the managers to renew the section; that is the responsibility of the RC. However, managers are expected to conduct a review of detention whenever it is renewed (see para 18.2.3).

Chapter 9

Medical Treatment Authorised under Part IV of the Mental Health Act 1983

9.1 INTRODUCTION

Following admission to hospital, the authority to treat the mental disorder of a patient detained under the MHA 1983 generally comes from Part IV, and any treatment must therefore be in accordance with its provisions. In outline, Part IV provides the general authority to treat a patient without his consent, identifies certain types of treatment in respect of which special safeguards must apply, and identifies circumstances in which those special safeguards can be temporarily overlooked. Each of these aspects of the provisions in Part IV is considered in this chapter.

9.2 PATIENTS TO WHOM PART IV OF THE MENTAL HEALTH ACT 1983 APPLIES

Section 56 of the MHA 1983 identifies the patients to whom Part IV applies. Virtually all patients detained under the Act (whether under the civil or criminal detaining sections) are subject to its provisions. The small category of detained patients who are not, are those detained under the Act's short-term sections, that is sections 4, 5, 35, 37(4), 45A(5), 135 and 136 (section 56(3)). Any such patients may not be treated under the authority of the Act and may only, therefore, be treated with their consent or, if they lack capacity, in accordance with the MCA 2005.

It should be noted that there is a very small category of voluntary or informal patients to whom Part IV of the MHA 1983 also applies. This category consists of patients receiving certain types of treatment for mental disorder which are serious enough to merit special safeguards even though the patient consents and is not detained under the Act. It includes patients receiving neurosurgery or surgical implantation of hormones (section 57), and patients aged under 18 receiving electroconvulsive therapy (ECT) treatment (section 58A). Even though the patient is not detained under the Act, any treatment must be in accordance with the relevant provisions of Part IV.

9.3   TREATMENT UNDER THE MENTAL CAPACITY ACT 2005

Before looking at the provisions concerning treatment under the MHA 1983, it is worth briefly considering the alternative possibility of treatment under the MCA 2005.

9.3.1   Use of the Mental Capacity Act 2005 where patients are not detained under the Mental Health Act 1983

A patient who is 16 or older and is admitted to hospital on an informal basis (that is, he is not detained under the MHA 1983), but who lacks the capacity to consent to treatment, may be treated for any mental disorder under the MCA 2005. Decisions regarding treatment would need to be taken in accordance with the general principles set out in Chapter 22. Where a patient requires treatment for mental disorder, however, clinicians should avoid treating under the MCA 2005 when treatment under the MHA 1983 would be more appropriate. Treatment for mental disorder may be authorised under either Act, and the MHA 1983 should only be used where it is necessary, but, as a general rule, if a patient meets the criteria for detention under the MHA 1983 and is objecting to any treatment for the mental disorder, then the MHA 1983 should be used, not the MCA 2005 (*GJ v Foundation Trust* [2009] EWHC 2972 (Fam)).

9.3.2   Use of the Mental Capacity Act 2005 where patients are detained under the Mental Health Act 1983

The MCA 2005 may not be used to authorise treatment for mental disorder where the patient's treatment is already regulated by the MHA 1983 (section 28(1) of the MCA 2005). Generally speaking, this means that the MCA 2005 may not be used to treat the mental disorder of a patient who is already detained under the MHA 1983; authority for treatment should come from the MHA 1983 itself. As already seen, however (para 9.2), there are certain patients detained under the MHA 1983 to whom Part IV does not apply and whose treatment is not therefore regulated by that Act. These patients may receive treatment for their mental disorder under the MCA 2005 even though detained under the MHA 1983.

The provisions in Part IV of the MHA 1983 only apply to treatment for *mental disorder* and, therefore, the MCA 2005 may be used to authorise other types of treatment for a detained patient, for example treatment for a physical disorder.

9.4 THE EUROPEAN CONVENTION ON HUMAN RIGHTS AND TREATMENT UNDER THE MENTAL HEALTH ACT 1983

Whatever treatment may be authorised under Part IV of the MHA 1983, the clinician who administers it must bear in mind that he is performing a role as a public body and is taking actions which are subject to the provisions of the ECHR.

As already noted (see para 2.7), Article 3 of the ECHR provides that, 'no one shall be subjected to torture or to inhuman or degrading treatment or punishment', and it has been held in various cases, for example, *Herczegfalvy v Austria* (Application No 10533/83) [1992] ECHR 83, that the compulsory administration of treatment to a detained patient could conceivably constitute inhuman or degrading treatment for these purposes. In the *Herczegfalvy* case, the treatment complained of was the forcible administering of food and neuroleptics while the patient was isolated and handcuffed to a security bed. The ECtHR ruled that, as a matter of principle, treatment which is therapeutically necessary cannot be regarded as inhuman or degrading. The court also ruled, however, that therapeutic necessity must have been 'convincingly shown to exist'. On the facts, although the court was worried, in particular, by the length of time over which the treatment was applied, it concluded that the evidence before it was not sufficient to disprove the argument from the Austrian government that it was justified by medical necessity.

In *R (on the application of N) v Doctor 'M' and others* [2002] EWCA Civ 1789, the Court of Appeal held that whether therapeutic necessity had been 'convincingly shown to exist' depended on a number of factors (at [19]):

> including (a) how certain is it that the patient does suffer from a treatable mental disorder; (b) how serious a disorder is it; (c) how serious a risk is presented to others; (d) how likely is it that, if the patient does suffer from such a disorder, the proposed treatment will alleviate the condition; (e) how much alleviation is there likely to be; (f) how likely is it that the treatment will have adverse consequences for the patient; and (g) how severe may they be.

As well as engaging Article 3 of the ECHR, treatment against a patient's will also engages Article 8 (see *Glass v UK* (Application No 61827/00) [2004] ECHR 103 and *X v Finland* (Application No 34806/04) [2012] ECHR 1371.

9.5   SECTION 63 OF THE MENTAL HEALTH ACT 1983 – GENERAL AUTHORITY TO TREAT WITHOUT CONSENT

Part IV of the MHA 1983 authorises treatment of a patient without consent. The authority comes from section 63, which provides that the 'consent of a patient shall not be required for any medical treatment given to him for the mental disorder from which he is suffering ... if the treatment is given by or under the direction of the approved clinician in charge of the treatment'.

The scope of this general authority to treat under section 63 of the MHA 1983 is considerable. It is subject to statutory safeguards in respect of certain types of treatment (considered in this chapter), but what is striking is how few statutory safeguards the Act creates. Seclusion, force-feeding (see para 9.5.3), the administration of medicine for up to 3 months, even the administration of a Caesarean section (see para 9.5.2) are all examples of treatment which may be carried out under the general authority of section 63, and in respect of which no additional statutory safeguards apply.

9.5.1   Treatment by consent under the Mental Health Act 1983

The fact that section 63 of the MHA 1983 authorises treatment without the patient's consent does not alter the fact that a patient may consent to treatment even though detained. Such consent will then provide lawful authority for the treatment as long as it is informed consent, as long as the patient has capacity to give it, and as long as any other particular safeguards stipulated by the Act have been complied with. The 1983 Code indicates (para 23.42) that the formulation of a treatment plan in respect of all detained patients is essential, and that the patient's consent should be sought before any treatment is given (para 23.37).

9.5.2   Defining medical treatment for the purposes of section 63 of the Mental Health Act 1983

Section 63 of the MHA 1983 provides that the patient's consent is not required for 'any medical treatment given to him for the mental disorder from which he is suffering'. What then constitutes medical treatment for the mental disorder? The answer is that there is no catch-all definition.

Very often, it means the administration of medicine. ECT would also fall within the definition, as would psychological therapy, although, practically speaking, it is difficult to imagine this type of therapy being delivered without consent.

Section 145(1) of the MHA 1983 offers some help by clarifying that treatment includes 'nursing, psychological intervention and specialist mental health habilitation, rehabilitation and care'. In this context, 'habilitation' means 'equipping someone with skills and abilities they never had' and 'rehabilitation' means 'helping them recover skills and abilities they have lost' (1983 Code, para 6.2).

The definition covers treatment which 'consists only of nursing and specialist day-to-day care under the clinical supervision of an approved clinician, in a safe and therapeutic environment with a structured regime' (1983 Code, para 6.16). In other words, there may be some patients for whom the therapeutic input is relatively minor. However, the definition of treatment does not extend to cover detention simply for its own sake.

The definition will extend to cover the management and control of patients as part of their overall treatment. The power to restrain a patient for the purposes of, for example, preventing disturbed or violent behaviour, or administering medicine, is not referred to explicitly in the MHA 1983, but is confirmed in Chapter 15 of the 1983 Code, while in *R v Ashworth Hospital Authority (now Mersey Care NHS Trust) ex parte Munjaz* [2005] UKHL 58, Lord Bingham offered the view that, 'the power to seclude a patient within the hospital is implied from the power to detain as a "necessary ingredient flowing from a power of detention for treatment"' (quoting Auld J in *R v Broadmoor Special Hospital Authority ex parte S, H and D* 5 February 1998 (unreported)).

9.5.3 Treatment for physical disorder under the Mental Health Act 1983

Section 145(4) of the MHA 1983 takes the definition of treatment further. It provides that:

> Any reference in this Act to medical treatment, in relation to mental disorder, shall be construed as a reference to medical treatment the purpose of which is to alleviate, or prevent a worsening of, the disorder or one or more of its symptoms or manifestations.

Applying this definition, treatment under section 63 of the MHA 1983 may extend to cover certain types of physical treatment.

In *B v Croydon Health Authority* [1995] 1 All ER 683, Lord Hoffmann held that section 63 of the MHA 1983 covers acts of physical treatment to include 'nursing and care concurrent with the care treatment or as a necessary pre-requisite to such treatment or to prevent the patient from causing harm to himself or to alleviate the consequences of the disorder'. He noted that (at pp 687–688):

> it would seem to me strange if a hospital could, without the patient's consent, give him treatment directed to alleviating a psychopathic disorder showing itself in suicidal tendencies, but not without such consent be able to treat the consequences of a suicide attempt.

Applying that logic, Lord Hoffmann agreed that section 63 of the MHA 1983 was a lawful basis for authorising naso-gastric feeding of a patient who, as a result of borderline personality disorder, was refusing to eat.

Treatment for physical health problems, for example the consequences of a suicide attempt or of a refusal to eat, therefore, falls within the definition of treatment for mental disorder, but only on the basis that the physical health problems are caused by the mental disorder.

Treatment for the physical consequences of a mental disorder must be distinguished, however, from treatment for a physical disorder which exists alongside the mental disorder but has no connection with it. Generally speaking, section 63 of the MHA 1983 does not authorise treatment without consent for a concurrent but unrelated physical disorder, even where the patient's refusal to accept treatment for that physical disorder is caused by mental disorder. In *B v Croydon Health Authority* [1995] 1 All ER 683, for example, Lord Hoffmann distinguished the facts with which he was dealing from those in *Re C* [1994] 1 WLR 290, the famous case of a patient with schizophrenia who refused treatment for a gangrenous leg. In *Re C*, the gangrene was entirely unconnected to the mental disorder, and so section 63 did not apply, even though the refusal to accept treatment was a consequence of the mental disorder.

The point was subsequently confirmed in *GJ v The Foundation Trust* [2009] EWHC 2972 (Fam), a case in which it was also held that the only circumstances in which treatment of an unrelated physical disorder might fall within section 63 of the MHA 1983 are those where treatment of the physical disorder could have a direct impact on the mental disorder itself. Reference was made to *Tameside and Glossop Acute Services Trust v CH* [1996] 1 FLR 762, in which Wall J held that a Caesarean section operation could be authorised under section 63 as treatment for mental disorder after concluding that the 'achievement of a successful outcome of her pregnancy is a necessary part of the overall treatment of her mental disorder'. Wall J, like Lord Hoffmann, distinguished the facts in his case from those in *Re C* [1994] 1 WLR 290. Whereas the safe delivery of the child was likely to have a positive impact on the mother's mental health, the successful treatment of the gangrenous leg was likely to have no impact at all on C's mental health.

Of course, where treatment is considered necessary for a physical disorder which is not covered by section 63 of the MHA 1983, clinicians may consider the use of the MCA 2005.

9.6   STATUTORY SAFEGUARDS IN RESPECT OF CERTAIN TYPES OF TREATMENT

Whatever general authority is supplied by section 63 of the MHA 1983, it is subject to the specific safeguards created in respect of certain types of treatment by sections 57, 58 and 58A. Each is considered below.

9.6.1   Section 57 of the Mental Health Act 1983 – safeguards for neurosurgery and surgical implantations of hormones

Neurosurgery and the surgical implantation of hormones (the purpose of which is to reduce the male sex drive), two very rare forms of treatment for mental disorder, may only be given where special safeguards are in place. According to section 57(2) of the MHA 1983, such treatment is only permissible where the patient consents *and*:

(a)   a registered medical practitioner appointed for the purposes of this Part of this Act by the regulatory authority (not being the responsible clinician (if there is one) or the person in charge of the treatment in question) and two other persons appointed for the purposes of this paragraph by the regulatory authority (not being registered medical practitioners) have certified in writing that the patient is capable of understanding the nature, purpose and likely effects of the treatment in question and has consented to it; and

(b)   the registered medical practitioner referred to in paragraph (a) above has certified in writing that it is appropriate for the treatment to be given.

In fact, the safeguards apply to this type of treatment whether or not the patient is detained under the MHA 1983 (section 56(1)).

9.6.2   Section 58 of the Mental Health Act 1983 – safeguards for the administration of medicine

Administration of medicine to a detained patient without that patient's consent is authorised in the short term under the general provisions of section 63 of the MHA 1983. The administration of medicine beyond 3 months, however, must be in accordance with the safeguards set out in section 58.

The safeguards apply 'if three months or more have elapsed since the first occasion in that period when medicine was administered to him by any means for his mental disorder' (section 58(1)(b)). They apply, therefore, whether the type of medicine has changed, whether the form of administration (e.g. oral to depot) has changed, and also whether or not the medicine has been administered regularly throughout the 3-month period. The requirement is simply that there has been a 3-month period since the first administration of medicine however many (or few) administrations there have been in the meantime.

The safeguards

According to section 58(3) of the MHA 1983, no medicine for the mental disorder may be given to the patient beyond the 3-month period unless either:

(a)   he has consented to that treatment and either the approved clinician in charge of it or a registered medical practitioner appointed for the purposes of this Part of this Act by the regulatory authority has certified in writing that the patient is capable of understanding its nature, purpose and likely effects and has consented to it; or

(b)   a registered medical practitioner appointed as aforesaid (not being the responsible clinician or the approved clinician in charge of the treatment in question) has certified in writing that the patient is not capable of understanding the nature, purpose and likely effects of that treatment or being so capable has not consented to it but that it is appropriate for the treatment to be given.

In other words, medicine may only be given beyond the 3-month period if the patient provides informed consent or, where he cannot or will not provide informed consent, a second opinion appointed doctor (SOAD) certifies that the treatment is appropriate.

The following changes in legal status will have no bearing on the requirement to apply the safeguards under section 58 of the MHA 1983 3 months from the first administration of the medicine:

- the patient's section changes (e.g. from section 2 to section 3);
- the patient is granted leave under section 17;
- the patient is transferred from one hospital to another under section 19;
- the patient's section is renewed;
- the patient is placed on a CTO;
- the patient's CTO is revoked.

Form T2

Form T2 (regulation 27(2) of the Mental Health Regulations 2008) must be completed in all cases where treatment beyond 3 months is authorised under section 58(3)(a) of the MHA 1983 on the basis of the patient's consent.

Form T2 should be completed and signed, either by the approved clinician or by a SOAD (usually the former), who will certify that the patient has the capacity to consent to the treatment, and will describe the particular type of treatment to which the patient has consented. Once completed, Form T2 provides authority to treat the patient beyond the 3-month period, in theory for an indefinite period, although the 1983 Code advises (para 24.72) that, 'it is good practice for the clinician in charge of the treatment to review them at regular intervals'.

Form T2 remains valid as long as the patient continues to consent to the treatment described. If consent to treatment is withdrawn by the patient then Form T3 will be required (see below). If treatment changes, a new authority will be required, either a new Form T2, if the patient consents, or Form T3 otherwise. A new authority for treatment will also be required if the approved clinician in charge of treatment changes.

Form T3

Form T3 (regulation 27(2) of the Mental Health Regulations 2008) must be completed in all cases where treatment beyond 3 months is authorised under section 58(3)(b) of the MHA 1983 on the basis of a SOAD's agreement because the patient cannot or will not consent.

Before issuing Form T3, the SOAD must consult two others professionally concerned with the patient's treatment, neither of whom may be the RC or approved clinician in charge of treatment. One must be a nurse. The other must be someone other than a nurse or RMP (section 58(4) of the MHA 1983). The 1983 Code reminds (para 24.56) SOADs that they must 'act as independent professionals and must reach their own judgement about whether the proposed treatment is appropriate'.

If treatment is authorised under Form T3, it will be for an indefinite period, although may also be time limited. The CQC recommends that, 'Forms T3 should not normally be extant for more than two years' (*Guidance Note for Commissioners on consent to treatment and the Mental Health Act 1983*, CQC, September 2008).

Treatment authorised under Form T3 may continue if there is a subsequent change of approved clinician.

Where Form T3 authorises treatment on the basis of lack of capacity, it cannot then be used to authorise treatment if the patient regains capacity. Where Form T3 authorises treatment on the basis of lack of consent, it cannot then be used to authorise treatment if the patient subsequently loses capacity.

9.6.3   Section 58A of the Mental Health Act 1983 – safeguards for electroconvulsive therapy treatment

Section 58A of the MHA 1983 establishes safeguards in respect of ECT treatment for:

- any detained patient;
- any other patient under the age of 18 who 'is capable of understanding the nature, purpose and likely effects of the treatment'.

Alternative sources of authority for electroconvulsive therapy when section 58A of the Mental Health Act 1983 does not apply

For any other category of patient, that is, informal adult in-patients, or informal in-patients aged under 18 who are not 'capable of understanding the nature, purpose and likely effects of treatment', authority for ECT treatment will need to come from elsewhere. For *informal adult patients*, this may be the patient's consent or the MCA 2005. For *informal 16 or 17 year olds* without the capability to 'understand the nature, purpose and likely effects of treatment', this may be the MCA 2005. For *informal under 16 year olds* without that capability, this may be the consent of those with parental responsibility (depending on the arguable point of whether ECT treatment could fall within the zone of parental control (see para 24.3.2)), or the High Court.

Safeguards under section 58A of the Mental Health Act 1983

For those to whom section 58A of the MHA 1983 applies, the safeguards provided by the Act can be summarised as follows:

- detained adult patients who are capable of understanding the nature, purpose and likely effects of the treatment may only be treated with their consent (section 58A(3));
- detained adult patients who are not capable of understanding the nature, purpose and likely effects of treatment may only be treated with the authorisation of a SOAD (section 58A(5));
- detained under 18 year olds who are capable of understanding the nature, purpose and likely effects of the treatment may only be treated with their consent *and* the authorisation of a SOAD (section 58A(4));

- detained under 18 year olds who are not capable of understanding the nature, purpose and likely effects of the treatment may only be treated with the authorisation of a SOAD (section 58A(5));
- informal under 18 year olds who are capable of understanding the nature, purpose and likely effects of the treatment may only be treated with their consent *and* the authorisation of a SOAD (section 58A(4)).

Table 9.1 summarises the various sources of authority for ECT treatment depending on the patient's age, legal status and capacity to consent.

9.7   SECTION 62 OF THE MENTAL HEALTH ACT 1983 – URGENT TREATMENT WHERE THE STATUTORY SAFEGUARDS NEED NOT APPLY

Sections 57, 58 and 58A of the MHA 1983 are all expressly subject to section 62 which provides that in certain urgent cases, the safeguards in each of those sections need not apply. To justify forgoing the safeguards, there must be the immediate necessity of treatment in order to avoid very serious consequences. As the 1983 Code puts it (para 24.34), these are strict tests and 'it is not enough for there to be an urgent need for treatment or for the clinicians involved to believe that treatment is necessary or beneficial'. Furthermore, treatment without the statutory safeguards may only continue for as long as it remains immediately necessary.

9.7.1   Urgent treatment under section 57 or section 58 of the Mental Health Act 1983

According to section 62(1) of the MHA 1983, the normal safeguards provided by section 57 and section 58 need not apply to any treatment:

(a)   which is immediately necessary to save the patient's life;

(b)   which (not being irreversible) is immediately necessary to prevent a serious deterioration of his condition; or

(c)   which (not being irreversible or hazardous) is immediately necessary to alleviate serious suffering by the patient; or

(d)   which (not being irreversible or hazardous) is immediately necessary and represents the minimum interference necessary to prevent the patient from behaving violently or being a danger to himself or to others.

Table 9.1   Authority for electroconvulsive therapy treatment

Age of patient	Legal status	'Capacity'	Consent?	Authority for treatment
Adult	Detained	Yes	Yes	Approved clinician or SOAD certifies capacity and consent (section 58A(3))
Adult	Detained	Yes	No	None
Adult	Detained	No	N/A	SOAD certifies lack of capacity and that treatment is appropriate and does not conflict with advance decision or decision of donee or deputy (section 58A(5))
Adult	Informal	Yes	Yes	Patient
Adult	Informal	Yes	No	None
Adult	Informal	No	N/A	MCA 2005
16/17	Detained	Yes	Yes	SOAD certifies capacity, consent and that treatment is appropriate (section 58A(4))
16/17	Detained	Yes	No	None
16/17	Detained	No	N/A	SOAD certifies lack of capacity and that treatment is appropriate and does not conflict with advance decision or decision of donee or deputy (section 58A(5))
16/17	Informal	Yes	Yes	SOAD certifies capacity, consent and that treatment is appropriate (section 58A(4))
16/17	Informal	Yes	No	None
16/17	Informal	No	N/A	MCA 2005 or with consent from those with parental responsibility (if in zone of parental control) or High Court
Under 16	Detained	Yes	Yes	SOAD certifies consent, capacity and that treatment is appropriate (section 58A(4))
Under 16	Detained	Yes	No	None
Under 16	Detained	No	N/A	SOAD certifies lack of capacity and that treatment is appropriate (section 58A(5))
Under 16	Informal	Yes	Yes	SOAD certifies capacity, consent and that treatment is appropriate (section 58A(4))
Under 16	Informal	Yes	No	None
Under 16	Informal	No	N/A	Consent of those with parental responsibility (if within zone of parental control) or High Court

9.7.2   Urgent treatment under section 58A of the Mental Health Act 1983

According to section 62(1A) of the MHA 1983, the normal section 58A safeguards in respect of ECT treatment need not apply if it is:

(a)   immediately necessary to save the patient's life; or

(b)   (not being irreversible) is immediately necessary to prevent a serious deterioration of his condition.

9.8   COMMUNITY TREATMENT ORDER PATIENTS RECALLED TO HOSPITAL

Section 62A of the MHA 1983 sets out the provisions concerning the treatment of CTO patients who are recalled for up to 72 hours or whose CTO is revoked. Although contained within Part IV, these provisions are considered in the context of CTOs generally in Chapter 20.

Part Four

Criminal Admissions under the Mental Health Act 1983

Chapter 10

Criminal Court Orders under Part III of the Mental Health Act 1983

10.1 INTRODUCTION

The alternative to a hospital admission under the civil provisions in Part II of the MHA 1983 is an admission from the criminal justice system. Part III applies. It sets out the powers available to criminal courts to order detention in hospital for assessment or treatment, and to the SSJ to order transfer from prison to hospital for similar reasons.

The range of orders that a criminal court may make in respect of a mentally disordered offender, or suspected offender, is considered in this chapter. There is particular emphasis on the most common, a hospital order under section 37 of the MHA 1983, but the chapter summarises all powers available to magistrates and the Crown Court in respect of all defendants, whether sentenced or not. The powers of transfer available to the SSJ are considered in Chapter 12.

Two particular types of sentence, a restriction order under section 41 of the MHA 1983 and a hospital direction under section 45A, are considered separately, in Chapters 11 and 13, respectively.

10.2 HOSPITAL ORDERS UNDER SECTION 37 OF THE MENTAL HEALTH ACT 1983

Section 37 of the MHA 1983 provides the Crown Court and magistrates with the power to order that a defendant is sent to hospital for treatment for mental disorder. The power is available in either court as a sentence following conviction (see para 10.2.1) and, in the magistrates' court, when mental disorder means that the defendant is too unwell to plead (see para 10.2.6). The effect of the order is that, in most respects, the defendant is treated as though subject to section 3 from the moment he begins his sentence.

10.2.1   Offences punishable by imprisonment

Subject to the relevant criteria being met (see para 10.2.2), the magistrates' court and Crown Court may impose a hospital order on any person convicted of any offence punishable with imprisonment, except murder (section 37(1)).

10.2.2   Criteria

Before a court makes the order, section 37(2)(a)(i) of the MHA 1983 requires it to be satisfied that:

- the offender is suffering from a mental disorder of a nature or degree which makes it appropriate for him to be detained in hospital for medical treatment; and
- appropriate medical treatment is available for him.

These criteria are, of course, similar to the criteria in section 3 of the MHA 1983, but section 37 does not require treatment to be 'necessary'. It is enough that the offender has committed a criminal act and is suffering from a mental disorder of a nature or degree which makes treatment 'appropriate'.

The requirement is that the offender 'is suffering' from a mental disorder. What is relevant, therefore, is his mental state at the time of sentence, not at the time of the offence. It follows that a link between mental illness and the offence itself 'is not a pre-condition for the making of a hospital order' (Keene LJ in *R v Smith* [2001] EWCA Crim 743). As with civil admissions, the words 'is suffering' do not mean that the offender must be symptomatic.

10.2.3   Most suitable method of disposal of the case

That the criteria are met does not mean that a hospital order must be imposed. A court has a discretion and must be of the opinion (section 37(2)(b)):

> (b)   … having regard to all the circumstances including the nature of the offence and the character and antecedents of the offender, and to the other available methods of dealing with him, that the most suitable method of disposing of the case is by means of an order under this section.

The first issue will be whether the case is serious enough for a hospital order. Although not a punishment, a hospital order is a form of detention and should only be used, therefore, as an alternative to another form of detention. A case is not serious enough for a hospital order if it is not otherwise serious enough for a custodial sentence (*R v Birch* (1989) 11 Cr App R (S) 202).

Assuming the case to be serious enough, a court may have little difficulty in concluding that a hospital order is the most suitable method of disposing of the case, where, perhaps, the link between the offence and the mental disorder is very strong, and/or where the evidence suggests that the risk of further offending is best addressed by treatment for the disorder in hospital. However, there is no presumption in favour of hospital and no reason in principle why a mentally disordered offender should not go to prison. In *R v Drew* [2003] UKHL 25, for example, Lord Bingham confirmed that, 'it cannot, as a matter of national law, be stigmatised as wrong in principle to pass a sentence of imprisonment on a mentally disordered defendant who is criminally responsible and fit to be tried'.

In *R v Birch* (1989) 11 Cr App R (S) 202, Mustill LJ suggested that there are two particular (separate) reasons why prison may be preferred to hospital. Firstly, the offender is 'dangerous and no suitable secure hospital is available'. Secondly, there is 'an element of culpability in the offence which merits punishment'.

Dangerousness

The offender's dangerousness ought not to be a reason for the imposition of a prison sentence without the court having first considered its power under section 41 of the MHA 1983 to impose a restriction order to accompany a hospital order (see Chapter 11). The restriction order may be imposed when there is a risk of serious harm to the public from a mentally disordered offender. The consequences for the offender are significant (see para 11.6). He is likely to be in hospital for significantly longer than he would be if on a straightforward hospital order, and, when discharged, is likely to be liable to recall to hospital for several years. Added to that, he will, of course, unlike in prison, receive treatment for his mental disorder. The hospital order with restrictions may therefore be sufficient to meet the heightened risk and may, in fact, be a more appropriate sentence in the long term (see para 11.4 for a further discussion on this point).

Culpability

The offender may, however, be culpable to the extent that he deserves a prison sentence. This may be because the commission of the offence had nothing to do with the offender's mental disorder, or because the offender's responsibility for the offence is reduced by his mental disorder, but not 'wholly extinguished' by it (*R v Birch* (1989) 11 Cr App R (S) 202).

In *R v Khelifi* [2006] 1 MHLR 257, the Court of Appeal noted that while the needs of the offender were an important consideration, they could not override 'strong reasons why justice would neither be done nor appear to be done if no prison sentence were imposed'. The defendant had been involved to a major extent in a serious and sophisticated fraud, and although the mental illness from which he suffered had been prevalent at the time of the offence, it was 'clearly not so severe as to disable him from participation in serious crime'. The court also had in mind that if he were made subject to a hospital order and responded well to treatment, the defendant might be 'within months discharged from hospital and wholly at liberty, notwithstanding the seriousness of the offence'.

See also *R v Khan* [2010] EWCA Crim 2880.

10.2.4   Procedural requirements

Obtaining a medical report if considering custody

A court should obtain a medical report in order to guide the exercise of its discretion. There is a requirement that a medical report will be obtained where custody is being considered in respect of an offender who is or appears to be suffering from a mental disorder (section 157(1) of the Criminal Justice Act 2003), although this does not apply where the sentence is fixed by law (murder) or where 'in the circumstances of the case, the court is of the opinion that it is unnecessary to obtain a medical report' (section 157(2)).

Medical evidence as to the relevant criteria

If it proposes to make the order, the court must be satisfied as to the relevant criteria by evidence from two RMPs, one of whom must be approved under section 12 of the MHA 1983 (section 54(1)). A court need not hear oral evidence, however, and can sentence on the basis of written reports alone.

Evidence of arrangements for admission of the defendant to hospital

A court must also be satisfied by written or oral evidence (from the approved clinician who will have overall responsibility for the offender's case or someone representing the relevant hospital managers) that arrangements are in place to admit him to hospital within 28 days of the order (section 37(4) of the MHA 1983). Where there is such evidence, the court may order that he is detained at a place of safety in the meantime. For these purposes, the definition of a place of safety can be found in section 55(1) of the MHA 1983 and section 107 of the Children and Young Persons Act 1933.

10.2.5   Which hospital?

Responsibility for providing a hospital bed rests with the clinical commissioning group (CCG) for the area in which the offender resides, or last resided at the time of sentence. If the offender has no permanent address then the responsible CCG will be the one for the area in which he is registered with a GP. Failing that, it will be the CCG for the area in which the offence was committed (1983 Code, para 33.24).

Before making the hospital order, the court may request that the relevant CCG furnish information 'with respect to the hospital or hospitals, if any, in their area or elsewhere at which arrangements could be made for the admission of that person in pursuance of the order' (section 39 of the MHA 1983).

10.2.6   Imposing a hospital order without conviction

Magistrates' court

Section 37(3) of the MHA 1983 entitles a magistrates' court to impose a hospital order *without convicting* a defendant where it is satisfied that he 'did the act or made the omission charged' and where the court would have power, on convicting him of that offence, to make a hospital order. The court need not take a plea, nor conduct a formal trial. The issues of fitness to plead and insanity will therefore rarely need to be resolved in magistrates' court proceedings (see paras 25.6.2 and 25.7.2).

In *Blouet v Bath and Wansdyke Magistrates' Court* [2009] EWHC 759 (Admin), it was suggested that the procedure to adopt in the magistrates' court in cases where there is an issue as to the defendant's mental disorder is as follows:

- Obtain up-to-date evidence as to the defendant's state of mind.
- If there is the possibility of a hospital order, the court should hold a fact-finding exercise to determine whether the defendant did the act or made the omission.
- If the court is satisfied that the defendant did the act or made the omission, it should then consider adjourning for further medical reports unless existing reports are sufficient, in which case, if all parties agree, the court should then proceed to sentence.

Crown Court

The Crown Court may also impose a hospital order without convicting a defendant. The power to do so, however, comes from section 5 of the Criminal Procedure (Insanity) Act 1964, not section 37(3) of the MHA 1983. The power arises following a finding that the defendant is unfit to plead (see para 25.6.1) or a finding that the defendant is insane (see para 25.7.1).

10.2.7   Effect of a hospital order

It is stated in *R v Birch* (1989) 11 Cr App R (S) 202 at page 210, that:

> A hospital order is not a punishment ... the sole purpose of the order is to ensure that the offender receives the medical care and attention he needs in the hope and expectation that the result will be to avoid the commission by the offender of further criminal acts.

Section 40(4) of the MHA 1983 confirms this point. It provides that a patient admitted under a hospital order will be treated as if admitted to hospital under section 3. This means:

- the authority to detain the patient will expire unless it is renewed after 6 months and then periodically in accordance with the provisions of section 20;
- the patient may be discharged at the discretion of the RC or the hospital managers (section 23);
- the patient may be granted leave by the RC (section 17);
- the patient may apply to the MHT for discharge (section 66);
- the patient can be treated without his consent under the provisions of Part IV.

Section 40(4) of the MHA 1983 is expressly subject to Schedule 1, Part I (Application of certain provisions to patients subject to hospital orders and guardianship orders), which clarifies exactly how the provisions of the Act apply to unrestricted section 37 patients and confirms the following as the only areas where a patient under section 37 is to be treated differently from his section 3 counterpart:

- he may not apply to the MHT for discharge during the first 6 months of his detention (although he may be discharged by the RC or apply to the hospital managers for discharge during this period);
- he is not entitled to be discharged by his nearest relative under section 23 (but the nearest relative does have the right – separate to that of the patient – to apply to the MHT for his discharge (section 69(1));
- his initial 6-month detention runs from the date of the order and not from the date of admission to hospital;
- there will be no reference of his case to the MHT under section 68(2) after 6 months.

10.3   RESTRICTION ORDERS – SECTION 41 OF THE MENTAL HEALTH ACT 1983

Whenever the Crown Court imposes a hospital order, it may also direct that it is accompanied by a restriction order under section 41 of the MHA 1983. The criteria to be met for the imposition of a restriction order, and the consequences for the defendant, are considered in Chapter 11.

10.4   OTHER COURT ORDERS – PRE-SENTENCE

10.4.1   Remand of accused person for report on mental condition – section 35 of the Mental Health Act 1983

Magistrates or the Crown Court may remand an 'accused person' to hospital for a report on his mental condition at any point prior to sentence. In the Crown Court, the power is available when a defendant is awaiting trial in respect of an offence punishable by imprisonment, or has been arraigned in respect of an offence punishable by imprisonment and has not yet been sentenced (section 35(2)(a) of the MHA 1983). Before magistrates, the power is available when a defendant has been convicted of an offence punishable by imprisonment, or charged with an offence and the court is satisfied that he did the act or made the omission charged or he has consented to the remand (section 35(2)(b)).

The Crown Court power is not available in respect of a defendant facing a charge of murder once he has been convicted (section 35(3) of the MHA 1983).

The relevant criteria

In order for a court to remand the accused person to hospital for a report, section 35(3) of the MHA 1983 requires it to be satisfied that:

(a)   … there is reason to suspect that the accused person is suffering from mental disorder; and

(b)   … it would be impracticable for a report on his mental condition to be obtained if he were remanded on bail.

Procedure

The decision to remand need only be based on the evidence of one RMP, who must, however, be approved under section 12 of the MHA 1983 (section 54(1)).

The court will need to be satisfied (on the evidence of the approved clinician who would be responsible for making the report, or someone else representing the hospital managers) that arrangements are in place for the admission of the person to hospital within 7 days (section 35(4)). If so satisfied, the court may order detention in a place of safety in the meantime (section 35(4)).

Effect

The remand can be for no more than 28 days at a time, up to a maximum of 12 weeks (section 35(7) of the MHA 1983). The provisions in Part IV do not apply. If the patient therefore requires treatment during his hospital admission, consideration would have to be given to an application for detention under section 2 or section 3 to run concurrently with the remand under section 35. The power to grant leave under section 17 does not apply to patients under section 35. Section 35 itself contains no such power and the patient may not, therefore, be granted leave from the hospital. The Act provides no right to a patient under section 35 to apply to the MHT.

10.4.2   Remand of accused person to hospital for treatment – section 36 of the Mental Health Act 1983

Section 36 of the MHA 1983 gives the Crown Court (not magistrates) the power to remand an accused person to hospital for treatment. The power is appropriate for circumstances in which a defendant who would otherwise be remanded in custody needs treatment for mental disorder, and is an alternative to the power of the SSJ to order the transfer of an unsentenced prisoner to hospital for treatment under section 48 (see Chapter 12).

The power is available in respect of any defendant in custody awaiting trial for an offence punishable with imprisonment (other than murder) or who at any time before sentence is in custody in the course of a trial before that court for such an offence (section 36(2) of the MHA 1983).

Criteria

In order for the Crown Court to remand the accused person to hospital for treatment, section 36(1) of the MHA 1983 requires it to be satisfied that:

    (a)   he is suffering from mental disorder of a nature or degree which makes it appropriate for him to be detained in a hospital for medical treatment; and

    (b)   that appropriate medical treatment is available for him.

Procedure

The court must be satisfied as to the criteria on the evidence of two RMPs (section 36(1) of the MHA 1983), at least one of whom must be approved under section 12 (section 54(1)), and must be satisfied (on the evidence of the approved clinician who would have overall responsibility for the case, or some other person representing the managers of the hospital) that arrangements are in place to admit the accused person to hospital within 7 days. If so satisfied, it may order detention in a place of safety in the meantime (section 36(3)).

Effect

The remand can be for no more than 28 days at a time, up to a maximum of 12 weeks (section 36(6) of the MHA 1983). The patient is subject to Part IV and may be treated without his consent (section 56(3)). The power to grant leave under section 17 does not apply to section 36 patients, section 36 itself contains no such power and the patient may not therefore be granted leave from the hospital. The Act provides no right to a section 36 patient to apply to the MHT.

10.4.3   Interim hospital orders – section 38 of the Mental Health Act 1983

When a court is considering whether or not to make a hospital order under section 37 of the MHA 1983 (see para 10.2), section 38 provides it with the power to make an interim order for hospital assessment before deciding what sentence to impose. It is a power available to both magistrates and the Crown Court, and is available whenever a person is convicted of an offence punishable by imprisonment (other than murder) (section 38(1)).

Which should be used, section 36 or section 48 of the MHA 1983? Both sections achieve the same outcome, namely the transfer of an unsentenced defendant to hospital for treatment for a mental disorder, although section 48 requires the person to be in 'urgent' need of treatment (see para 12.3.2).

From the defendant's point of view, section 48 may be marginally preferable. A patient transferred under section 48 is eligible for leave under section 17, whereas a patient remanded under section 36 is not (although this advantage should not be over-stated as the transfer under section 48 is bound to be accompanied by a transfer direction under section 49 and leave will therefore require the consent of the SSJ). Additionally, a patient under section 48 has the right to apply to the MHT whereas one under section 36 does not, although the MHT powers are limited (see para 17.3.2).

Criteria

In order to make an interim hospital order, section 38(1) of the MHA 1983 requires the court to be satisfied:

    (a)   that the offender is suffering from mental disorder; and
    (b)   that there is reason to suppose the mental disorder from which the offender is suffering is such that it may be appropriate for a hospital order to be made in his case.

Procedure

The court must be satisfied as to the criteria on the evidence of two RMPs, one of whom must be approved under section 12 of the MHA 1983 (section 54(1)), and one of whom must be 'employed at the hospital which is to be specified in the order' (section 38(3)). The court must also be satisfied on oral or written evidence from the approved clinician who would have overall responsibility for the offender's case, or from some other person representing the managers of the hospital, that arrangements are in place for the admission to hospital within 28 days. If so satisfied, the court may direct detention in a place of safety in the meantime (section 38(4)).

Effect

The order may initially be for any period of up to 12 weeks, but is renewable for further periods of 28 days at a time, subject to a maximum period of 12 months (section 38(5) of the MHA 1983). While detained, the patient is subject to Part IV and may, therefore, be treated without his consent. As with sections 35 and 36, the power to grant leave under section 17 does not apply to this category of patients, section 38 itself contains no power to grant leave, and the patient may not, therefore, be granted leave. He is not entitled to apply to the MHT.

10.5   OTHER COURT ORDERS – SENTENCE

10.5.1   Guardianship orders – section 37 of the Mental Health Act 1983

As well as entitling magistrates and the Crown Court to impose a hospital order, section 37 of the MHA 1983 also entitles either court to impose a guardianship order. The power is available in respect of the same group of defendants who would be eligible to receive a hospital order, namely those convicted of an offence punishable by imprisonment (section 37(1)), and (in the magistrates' court) those charged with such an offence where the court is satisfied that the 'accused did the act or made the omission charged' (section 37(3)). The effect is largely the same as a civil admission to guardianship under section 7 (see Chapter 21). The order will place the defendant under the guardianship of a LSSA or 'such other person approved by a LSSA' (section 37(1)).

Criteria

To make the order in respect of a defendant convicted of an offence, section 37(2)(a)(ii) of the MHA 1983 requires the court to be satisfied that an offender is:

- aged 16 years or older; and
- suffering from a mental disorder of a nature or degree which warrants his reception into guardianship.

Court's discretion

As with a hospital order, even where the criteria are met the court will only impose the order when satisfied (section 37(2)(b) of the MHA 1983):

> (b)   … having regard to all circumstances including the nature of the offence and the character and antecedents of the offender, and to the available methods of dealing with him, that the most suitable method of disposing of the case is by means of an order under this section.

Procedure

The court must be satisfied as to the relevant criteria by evidence from two RMPs, at least one of whom should be approved under section 12 of the MHA 1983 (section 54). The order may not be made unless the court is satisfied that the LSSA or person proposed as guardian is willing to receive the offender into guardianship (section 37(6)).

Effect

The authority or person named in the order as guardian will have the same powers as a guardian would have following a guardianship application under section 7 of the MHA 1983 (section 40(2)), and an offender placed under a guardianship order shall be treated as though subject to guardianship following an application under section 7 (section 40(4)) (see Chapter 21). The nearest relative's power of discharge under section 23 is not available in respect of a patient who is subject to a guardianship order (Schedule 1, Part I).

Section 69(1)(b) of the MHA 1983 provides the patient (and his nearest relative) with the right to apply to the MHT for discharge.

No conviction

Magistrates have the power to impose a guardianship order without convicting the defendant under section 37(3) of the MHA 1983 when satisfied that he 'did the act or made the omission charged'. The procedure to be adopted in such cases is set out at para 10.2.6. There is no equivalent power in the Crown Court.

10.5.2 Hospital directions – section 45A of the Mental Health Act 1983

Section 45A of the MHA 1983 gives the Crown Court the power to impose a prison sentence following conviction and, at the same time, direct that the offender should immediately be transferred to hospital for treatment. The effect of the order is that, from the moment it is imposed, the offender is treated as though subject to a transfer direction imposed by the SSJ under section 47, with restrictions under section 49.

To better understand orders under section 45A, therefore, they are considered separately, in Chapter 13, following consideration of the powers under sections 47 and 49, which are set out in Chapter 12.

Chapter 11

Restriction Orders

11.1 INTRODUCTION

Whenever the Crown Court imposes a hospital order under section 37 of the MHA 1983, it may also impose a restriction order under section 41 to accompany it, the chief effect of which is to require key decisions regarding the patient to be made only with the approval of the SSJ. Whether to impose a restriction order is left to the discretion of the sentencing judge, but it will be used for those cases where concerns for public safety are such that future decisions regarding the patient ought not to be left to the clinical team alone. A restriction order has no life of its own and may only be imposed to accompany a hospital order. This chapter considers the factors which will impact on a court's decision to impose a restriction order, and the consequences of such an order for the offender.

11.2 MAGISTRATES' COURT

Magistrates have no power to impose a restriction order, but if dealing with an offence for which one appears suitable, they may commit the defendant for sentence to the Crown Court under section 43 of the MHA 1983. The power is available whenever magistrates are sentencing an offender over the age of 14 who has been convicted of an offence punishable on summary conviction with imprisonment, where the conditions for imposing a hospital order are satisfied and where it appears to the court that a restriction order should also be made. The power, therefore, allows magistrates to commit to the Crown Court for sentence in respect of summary-only offences, which would not normally be dealt with in the Crown Court at all.

A committal in this way is not binding on the Crown Court, which may deal with the offender in any other manner in which the magistrates might have dealt with him (section 43(2) of the MHA 1983).

11.3   DECISION TO IMPOSE A RESTRICTION ORDER

According to section 41(1) of the MHA 1983, the Crown Court may impose a restriction order to accompany a hospital order whenever it appears 'having regard to the nature of the offence, the antecedents of the offender and the risk of his committing further offences if set at large, that it is necessary for the protection of the public from serious harm so to do'.

When considering whether to add a restriction order to a hospital order, the court must ask itself whether the risks posed by the offender to the public are significant enough to warrant the serious consequences for him (summarised at para 11.6) of the imposition of the order. Given that this is an exercise in risk evaluation, decisions tend to be very case-specific. The individual weight to attach to each of the factors affecting risk (the nature of the offence, the antecedents of the offender, and the risk of further offences) is a matter for the sentencing judge, and may vary from case to case. A judge may, for example, impose a restriction order in respect of a minor offence where previous offences or the risk of further offences indicates a significant risk to the public (*R v Birch* (1989) 11 Cr App R (S) 202), and may decline to impose one in respect of a very serious offence where it is clear from other factors that the risk to the public is low (*Courtney* [1987] 9 Cr App R (S) 404).

The term 'public' used in section 41(1) of the MHA 1983 is not restricted to the general public and may refer to an individual person, and 'harm' is not limited to personal injury (see *R v Birch* (1989) 11 Cr App R (S) 202). The potential harm to the public or to an individual must, however, be serious. Even when there is evidence to suggest a 'high risk of re-offending involving violence', this does not necessarily justify a finding that the public would suffer serious harm (*R v Hurst* [2007] EWCA Crim 3436).

The fact that a hospital order patient without restrictions can be discharged onto a CTO (and is, therefore, liable to recall to hospital) may also now be a relevant consideration in deciding whether a restriction order is, in fact, necessary (*R v Goucher* [2012] 1 MHLR 107 and *R v Chiles* [2012] 1 MHLR 60).

11.4   RESTRICTION ORDERS AS AN ALTERNATIVE TO PRISON

The choice for the court may not, of course, be between a hospital order with restrictions and one without. It may be between a hospital order (with restrictions) and prison (see para 10.2.3). In this respect, the advantages of a hospital order with restrictions in allowing for the treatment of mental disorder should not be ignored (see, e.g. *R v Mbatha* (1985) 7 Cr App R (S) 373 and *R v*

Simpson [2007] EWCA Crim 2666 ('the best chance of minimising the danger lies in a hospital order rather than imprisonment')).

In *R v IA* [2005] 1 MHLR 336, the Court of Appeal confirmed that, 'judges are not required to ignore, but should on the contrary, give some appropriate weight to such differences as there are between the regime of custody for life ... and the regime of the hospital order with indefinite restrictions'. In that case, the court overturned a sentence of imprisonment and imposed a hospital order with restrictions having concluded on the evidence 'that the real risks are, in the case of this particular appellant, associated with conditions in respect of which medical treatment would be appropriate'.

A court may decide, however, that the risks presented by the offender extend beyond those linked to mental disorder, in which case it may conclude that any future decision regarding release into the community should be made by the Parole Board, not the MHT. In *R v Fort* [2013] EWCA Crim 2332, the Court of Appeal confirmed (at [61]) that if:

> the offender poses a significant risk of serious harm to members of the public occasioned by the commission of serious offences, even if his mental disorder were to be cured or substantially alleviated, then the sentence to be imposed must recognise and focus on that residual risk.

11.5 PROCEDURE

One of the two RMPs who have provided a recommendation for the purposes of the hospital order must give oral evidence if there is to be a restriction order (section 41(2) of the MHA 1983). A judge is bound neither to accept medical recommendations that a restriction order is required, nor to accept recommendations that it is not (see *R v Osker* [2010] EWCA Crim 955).

11.6 CONSEQUENCES OF A RESTRICTION ORDER

If an order under section 41 of the MHA 1983 is imposed, the offender will, of course, be subject to a hospital order under section 37. Unlike his unrestricted counterpart, however, he will also face the following short- and long-term consequences as a result of the restriction order.

11.6.1 Secure hospitals

Most restricted patients (that is, those subject to a restriction order) are treated within a forensic mental health service setting, and although there is no requirement in this respect, most will be located in a secure hospital. There are three types of secure hospital (*Good Practice Procedure Guide. The transfer and remission of adult prisoners under s47 and s48 of the Mental Health Act* (Department of Health, April 2011)):

- *High secure hospitals* for patients who pose (para 4.22):

  a grave and immediate danger to themselves and/or others and cannot be safely managed in a less secure environment

- *Medium secure hospitals* for patients who present (para 4.28):

  a serious but not grave and immediate danger to others. ... Admission criteria include ...:

  - risk predominantly to others including serious risk to the public
  - significant risk of and/or attempts to escape/abscond
  - present or history of violent behaviour that cannot be managed in less secure conditions

- *Low secure hospitals* for patients who (para 4.29):

  typically require treatment in conditions with a higher level of physical and relational security than open wards because of the level of risk they pose to themselves or others. ... Admission criteria may include

  - history of non-violent offending behaviour
  - low risk of abscond or escape
  - offending behaviour connected to mental disorder
  - risk of self-neglect, challenging behaviour and/or self-harm
  - risk of lower level violent offending e.g. common assault, actual bodily harm

11.6.2   Care teams

Whatever level of security, the care and treatment provided to restricted patients will be delivered by clinicians specialising in forensic psychiatry. The principal features of treatment will, therefore, be:

- A multi-disciplinary team approach, usually led by a forensic psychiatrist but also comprising nursing, social work, psychology and occupational therapy.
- Focus on risk assessment, often based around the Historical Clinical Risk Management–20, Version 3 (HCR-20V3), a 20-item checklist test used to assess the risk of future violent behaviour (Douglas, KS, Hart, SD, Webster, CD and Belfrage, H, *HCR-20V3: Assessing risk of violence –*

User guide (Mental Health, Law, and Policy Institute, Simon Fraser University, Burnaby, Canada, 2013)).

- Psychological work, including offender behaviour programmes, to address issues such as anger management, drug and alcohol addiction, and relapse prevention.
- A gradual, staged approach to leave under section 17 of the MHA 1983, beginning with escorted ground leave, then unescorted ground leave, then escorted community leave, and then unescorted community leave.
- A gradual, staged approach towards discharge.

11.6.3 Decision-making

Perhaps most significantly of all, decisions to grant the patient leave under section 17 of the MHA 1983, to transfer the patient under section 19 or to discharge the patient under section 23 may not be made without the consent of the SSJ (section 41(3)(c)). In this respect, the SSJ's decision-making authority is delegated to the mental health casework section (MHCS) of the Ministry of Justice (MOJ).

Any decision taken by the MHCS regarding a patient will depend to a large extent on advice received from the patient's clinical team, but in *R (on the application of PP) v SSJ* [2009] 1 MHLR 236, the High Court issued a reminder that the SSJ is not bound to accept clinical advice when exercising his discretion on whether to consent (in that case) to a transfer of a restricted patient to a different hospital. The SSJ has wider considerations than those of the RC and must be allowed to make his own judgement. Any decision must, however, follow general public law principles and may not be unreasonable or irrational (*R (on the application of X) v SSJ* [2009] 1 MHLR 250).

11.6.4 Renewal of detention

Unlike an unrestricted patient under section 37 of the MHA 1983, a restricted patient's detention is for an indefinite period and need not be renewed at 6-monthly and then annual intervals; it need not be renewed at all (section 41(3)(a) of the MHA 1983). A restricted patient's detention will never simply lapse, and will only come to an end when a positive decision to discharge the patient has been taken, either by the SSJ (see para 11.7) or by the MHT (see para 17.2).

11.6.5 Nearest relative

A restricted patient does not have a nearest relative for the purposes of the MHA 1983.

11.6.6   Mental health tribunals

A restricted patient's entitlement to apply to the MHT is set out in section 70 of the MHA 1983. The patient may not apply to the MHT within the first 6 months of his detention, but may apply within the second 6 months and within every 12-month period thereafter. The SSJ will be a party to any MHT proceedings (rule 1 of the Tribunal Procedure Rules 2008).

The discharge criteria to be applied by the MHT considering the patient's case are set out in section 73 of the MHA 1983 (see para 17.2). There is a presumption that any discharge will be conditional (section 73(2)).

11.6.7   Liability to recall

Assuming a restricted patient is conditionally (as opposed to absolutely) discharged, either by the MHT (see para 17.2) or the SSJ (see para 11.7), the restriction order remains in place following discharge. A patient will then remain liable to recall to hospital for as long as he is subject to the conditional discharge. Liability to recall ends only at the point at which the patient is discharged absolutely, either by the SSJ (section 42(2) of the MHA 1983) or by the MHT (section 75(3)).

While the patient is subject to a conditional discharge, recall is at the discretion of the SSJ (section 42(3) of the MHA 1983), but any decision to recall will mean further detention and must be based, applying *Winterwerp v The Netherlands* (Application No 6301/73) [1979] ECHR 4 (see para 2.7.2), on evidence of mental disorder, established by objective medical expertise, of a nature or degree warranting detention. Except in emergencies, therefore, the decision to recall must be based on up-to-date medical evidence which shows that the criteria for detention are met.

Policy regarding the exercise of this discretion is set out in guidance issued by the MHCS (*The recall of conditionally discharged restricted patients*, 4 February 2009), which states that, 'patients will be recalled where it is necessary to protect the public from the actual or potential risk posed by that patient *and* that risk is linked to the patient's mental disorder' (para 5). The guidance notes that, 'it is not possible to specify all the circumstances when recall will be appropriate but *public safety will always be the most important factor*' (para 5). It also makes the following points:

- Substance or alcohol misuse cannot of itself lead to recall, but it will lead to consideration of recall if there is evidence that misuse is known to have a detrimental effect on the patient's mental health.

- Non-compliance with medication will lead to consideration of recall. Relevant factors will include: whether there is a pattern of non-compliance, whether there is also evidence of general disengagement, the inter-relationship between non-compliance and relapse.
- Recall must be considered whenever there is any informal admission to a psychiatric hospital. Relevant factors will be: the likely length of admission, any evidence of increased risk to others, and whether the supervising psychiatrist would seek to detain the patient if he tried to leave. Admission for more than a few weeks is likely to trigger recall.
- Detention under section 2 or section 3 will 'almost invariably' lead to recall.
- Where a conditionally discharged patient receives a period of imprisonment, consideration to recall must be given when he is released from prison.

11.7   SECRETARY OF STATE FOR JUSTICE'S POWER OF DISCHARGE

Section 42(2) of the MHA 1983 provides the SSJ with his own discretionary power to discharge restricted patients, either conditionally or absolutely. Any patient subject to a restriction order is therefore provided with an alternative to the MHT as a route to discharge, although a relatively under-used one.

11.8   SECRETARY OF STATE FOR JUSTICE'S POWER TO REMOVE THE RESTRICTION ORDER

Under section 42(1) of the MHA 1983, the SSJ may direct that the patient should no longer be subject to a restriction order where he is satisfied that the order 'is no longer required for the protection of the public from serious harm'. The significance of this rarely used provision is that it is the only means by which a restriction order may be removed while allowing the underlying hospital order to continue. The MHT has no such power.

Chapter 12

Transfers from Prison to Hospital under Sections 47 and 48 of the Mental Health Act 1983

12.1 INTRODUCTION

The Department of Health acknowledges that, 'a large proportion of the prison population will experience some form of mental illness during their period in custody, either because of a relapse in a pre-existing condition or because they become unwell for the first time' (*Good Practice Procedure Guide. The transfer and remission of adult prisoners under s47 and s48 of the Mental Health Act* (Department of Health, 2011)). While the Department also suggests that the vast majority who experience mental illness while in prison are successfully treated by prison health services, there are a significant number for whom treatment in prison is not enough. Part III of the MHA 1983 therefore contains provisions which mean that once the criteria for admission to hospital under the Act are met, an application may be made to the SSJ for authorisation to transfer the prisoner to hospital for treatment. In the case of serving prisoners, the transfer will be under section 47; in the case of remand prisoners, the transfer will be under section 48. In either case, the transfer direction is almost certain to be accompanied by a restriction direction under section 49. These provisions are considered in this chapter.

12.2 TRANSFER OF SENTENCED PRISONERS UNDER SECTION 47 OF THE MENTAL HEALTH ACT 1983

12.2.1 Prisoners to whom section 47 of the Mental Health Act 1983 applies

The SSJ's power of transfer under section 47 of the MHA 1983 applies in respect of a person who is 'serving a sentence of imprisonment' (section 47(1)), a term which is confirmed by section 47(5) to include references to prisoners:

(a)   ... detained in pursuance of any sentence or order for detention made by a court in criminal proceedings or service disciplinary proceedings (other than an order made in consequence of a finding of insanity or unfitness to stand trial or a sentence of service detention within the meaning of the Armed Forces Act 2006);

(b)   ... committed to custody under section 115(3) of the Magistrates' Court Act 1980 (which relates to persons who fail to comply with an order to enter into recognisances to keep the peace or be of good behaviour); and

(c)   ... committed by a court to a prison or other institution to which the Prison Act 1952 applies in default of payment of any sum adjudged to be paid on his conviction.

12.2.2 Relevant criteria

According to section 47(1) of the MHA 1983, the SSJ may order the transfer of any such prisoner if satisfied:

(a)   that the said person is suffering from mental disorder; and

(b)   that the mental disorder from which that person is suffering is of a nature or degree which makes it appropriate for him to be detained in a hospital for medical treatment; and

(c)   that appropriate medical treatment is available for him.

12.2.3 Secretary of State for Justice's discretion

Assuming the relevant criteria are met, transfer is at the discretion of the SSJ, who may direct it 'if he is of the opinion having regard to the public interest and all the circumstances that it is expedient so to do' (section 47(1)). The Department of Health guidance (*Good Practice Procedure Guide. The transfer and remission of adult prisoners under s47 and s48 of the Mental Health Act* (Department of Health, 2011)) notes that the SSJ in reaching his decision should take account of factors such as (para 3.26):

- any risks associated with the prisoner (escape risk, nature and history of offending, notoriety, victim issues), and the public protection implications
- whether public confidence could be undermined by allowing the transfer
- the court's intention at the time of sentencing to imprisonment
- the effect of any pending appeal
- whether appropriate treatment can be provided in prison
- the length of time the prisoner still has to serve, behaviour and current security category
- medical opinion, past and present presenting symptoms and level of clinical risk (e.g. actively suicidal, assaultive).

12.2.4 Procedure

The decision regarding transfer will be made by the MHCS. Section 47(1) of the MHA 1983 requires evidence as to the relevant criteria to be provided in the form of reports from at least two RMPs, at least one of whom will need to be approved under section 12 (section 54(1)). Any transfer direction will cease to have effect if the person is not received into the hospital within 14 days of the date of the direction (section 47(2)).

12.2.5 Effect of a transfer direction under section 47 of the Mental Health Act 1983

If a transfer direction is made, it will have the same effect as a hospital order under section 37 of the MHA 1983 (section 47(3)). However, section 49 gives the SSJ the power to attach a restriction direction to any transfer direction. There is no requirement that he must, but MOJ policy is that he will do so, in virtually every case. The vast majority of patients transferred under section 47, therefore, have a restricted status as a result of the restriction direction. The consequences of this for the patient are considered at para 12.4. In the unlikely event, however, that no restriction direction is attached to a transfer direction and that a prisoner is transferred under section 47 alone, the effects are that:

- He will not be able to be returned to prison. An unrestricted transfer direction means that the prisoner 'passes out of the penal system and into the hospital regime' (Mustill LJ in *R v Birch* (1989) 11 Cr App R (S) 202).
- He need not serve the equivalent of his prison term. He is no longer treated as though serving a sentence and instead is treated as though serving a hospital order.
- He will not be discharged from hospital if he remains there at the point at which he has served the equivalent of his prison term. He will remain in hospital until he is discharged under section 23 or by the MHT.
- He will be discharged by his RC or by hospital managers (section 23) as soon as the criteria for detention are no longer met.
- The transfer direction will last initially for up to 6 months and will then need to be renewed periodically (as per section 20) if his detention is to continue.
- He may apply to the MHT for discharge (section 69(2)(b)).

12.2.6 Late transfers

The effect of section 47 of the MHA 1983 is that, whether accompanied by a restriction direction or not, the prisoner need not be released from hospital at the end of his sentence, but may be kept there instead until he no longer meets the criteria for detention under the Act. Prisoners transferred are therefore at real risk of being detained for a period longer than their prison sentence. Section 47 should not be used, however, as a way of keeping a dangerous prisoner detained for longer than his sentence would otherwise allow.

In *R (on the application of TF) v SSJ* [2008] 1 MHLR 370, the court's view was that any decision taken by the SSJ to transfer under section 47 of the MHA 1983 towards the end of a prison sentence should only be 'in very exceptional circumstances' and 'cannot simply be taken on the grounds that a convicted person will be a danger to the public if released'. As an alternative, the use of section 2 or section 3 should be considered at the end of a prison sentence, and where 'a prisoner is sufficiently close to their release date that admission to hospital could be appropriately achieved using civil powers … it is unlikely that directing transfer under 47 can be justified' (*Good Practice Procedure Guide. The transfer and remission of adult prisoners under s47 and s48 of the Mental Health Act* (Department of Health, 2011), para 3.10).

12.3   TRANSFER OF UNSENTENCED PRISONERS UNDER SECTION 48 OF THE MENTAL HEALTH ACT 1983

Section 48 of the MHA 1983 provides the SSJ with a similar power to transfer *remand prisoners* to hospital for treatment for mental disorder.

12.3.1   Prisoners to whom section 48 of the Mental Health Act 1983 applies

Under section 48(2) of the MHA 1983 the following unsentenced prisoners are eligible for transfer:

(a)   persons detained in a prison or remand centre, not being persons serving a sentence of imprisonment …;

(b)   persons remanded in custody by a magistrates' court;

(c)   civil prisoners, that is to say, persons committed by a court to prison for a limited term who are not persons falling to be dealt with under section 47 above;

(d)   persons detained under the Immigration Act 1971 or under section 62 of the Nationality Immigration and Asylum Act 2002 … .

By far the majority will be in either of the first two of these categories.

12.3.2 Relevant criteria

Section 48(1) of the MHA 1983 provides that the SSJ may direct transfer if satisfied that:

(a)   that person is suffering from mental disorder of a nature or degree which makes it appropriate for him to be detained in a hospital for medical treatment; and

(b)   he is in urgent need of such treatment; and

(c)   appropriate medical treatment is available for him.

Unlike in cases under section 47 of the MHA 1983, the person must, therefore, be in urgent need of treatment.

12.3.3 Secretary of State for Justice's discretion

Although the relevant criteria may be met, the SSJ's power is again discretionary, and again, therefore, he will need to be satisfied, having regard to the public interest and all the circumstances, that it is 'expedient' to make the direction (section 47(1) of the MHA 1983). Factors to be taken into account by the MHCS in cases under section 48 are, in the main, identical to those in cases under section 47, save, of course, that the medical evidence will also need to support the proposition that transfer is an urgent necessity.

12.3.4 Procedure

There must be evidence as to the relevant criteria in the form of reports from at least two RMPs (section 48(1) of the MHA 1983), and one of the RMPs must be approved under section 12 (section 54(1)). The transfer direction will cease to have effect if the prisoner is not received into the hospital within 14 days of the direction (section 48(3)).

12.3.5 Effect

Were the transfer direction to be made without a restriction direction, the effect would be as it would be for an unrestricted case under section 47 of the MHA 1983, and the patient would be treated as though subject to a hospital order (section 48(3)) (see para 12.2.5). Again, however, this is highly unlikely to occur. Virtually all patients under section 48 will be restricted as a result of section 49(1), which provides that where the prisoner is one to whom section 48(2)(a) or (b) applies, that is 'detained in a prison or remand centre, not being (a person) serving a sentence of imprisonment' or 'remanded in custody by a magistrates' court' (in other words, the vast majority of cases under section 48), the SSJ *must* attach a restriction direction to the transfer direction. Unlike in cases under section 47, therefore, the SSJ has no discretion.

12.4   RESTRICTION DIRECTIONS UNDER SECTION 49 OF THE MENTAL HEALTH ACT 1983

12.4.1   Introduction

In cases under section 47 of the MHA 1983, the SSJ may impose a restriction direction whenever a transfer direction takes place and will, as a matter of policy, impose one on nearly every occasion. In cases under section 48, the SSJ must impose a restriction direction, as a matter of law, in the vast majority of cases and will likely impose one as a matter of policy in all other cases. Virtually all prison transfers will, therefore, result in a restriction direction under section 49 running alongside the transfer direction. This should come as no surprise. One of the main effects (see para 12.4.2) of a restriction direction is that it allows for the prisoner to be remitted to prison when hospital treatment is no longer called for, and, given that all those transferred have been charged with, or convicted of, a criminal offence for which they have either been remanded in custody or given a term of imprisonment, it would be odd if the SSJ did not take the view that they should, generally, be returned to prison when the time for treatment was over. In *R (on the application of T) v Home Secretary* [2003] 1 MHLR 239, Maurice Kay J therefore endorsed the view that a Home Office policy to impose a restriction direction at the same time as a transfer direction was justified, noting that it was reasonable 'to have a policy which is designed to ensure that [a prisoner transferred to hospital] does not regain his liberty before the envisaged date'.

12.4.2   Effect of restriction direction

Whenever a restriction direction is attached to a transfer direction under section 47 or section 48 of the MHA 1983, there are three main consequences, all of which mean that the legal status of the patient is significantly different to that of an unrestricted transfer patient.

Firstly, the restriction direction 'shall have the same effect as a restriction order under section 41' (section 49(2) of the MHA 1983). The effect of a restriction order on the treatment of a patient is looked at in more detail in Chapter 11, but, in summary, the patient is likely to be detained in a forensic setting, the clinical team will be unable to make any significant decisions (e.g. regarding leave or transfer) without the approval of the SSJ, detention need not be periodically renewed, and the patient has no nearest relative for the purposes of the Act.

Secondly, although a patient subject to a restriction direction may apply to the MHT, the MHT's powers, set out in section 74 of the MHA 1983 (and considered in more detail in Chapter 17), are strictly limited; the patient may not be discharged by the MHT without the agreement of the SSJ.

Thirdly, the restriction direction allows for the return of the patient to prison at the point when he is deemed to no longer require treatment in hospital for mental disorder, or where no effective treatment for the disorder may be given at the hospital to which he has been removed. Section 50(1) of the MHA 1983 authorises the SSJ by warrant to direct that the patient under section 47 be remitted to prison upon the recommendation of the RC, another approved clinician or the MHT, and section 51(3) provides a similar power in respect of patients under section 48.

12.4.3 How will a restriction direction come to an end?

Cases under section 47 and section 48 of the Mental Health Act 1983 – the patient is returned to prison

In cases under both sections 47 and 49 and sections 48 and 49, the restriction direction will end at the point at which the patient is returned to prison because no further treatment for mental disorder is required or can be effective (sections 50(1) and 51(3)). The patient will then either serve out his sentence in prison or remain there until the conclusion of the criminal proceedings.

Cases under section 48 of the Mental Health Act 1983 – the criminal proceedings come to an end or bail is granted

If a patient under section 48 of the MHA 1983 is not returned to prison under section 51(3), the transfer direction will last as long as the criminal proceedings in which the patient is involved (section 51(2)), and the restriction direction under section 49 will last as long as the transfer direction. For all of the time that the patient is in hospital pending the conclusion of the criminal proceedings, he will therefore be a restricted patient. The transfer direction will end with the criminal proceedings, and so, automatically, will the restriction direction. What happens at the conclusion of the proceedings will depend on what sentence, if any, is imposed by the court.

The transfer direction and accompanying restriction direction of a patient under section 48 or section 49 of the MHA 1983 will also end if the patient is granted bail in the criminal proceedings (section 51(4)).

Either the RC or the MHT may notify the SSJ that a patient no longer needs treatment in hospital or that no effective treatment can be given, following which the SSJ may exercise his discretion to remit the patient to prison. A patient who wishes to return to prison against the wishes of his RC should therefore consider applying to the MHT for an appropriate recommendation to the SSJ. A patient who wishes to remain in hospital against the wishes of his RC should also consider applying to the MHT. Where the MHT considers that the criteria for detention in hospital remain in place, and that the patient ought therefore to remain there, any subsequent decision by the RC to notify the SSJ that the patient should be remitted to prison may be in breach of the rule of law which requires that, 'effect should be loyally given to the decision of legally-constituted tribunals' (*R (on the application of von Brandenburg) v East London and the City Mental Health NHS Trust and Another* [2003] UKHL 58, [2004] 2 AC 280).

Cases under section 47 of the Mental Health Act 1983 – the prison sentence comes to an end

If a patient under section 47 of the MHA 1983 is not returned to prison to serve out his sentence, the direction under section 49 will continue until the patient's prison sentence comes to an end, that is until his 'release date' (section 50(2)). For these purposes, 'release date' is defined as being the date upon which the patient would be 'entitled to be released', disregarding any discretionary power of release available to either the Parole Board or the SSJ (section 50(3)).

The restriction direction of a patient under section 47 of the MHA 1983 serving a *fixed term of imprisonment* will, therefore, come to an end at the point at which the patient would automatically have been entitled to release from prison had he still been there. The end of the restriction direction does not mean that the patient is discharged. From that point on, the patient, if still detained, will be unrestricted (see para 12.4.4).

For a patient under section 47 of the MHA 1983 who is serving a *life or indeterminate sentence*, the restriction direction will never come to an end while he is in hospital. Release from prison would always be at the discretion of the Parole Board, the patient would never therefore be 'entitled to release' and never has a 'release date' for the purposes of section 50(2).

12.4.4   Importance of the difference between fixed term and indeterminate prison sentences in cases under section 47 of the Mental Health Act 1983

The importance of the difference between a fixed term and an indeterminate term of imprisonment in cases under section 47 of the MHA 1983 should not be underestimated.

Where the patient is serving a fixed term of imprisonment, he will have a restricted status until his prison release date is reached. Once that point is reached, the restriction direction under section 49 of the MHA 1983 falls away, but the patient is not necessarily released from hospital. While no longer a restricted patient, his transfer direction remains in place, and he is liable to be detained until he no longer meets the criteria for detention. His position is, however, significantly improved. He is no longer liable to return to prison. He is treated as though subject to section 37 and is known as a 'notional hospital order' patient. Decisions are no longer subject to the intervention of the SSJ, he may be granted leave by his RC, his detention must be renewed periodically if it is to continue, he may be discharged by his RC or hospital managers under section 23 and he may apply to the MHT for discharge. Any application to the MHT is considered according to the normal section 3 discharge criteria (see para 16.3).

Where the patient is serving an indeterminate sentence, on the other hand, he never reaches a release date and therefore never stops being a restricted patient for as long as he is in hospital. He always remains liable to return to prison. He may never be discharged at the discretion of his RC or hospital managers alone, and, crucially, the powers of the MHT (considered in detail at para 17.3) will always be limited. Section 74 of the MHA 1983 always applies, which means that the MHT will never have the power to discharge the patient. His release from detention will always be at the discretion of the SSJ, usually in the form of the Parole Board.

Chapter 13

Hospital Directions under Section 45A of the Mental Health Act 1983

13.1 INTRODUCTION

This chapter considers section 45A of the MHA 1983, which provides a relatively under-used sentencing option for the Crown Court dealing with a mentally disordered offender. It allows for the imposition of a prison sentence in the normal way, together with a direction that the offender should immediately be sent to hospital for treatment. The offender is then treated as if subject to a transfer and restriction direction under section 47 and section 49.

The sentence might be thought an attractive option to sentencing judges in that it allows for a mentally disordered offender to be sent to prison, perhaps to reflect a degree of culpability associated with the offending, but also provides the re-assurance that the offender will receive treatment for his mental disorder during the course of his sentence. It is, therefore, perhaps surprising that it is used as infrequently as it is (see Appendix 7).

Until the amendments made by the MHA 2007, the sentence was only available in respect of offenders with a psychopathic disorder. Since then, it has been available for offenders with any form of mental disorder.

13.2 WHICH OFFENDERS?

The order may be imposed whenever an offender is convicted of an imprisonable offence (except murder) in the Crown Court (section 45A(1)). It can only, therefore, be imposed in respect of offenders who are 21 years or over, a sentence of imprisonment being unavailable in respect of anyone any younger (*AG's reference (No 54 of 2011)* [2011] EWCA Crim 2276 and *R v Fort* [2013] EWCA Crim 2332).

13.3   CRITERIA

According to section 45A(2) of the MHA 1983, the Crown Court may impose the sentence whenever it is satisfied that:

(a)   the offender is suffering from mental disorder;

(b)   the mental disorder from which the offender is suffering is of a nature or degree which makes it appropriate for him to be detained in a hospital for medical treatment; and

(c)   appropriate medical treatment is available for him.

13.4   THE COURT'S DISCRETION

A court may impose the sentence whenever the criteria are met, but it is not required to do so. That would make no sense, as the criteria are exactly the same as those for the imposition of a hospital order under section 37 of the MHA 1983. The point is simply to provide a court with the discretion to choose a third way as an alternative, where appropriate, to the stark choice between a prison and hospital. The court is given the opportunity to impose a prison sentence to reflect, for example, culpability or risks which make a hospital order inappropriate (see, e.g. *R v Jenkin* [2012] EWCA Crim 2557), but at the same time, where there is clear evidence of mental disorder, the court can give itself the security of knowing that the offender will receive treatment in hospital without having to rely on the SSJ to transfer under section 47.

The court must in fact have considered making a hospital order under section 37 of the MHA 1983 and decided against it before it is able to exercise its power under section 45A (section 45A(1)(b)).

13.5   PROCEDURAL REQUIREMENTS

The court must be satisfied as to the relevant criteria by evidence from two RMPs (section 45A(2) of the MHA 1983), at least one of whom must have given oral evidence (section 45A(4)). One of the RMPs must be approved under section 12 (section 54(1)). The court must also be satisfied on the written or oral evidence of the approved clinician who would have overall responsibility for the offender's case, or of some other person representing the managers of the hospital, that arrangements have been made for the offender's admission to hospital within 28 days of the order being made. Assuming that to be the case, the offender may be moved to a place of safety pending admission to the hospital concerned (section 45A(5)).

The court may make an interim hospital order under section 38 of the MHA 1983 while considering whether to make an order (section 45A(8)).

13.6 HOSPITAL DIRECTIONS AND LIMITATION DIRECTIONS

The court will impose a sentence of imprisonment (section 45A)(1)(b) of the MHA 1983) in the normal way and according to the normal sentencing rules. At the same time, however, the court will give *both* of the following directions:

- that instead of being removed and detained in a prison, the offender is removed to and detained in such hospital as may be specified (section 45A(3)(a)) – the hospital direction;
- that the offender be subject to the special restrictions set out in section 41 (section 45A(3)(b)) – the limitation direction.

The court has no discretion so far as the limitation direction is concerned. If it decides to impose a hospital direction then it must impose a limitation direction. All patients under section 45A of the MHA 1983 will, therefore, be restricted.

13.7 EFFECT

The effect is that from the moment the sentence is imposed, the offender is treated as though he had been made subject to a transfer direction under section 47 of the MHA 1983 and a restriction direction under section 49 (section 45B(2)). He is a serving prisoner who has been moved to hospital for treatment for his mental disorder. There is no difference of any significance between the legal status of a patient under section 45A and a patient under section 47 or section 49.

The legal status of a patient under section 47 or section 49 of the MHA 1983 is considered in Chapter 12, and the points made there apply equally to patients under section 45A. To summarise, the effect of the *hospital direction* (the equivalent of the transfer direction) is, quite simply, that the patient is transferred to hospital. The effect of the *limitation direction* (the equivalent of the restriction direction) is threefold:

- the patient is treated as though subject to a restriction order under section 41 (section 45B(2) and section 49(2));
- the patient may apply to the MHT, but the tribunal's powers, set out in section 74, are strictly limited; there is no power of discharge;

- the patient may be remitted to prison when he no longer requires treatment for mental disorder or no effective treatment can be given (section 50(5)(a)).

Rules governing the length of the limitation direction under section 45A of the MHA 1983 are the same as those governing the length of the restriction direction under section 49 (see para 12.4.3). The sentence imposed by the court when making the order under section 45A may have been of fixed term or indeterminate. If fixed term, the limitation direction will last until the patient's 'release date', that is the point at which he would be automatically entitled to release from prison (section 50(5)(b)). If indeterminate, the patient does not have a 'release date' for the purposes of the Act, and his limitation direction will never come to an end while he remains a hospital patient (section 50(5)(c)).

For a person serving a fixed term sentence, the point at which the release date is reached means the point at which he loses his restricted status. The underlying hospital direction remains in place, however, and, although now unrestricted, he remains in hospital as a notional hospital order patient until he no longer meets the criteria for detention (see para 12.4.4).

Part Five

Tribunals and Discharge

Chapter 14

Challenging the Lawfulness of Detention – Mental Health Tribunals, etc

14.1 INTRODUCTION

Article 5(4) of the ECHR requires that a patient detained under the MHA 1983 should have the opportunity to take proceedings by which the 'lawfulness of his detention shall be decided speedily by a court and his release ordered if the detention is no longer lawful'. For these purposes, the ECtHR, in *X v UK* (Application No 7215/75) [1981] ECHR 6, following the judgment in *Winterwerp v The Netherlands* (Application No 6301/73) [1979] ECHR 4 (see para 2.7.2), confirmed that 'lawfulness' should be interpreted to cover both procedural and substantive issues.

In respect of civil detentions, a patient is able to challenge the *procedural* lawfulness of his detention (e.g. whether the detaining authority has exceeded its powers or whether an essential procedural requirement has been overlooked) by means of a writ of habeas corpus or judicial review proceedings. These remedies are considered briefly at para 14.2.

Quite separately, however, all patients are able to challenge the *substantive* lawfulness of their detention (whether the detention is justified on the merits, whether the criteria for detention are made out) by applying to the MHT for discharge. The bulk of this chapter, therefore, considers the rules set out in Part V of the MHA 1983, which govern when a patient may make an application to the MHT or when the case of a patient must be referred to the MHT. Procedural issues concerning MHT hearings are then considered in Chapter 15, and the statutory criteria to be applied by MHTs when deciding on the substantive lawfulness of detention are considered in Chapters 16–18.

14.2   CHALLENGING THE FORMAL LAWFULNESS OF DETENTION

14.2.1   Habeas corpus

A writ of habeas corpus is one potential remedy available to anyone who wishes to challenge the formal lawfulness of his detention. The basis of the claim will be that there is no legal authority to detain the individual in question and that the detaining authority or individual has acted outside their lawful powers. Where such a claim is made, the person or body responsible for the individual's detention can be required to justify to a court that the detention is in fact in accordance with the law. As put by Sir Thomas Bingham MR in *Re S-C* [1995] EWCA Civ 60, 'the ordinary form of a writ of habeas corpus requires a custodian to produce the body of an applicant and show cause justifying the detention'.

Any application for a writ of habeas corpus will be made to the High Court. Procedure is governed by Schedule 1 to the Civil Procedure Rules 1998 (SI 1998/3132), incorporating Order 54 of the Rules of the Supreme Court 1965 (SI 1965/1776). The remedy sought will be the release of the individual concerned.

In *X v UK* (Application No 7215/75) [1981] ECHR 6, the ECtHR described the scope of habeas corpus thus (at paragraph 56):

> In habeas corpus proceedings, in examining an administrative decision to detain, the court's task is to inquire whether the detention is in compliance with the requirements stated in the relevant legislation and with the applicable principles of the common law. According to these principles, such a decision – even though technically legal on its face – may be upset, inter alia, if the detaining authority misused its powers by acting in bad faith or capriciously or for a wrongful purpose, or if the decision is supported by no sufficient evidence or is one which no reasonable person could have reached in the circumstances.

Somewhat more concisely, in *R v Secretary of State for the Home Department ex parte Cheblak* [1991] 2 All ER 319, Lord Donaldson suggested that, 'a writ of habeas corpus will issue where someone is detained without any authority or the purported authority is beyond the powers of the person authorising the detention and so is unlawful'.

As to the type of mental health cases where an application for a writ of habeas corpus will be appropriate, the Court of Appeal in *Re S-C* [1995] EWCA Civ 60, cited the principle from *R v Secretary of State for the Home Department ex parte Muboyayi* [1992] QB 244, namely that (at page 7):

where the power to detain is dependent upon the existence of a particular state of affairs ('a precedent fact') and the existence of that fact is challenged by or on behalf of the person detained, a challenge to the detention may be mounted by means of an application for a writ of habeas corpus.

In *Re S-C* [1995] EWCA Civ 60, the complaint was that the application for detention had been made without consultation with the patient's nearest relative, a 'precedent fact' upon which a lawful application was dependent. It was claimed, therefore, that there was an absence of any jurisdiction to apply for detention. Habeas corpus was held to be an appropriate remedy in such circumstances.

Similarly, the remedy successfully claimed in *GD v Edgware Community Hospital and London Borough of Barnet* [2008] EWHC 3572 (Admin), [2008] 1 MHLR 282 (inadequate consultation with nearest relative) and in *R (on the application of GP) v Derby City Council* [2012] EWHC 1451 (Admin) (failure by the AMHP to consult the nearest relative at all before the application under section 3 (see para 5.3.4)) was a writ of habeas corpus.

In *Re AR (Habeas Corpus: Medical Recommendation)* [2001] EWHC 792 (Admin), although an unsuccessful application on the facts, habeas corpus was accepted as the appropriate remedy in a case where it was alleged that neither of the two RMPs who provided medical recommendations in support of detention had 'previous acquaintance' with the patient, as required by section 12(2) of the MHA 1983.

In *Barker v Barking, Havering and Brentwood Community Healthcare NHS Trust (Warley Hospital) and Another* [1998] EWCA Civ 1347, Lord Woolf, referring to *Re S-C* [1995] EWCA Civ 60, disagreed that a writ of habeas corpus was the only appropriate remedy on the facts, and suggested that judicial review was equally, perhaps, more appropriate. He noted the distinction drawn between a case where 'what is in issue is whether some precedent fact going to jurisdiction is in issue … when an application for habeas corpus is appropriate' and a case 'where what is in issue is the propriety of some prior administrative act', where judicial review proceedings would be more appropriate. He also noted that the 'distinction between the two categories of situations is not always easy to distinguish and that is another reason why it is preferable to usually … proceed by way of judicial review'.

14.2.2   Judicial review proceedings

Judicial review proceedings provide an alternative potential remedy for those challenging the formal lawfulness of their detention. Unlike habeas corpus proceedings, where the issue is simply whether there was ever any lawful authority to detain, the issue for judicial review proceedings is whether detention is rendered invalid as a consequence of the quality of the decision-making process.

As put by Lord Donaldson in *R v Secretary of State for the Home Department ex parte Cheblak* [1991] 2 All ER 319 at page 323:

> the remedy of judicial review is available where the decision or action sought to be impugned is within the powers of the person taking it but, due to procedural error, a misappreciation of the law, a failure to take account of relevant matters, a taking account of irrelevant matters or the fundamental unreasonableness of the decision or action, it should never have been taken.

Put another way, the court's function in judicial review proceedings is 'to review decisions of statutory and other public authorities to see that they are lawful, rational and reached by a fair and due process' (per May LJ in *St Helens Borough Council v Manchester Primary Care Trust & Anor* [2008] EWCA Civ 931).

Such summaries of the function of judicial review proceedings are based on the judgment of Lord Diplock in *Council of Civil Service Unions v Minister for the Civil Service* [1983] UKHL 6, and his summary therein of the three bases upon which administrative action may be subject to control by judicial review: illegality, irrationality and procedural impropriety. Additionally now, section 7 of the HRA 1998 allows for judicial review proceedings to be brought on the basis that a public authority has acted in a way which is incompatible with a Convention right.

As to when judicial review proceedings are the appropriate vehicle in respect of any complaint regarding the formalities of detention, reference has already been made to the judgment in *Barker v Barking* [1998] EWCA Civ 1347. In that case, Lord Woolf expressed the view that judicial review proceedings might have been more appropriate in *Re S-C* [1995] EWCA Civ 60, when the complaint was of a failure to consult the patient's nearest relative before applying for detention under section 3 of the MHA 1983, and in *R (on the application of C) v South London & Maudsley NHS Trust & Anor* [2001] EWHC Admin 1025, where the complaint was, similarly, of a failure to consult the nearest relative – the case was brought, without criticism, as a judicial review claim, not as a habeas corpus one.

On the facts of *Barker v Barking* [1998] EWCA Civ 1347, the court expressed the clear view that judicial review proceedings were the most appropriate route where the complaint was that a consultant renewing a patient's detention could not properly have come to the conclusion that the patient met the criteria for renewal of detention under section 20 of the MHA 1983. A similar complaint formed the basis of a judicial review claim in the case of *R (on the application of DR) v Mersey Care NHS Trust* [2002] EWHC 1810 (Admin).

Judicial review was the appropriate way to challenge the decision of an ASW (see para 2.3.3) to apply for a patient's detention in hospital shortly after the patient had been discharged by a tribunal (*R (on the application of von Brandenburg) v East London and the City Mental Health NHS Trust and Another* [2003] UKHL 58, [2004] 2 AC 280), the argument being whether the ASW's decision was unlawful on the ground of irrationality. Also, it was the appropriate way to challenge a decision by the Home Secretary to recall a patient under section 42 of the MHA 1983 in *R (on the application of MM) v Secretary of State for the Home Department* [2007] EWCA Civ 687, the issue being whether, on the facts, the Home Secretary's decision was reasonable.

The rules governing judicial review proceedings in the High Court are contained in Part 54 of the Civil Procedure Rules 1998 (SI 1998/3132).

14.3 CHALLENGING THE SUBSTANTIVE LAWFULNESS OF DETENTION – THE LEGAL AND ADMINISTRATIVE FRAMEWORK FOR MENTAL HEALTH TRIBUNALS

14.3.1 Tribunals, Courts and Enforcement Act 2007

The Tribunals, Courts and Enforcement Act 2007 brought organisational coherence to the work of tribunals in all areas of law, creating a single, unified judicial structure encompassing them all. It created two types of tribunal, the First-tier Tribunal (or tribunal of first instance) and the Upper Tribunal (or appellate tribunal). It also grouped all tribunals into chambers covering broadly similar subject matter. There are six First-tier Tribunal Chambers and four Upper Tribunal Chambers.

14.3.2 Mental health tribunals

Any application or reference made by or in respect of a patient subject to the MHA 1983 will be considered by a First-tier Tribunal which specialises in mental health law, otherwise known as an MHT. The MHT is part of the Health, Education and Social Care Chamber, alongside tribunals dealing with care standards, special educational needs, and primary health lists. The Chamber issues procedural rules and guidance under which tribunals in these areas of law must operate. These are considered in Chapter 15. The administrative support for MHTs is provided by Her Majesty's Courts & Tribunals Service (HMCTS), an executive agency of the MOJ. Any appeal against the decision of an MHT will be considered by an Upper Tribunal in the Administrative Appeals Chamber (UT (AAC)).

14.3.3   Composition of mental health tribunals

In December 2009, the Senior President of Tribunals issued a Practice Statement ('Composition of Tribunals in relation to matters that fall to be decided by the Health, Education and Social Care Chamber on or after 18 January 2010'), the effect of which was to confirm that the MHT will comprise a judge (the legal member), an RMP (the medical member), and a third member who has substantial experience of health or social care matters (the specialist lay member). MHT members in any given case will be assembled by HMCTS from a pool of judges, medical members and specialist lay members all of whom are appointed by the Lord Chancellor through the Judicial Appointments Committee.

14.4   APPLICATIONS TO THE MENTAL HEALTH TRIBUNAL

According to rule 32(1) of the Tribunal Procedure Rules 2008, any application to the MHT must be:

    (a)   made in writing;
    (b)   signed (in the case of an application, by the applicant or any person authorised by the applicant to do so); and
    (c)   sent or delivered to the Tribunal so that it is received within the time specified in the Mental Health Act 1983 or the Repatriation of Prisoners Act 1984.

There is no prescribed application form, but HMCTS produces one of its own which is widely used.

A patient must have capacity to apply to the MHT, but in *MH v Secretary of State for Health and others* [2005] UKHL 60, Baroness Hale noted the 'very limited capacity required'.

14.4.1   Applications by an unrestricted patient

The rules governing applications to the MHT by patients under *Part II* of the MHA 1983 are set out in section 66. Those governing applications from *unrestricted patients under Part III* are set out in Schedule 1, Part I and section 69. In essence, the rules dictate when and how often a patient may apply to the MHT.

Table 14.1 sets out when an unrestricted patient may apply to the MHT, and how often, depending upon his detaining section.

Table 14.1   Applications to the mental health tribunal by unrestricted patients

Type of section	Period for submitting application	Authority
Section 2	The first 14 days of detention	Section 66(2)(a)
Section 3	Once in the first 6 months and once during each subsequent period of renewal	Section 66(2)(b) and (f)
Section 7 (guardianship)	Once in the first 6 months and once during each period of renewal	Section 66(2)(c) and (f)
Section 37 (hospital order)	Not in the first 6 months but once during each period of renewal	Schedule 1, Part I, paras 2 and 9, and section 66(2)(f)
Section 37 (guardianship order)	As for section 7	Section 69(1)(b)(i) and section 66(2)(f)
Section 47	Once in first 6 months following transfer and once during each period of renewal	Section 69(2)(b) and section 66(2)(f)
Section 48	As for section 47	As for section 47
Notional hospital order	Once in the first 6 months following the expiry of restriction or limitation direction and once during each period of renewal	Section 69(2)(a) and section 66(2)(f)
CTO (following detention under section 3)	Once in the first 6 months and once during each period of renewal	Section 66(2)(ca) and section 66(2)(fza)
CTO (following detention under Part III)	Once in the period between the end of 6 months starting with the date of the hospital order and 6 months from the start of the CTO, and once during each period of renewal	Section 69(4)
CTO revocation (following detention under section 3)	Once in the first 6 months from revocation, and once during each period of renewal	Section 66(2)(cb) and Section 66(2)(fza)
CTO revocation (following detention under Part III)	As above unless still within 6 months of the hospital order, in which case first 6-month period begins 6 months from date of hospital order	Section 69(4)

14.4.2   Applications by a restricted patient

The rules governing when and how often applications to the MHT may be made by restricted patients are set out in section 70 and section 75 of the MHA 1983.

The rules are summarised in Table 14.2.

Table 14.2   Applications to the mental health tribunal by restricted patients

Type of section	*Period for submitting application*	*Authority*
Section 37/41	No application in first 6 months, once in next 6 months and once in each subsequent 12-month period	Section 70
Section 45A	As above	As above
Section 47/49	As above	As above
Section 48/49	As above	As above
Conditionally discharged	No application in the first year following conditional discharge, once in the second year, and once in every subsequent 2-year period	Section 75(2)
Recalled conditionally discharged	As for section 37/41	Section 75(1)(b) and section 70

14.4.3   Applications by the nearest relative

Applications to the MHT may be made not just by the patient himself, but, in certain circumstances, by his nearest relative. Rules governing applications by the patient's nearest relative are set out in section 66 and section 69 of the MHA 1983. They are of no application to restricted patients, who have no nearest relative for the purposes of the Act.

The rules are summarised in Table 14.3.

Table 14.3   Applications to the mental health tribunal by the patient's nearest relative

Type of section	Period for submission	Authority
Patient is subject to section 2, section 3, CTO (following section 3), section 7 (guardianship), and nearest relative is displaced on grounds in section 29(3)(c) or (d)	Once in the first 12 months from displacement and once in any subsequent 12-month period while the order is in force	Section 66(2)(g)
Patient is subject to section 3 or CTO (following section 3) and RC has barred nearest relative's discharge of patient	Once in the 28-day period from date nearest relative is informed of the barring report	Section 66(2)(d)
Section 37 (hospital order)	Same entitlement as the patient	Section 69(1)(a)
Section 37 (guardianship order)	In the first 12 months of the order and in any subsequent 12-month period	Section 69(1)(b)(ii)
Section 47	As for section 37 (hospital order)	Section 69(1)(a) and section 47(3)
Section 48	As above	Section 69(1)(a) and section 48(3)
Notional hospital order	As above	Section 69(1)(a) and section 41(5)
CTO following section 37	Same entitlement as patient	Section 69(1)(a)

14.5   REFERENCES TO THE MENTAL HEALTH TRIBUNAL BY HOSPITAL MANAGERS AND SECRETARY OF STATE FOR JUSTICE

Regardless of the right of the patient or his nearest relative to apply to the MHT, Part V of the MHA 1983 stipulates that there are certain occasions when a patient's case must be referred to the MHT for consideration. Where the patient is unrestricted, responsibility for referring the case lies with hospital managers; where the patient is restricted, it lies with the SSJ.

14.5.1 References by hospital managers

Section 68 of the MHA 1983 places a duty on hospital managers to refer the cases of unrestricted patients under Part II in certain specified circumstances. A duty also applies in respect of certain unrestricted patients under Part III (Schedule 1, Part I, para 2). Managers have no power to refer the case of a restricted patient. The circumstances in which a reference must be made are summarised below. There is no power to refer in any other circumstances.

Six-month reference

Where the patient is detained under section 2 or section 3 of the MHA 1983, is subject to a CTO (following section 3), has had his CTO (following section 3) revoked or has been transferred from guardianship to hospital (section 19), his case must be referred to the MHT after the *expiry of 6 months* from the 'applicable day' (section 68(2)). The 'applicable' day is defined by section 68(5). For patients detained under section 2, it is the start date of that period of detention. For patients under section 3, it is the start date of that period of detention, or of any preceding detention under section 2. For CTO patients, it is the start date of the detention under section 3 which preceded the CTO, or of any detention under section 2 that preceded the section 3. For patients under section 19, it is the date of transfer.

The likelihood of a reference in cases under section 2 is exceedingly remote, and is only conceivable in circumstances when detention under section 2 has been extended (section 29(4)) pending the outcome of county court proceedings to displace the nearest relative.

A reference will not be required if during the 6-month period from the applicable day, the patient's case has already been considered by the MHT, for example, as a result of an application by the patient (section 68(3) of the MHA 1983). Hearings prompted by an application by a patient while detained for *assessment* (section 2) are, however, discounted for these purposes.

Three-year reference

The same categories of patients and, additionally, unrestricted patients under Part III of the MHA 1983 must also have their cases referred to the MHT whenever a period of 3 years has elapsed since their last tribunal hearing (section 68(6), and Schedule 1, Part I, paras 2 and 10).

Under 18 year olds

The duty to refer after 3 years under section 68(6) of the MHA 1983 (above) is modified in respect of under 18 year olds so that it arises whenever a period of one year has elapsed since the last tribunal hearing.

Community treatment order revocation

Hospital managers must also refer the case of any patient whose CTO is revoked (section 68(7) of the MHA 1983). The reference should be made 'as soon as possible' after revocation.

14.5.2   References by the Secretary of State for Justice

The equivalent duty on the SSJ to refer cases of restricted patients is set out in section 71 of the MHA 1983. As well as being under a duty to refer in the circumstances summarised below, the SSJ also has a discretion to refer a patient's case at any time (section 71(1)).

Three-year reference

The SSJ must refer the case of any restricted patient who is detained in hospital and whose case has not been considered by the MHT within the last 3 years (section 71(2) of the MHA 1983).

Recall from conditional discharge

The SSJ must refer the case of any conditionally discharged patient who is recalled to hospital (section 75(1) of the MHA 1983). The reference must be made within one month of the day on which the patient arrives back in hospital.

14.6   DISCRETIONARY REFERENCES TO THE MENTAL HEALTH TRIBUNAL BY THE SECRETARY OF STATE FOR HEALTH

Section 67 of the MHA 1983 gives the SSH the discretion to refer to the MHT for hearing the case of any unrestricted detained patient, any community patient or anyone subject to guardianship.

The SSH may be requested to exercise his discretion by the patient directly or by hospital managers on the patient's behalf. The 1983 Code advises (para 30.40) that managers should consider requesting a reference in respect of any patient whose rights under Article 5(4) of the ECHR may be at risk of being violated because he is unable to have his case considered speedily by the MHT. Requests are made most commonly when a patient under section 2 of the MHA 1983 misses the 14-day deadline for submission of an application, or when detention under section 2 has been extended under section 29(4).

In *R (on the application of Modaresi) v Secretary of State for Health and Others* [2013] UKSC 53, the Supreme Court upheld a Court of Appeal decision that it was lawful for the SSH to decline to refer a case to the MHT where the patient, having missed the 14-day deadline for an application under section 2, was now detained under section 3 and therefore able to exercise her entitlement to apply under that section, particularly since the SSH had held out the possibility of referring under section 67 once the entitlement under section 3 was used up.

14.7   CHANGES IN LEGAL STATUS

It may be several weeks between an application or reference being submitted and the hearing taking place, and it is not uncommon, therefore, for the patient's legal status to have changed by the time of the hearing. The following rules will apply in such cases:

- Where a patient under section 2 of the MHA 1983 becomes detained under section 3 before the hearing of his application under section 2, he is entitled to continue with that application notwithstanding his change of legal status, but the application will be determined according to the discharge criteria under section 3 (see *R v South Thames Mental Health Review Tribunal ex parte M* (1998) COD 38 and *KF, MO and FF v Birmingham & Solihull Mental Health NHS Foundation Trust* [2010] UKUT 185 (AAC)). The patient will retain his right to make an additional application pursuant to his detention under section 3.
- Where a patient under section 3 is discharged onto a CTO before the hearing of his application under section 3, the same principle will apply and the patient may proceed with that application, although it will be determined according to the CTO criteria (see *KF, MO and FF v Birmingham & Solihull Mental Health NHS Foundation Trust* [2010] UKUT 185 (AAC)). The patient will retain the right to an additional application pursuant to the imposition of the CTO.
- Where a CTO patient has had his CTO revoked, prompting an automatic reference under section 68(7), the reference will proceed even though the

patient is discharged onto a new CTO by the time of the hearing (see *PS v Camden & Islington NHS Foundation Trust* [2011] UKUT 143 (AAC)).

- As a matter of practice (confirmed, e.g. in *R (on the application of MN) v MHRT* [2008] EWHC 3383 (Admin)), a patient under section 47, 49 or 45A who applies under section 70 but whose restriction direction or limitation direction ends, and who has therefore become an unrestricted notional hospital order patient by the time of the hearing, will be allowed to proceed with that application (even though it is technically now invalid) and will not be required to submit a fresh application under section 69(2)(a).

Chapter 15

Mental Health Tribunals – Rules of Procedure

15.1 INTRODUCTION

MHT procedure is decided according to the Tribunal Procedure (First-tier Tribunal) (Health, Education and Social Care Chamber) Rules 2008 (SI 2008/ 2699). These Rules, which apply to all First-tier Tribunal hearings within that chamber, are divided into five parts, Parts 1, 2 and 5 being of general application, Part 4 of specific application to MHTs, and Part 3 of application to non-MHT cases. They are supplemented by Practice Directions, issued by the Senior President of Tribunals. This chapter identifies some of the more significant rules, and considers them alongside some fundamental common law principles which apply to the conduct of hearings.

15.2 OVERRIDING OBJECTIVE

Rule 2 of the Tribunal Procedure Rules 2008 provides that the overriding objective of the Rules 'is to enable the tribunal to deal with cases fairly and justly'. The MHT is expected to give effect to the overriding objective whenever exercising its powers, and parties are expected to help the MHT to achieve this. According to rule 2(2), this means:

>   (a)   dealing with the case in ways which are proportionate to the importance of the case, the complexity of the issues, the anticipated costs and the resources of the parties;
>   (b)   avoiding unnecessary formality and seeking flexibility in the proceedings;
>   (c)   ensuring so far as practical that the parties are able to participate fully in the proceedings;
>   (d)   using any special expertise of the Tribunal effectively;
>   (e)   avoiding delay, so far as compatible with proper consideration of the issues.

15.3 PRE-HEARING PROCEDURAL RULES

The following rules regarding pre-hearing procedure are of particular note.

15.3.1 Parties

The parties to MHT proceedings will be (rule 1(3) of the Tribunal Procedure Rules 2008):

> the patient, the responsible authority, the Secretary of State (if the patient is a restricted patient or in a reference under rule 32(8) (seeking approval under section 86 of the Mental Health Act 1983)), and any other person who starts a mental health case by making an application.

In the case of a detained patient, the responsible authority will be the hospital managers, in the case of a patient subject to guardianship, it will be the LSSA, and in the case of a CTO patient, it will be the managers of the hospital in which he was detained immediately before the CTO was made (rule 1(3) of the Tribunal Procedure Rules 2008). The nearest relative will only be a party to the proceedings if he makes the application himself.

The Tribunal Procedure Rules 2008 set out that anyone who is a party to the proceedings may:

- receive a copy of any application or reference (rule 32(3));
- appoint a representative to act in the proceedings (rule 11);
- receive a copy of any document provided to the tribunal by any other party (rule 32(3));
- apply to the MHT for a direction (rule 6);
- receive written notice of any direction made by the MHT (rule 6);
- attend the hearing (rule 36);
- receive reasonable notice of the time and place of the hearing (rule 37).

15.3.2 Case management powers

Under rule 5(1) of the Tribunal Procedure Rules 2008, the MHT is given the general power to regulate its own procedure. Under rule 5(2), it 'may give a direction in relation to the conduct or disposal of proceedings at any time, including a direction amending, suspending or setting aside an earlier direction'. Examples of directions that the MHT may make are provided in rule 5(3). They include:

- consolidating two or more sets of proceedings;
- dealing with an issue as a preliminary issue;
- holding a hearing to consider any matter;
- adjourning or postponing a hearing.

15.3.3   Provision of reports and other written material

The Tribunal Procedure Rules 2008 place no duty on the patient (or nearest relative) to submit any written material in support of any application or reference, but do require written material from the responsible authority and, in restricted cases, the SSJ.

Information to be supplied by the responsible authority

Written reports should be supplied by the responsible authority within 3 weeks of the application or reference (rule 32(6) of the Tribunal Procedure Rules 2008), or in cases under section 2, 'as soon as practicable' (rule 32(5)(b)). These reports will then form the written evidence for consideration at the hearing. Once received by the tribunal, and subject to rule 14(2) (see below), any reports should be circulated to all other parties. The reports to be supplied by the responsible authority are:

- a statement of information about the patient (to include name, date of birth, where the patient is detained, date of admission, name of RC, name of body responsible for aftercare services, name of care coordinator);
- a report from the patient's RC;
- a social circumstances report;
- a nursing report (where the patient is detained).

Guidance on the content of reports is found in the Practice Direction, 'First-tier Tribunal, Health, Education and Social Care Chamber, Statements and Reports in Mental Health Cases', last issued by the Senior President of Tribunals on 28 October 2013.

Information to be supplied by the Secretary of State for Justice

In addition, in all restricted cases, rule 32(7B) of the Tribunal Procedure Rules 2008 requires the SSJ to prepare:

- a summary of the offence or alleged offence;
- a record of any criminal convictions or findings recorded against the patient;

- full details of the patient's liability to detention under the MHA 1983 since the restrictions were imposed;
- any further information in the SSJ's possession that he considers relevant to the proceedings.

15.3.4 Timing of the hearing

Where a patient is *detained under* section 2, the hearing of the case 'must start within 7 days after the date on which the tribunal received the application notice' (rule 37(2) of the Tribunal Procedure Rules 2008). Where a *conditionally discharged* patient is recalled to hospital, the recall hearing will start at least 5 weeks but no more than 8 weeks from the date on which the tribunal received the reference under section 75(1) of the MHA 1983 (rule 37(2)). Otherwise, the Rules do not stipulate when a hearing must take place, but guidance from HMCTS is that an unrestricted case will be listed for hearing within 8 weeks of any application or reference, and a restricted case, 16 weeks.

15.3.5 Representation

Rule 11(1) of the Tribunal Procedure Rules 2008 provides that any party 'may appoint a representative (whether a legal representative or not) to represent that party in the proceedings'. Once appointed, the representative's name and address must be supplied in writing to the tribunal and to all parties to the proceedings (rule 11(2)). The representative may then do anything that would be permitted or required to be done by the party except for signing a witness statement (rule 11(3)).

Rule 11(7) of the Tribunal Procedure Rules 2008 provides that if a patient has not appointed a representative, the tribunal may appoint a legal representative for the patient where:

(a)   the patient has stated that they do not wish to conduct their own case or that they wish to be represented; or

(b)   the patient lacks the capacity to appoint a representative, but the Tribunal believes that it is in the patient's best interest for the patient to be represented.

15.3.6 Non-disclosure of material

The law

Rule 32(3) of the Tribunal Procedure Rules 2008, which states that when it receives a document, the tribunal must send a copy to every other party, is subject to rule 14(2), which provides that the tribunal may give a direction prohibiting the disclosure of a document or information to a person if it is satisfied:

(a)   … that such disclosure would be likely to cause that person or some other person serious harm; and

(b)   … having regard to the interests of justice, that it is proportionate to give such a direction.

Serious harm

Neither of the leading authorities on rule 14 of the Tribunal Procedure Rules 2008, *Dorset Healthcare NHS Foundation Trust v MH* [2009] UKUT 4 (AAC) and *RM v St Andrew's Healthcare* [2010] 1 MHLR 176, provides any assistance in defining what is meant by 'likely to cause that person or some other person serious harm'. However, in *Roberts v Nottinghamshire Healthcare NHS Trust* [2008] 1 MHLR 294, in relation to a similar test under the Data Protection (Subject Access Modification) (Health) Order 2000 (SI 2000/413), Cranston J stated that, 'the question is whether there may very well be a risk of harm to health even if the risk falls short of being more probable than not'.

Interests of justice

In *RM v St Andrew's Healthcare* [2010] 1 MHLR 176, HHJ Jacobs said (at [31]) that in applying the interests of justice test to decisions regarding disclosure 'justice and fairness generally requires openness'.

Disclosure to legal representative

Under rule 14(5) of the Tribunal Procedure Rules 2008, if the party has appointed a legal representative, then a direction preventing disclosure under rule 14(2) may also be accompanied by a direction that the relevant documents or information are disclosed to the representative, if the tribunal is satisfied that:

(a)   disclosure to the representative would be in the interests of the party; and

(b)   the representative will act in accordance with paragraph (6).

Rule 14(6) of the Tribunal Procedure Rules 2008 provides that documents or information provided to a representative in accordance with rule 14(5) must not 'be disclosed either directly or indirectly to any other person without the tribunal's consent'.

Most applications under rule 14 of the Tribunal Procedure Rules 2008 will be for non-disclosure of material to the patient. Assuming the patient to be legally represented, the normal procedure in such cases is as follows:

- the responsible authority will supply the usual information and reports to the tribunal (rule 32);
- in addition, the responsible authority will extract the sensitive information or document from any documents and will provide it to the tribunal as a separate document, together with reasons for its exclusion (rule 14(3));
- a judge will then take a preliminary view on whether disclosure should be allowed, applying the test in rule 14(2); a direction will be made accordingly;
- if disclosure is not allowed then, unless exceptional circumstances apply, the excluded material will be supplied to the patient's legal representative (rule 14(5)), along with the usual information and reports; the excluded material will be marked 'not for disclosure to the patient';
- in accordance with rule 14(6), the patient's legal representative is then prohibited from disclosing the document or the information (although not the fact of the prohibition itself) to the patient;
- the legal representative will be at liberty either before the hearing or at the hearing itself to invite the tribunal to reconsider the prohibition of disclosure under rule 14(2);
- if the prohibition remains in place, the tribunal will go ahead without the patient having had access to the excluded material.

15.3.7 Withdrawals of applications

According to rule 17(1) of the Tribunal Procedure Rules 2008, a party (invariably the patient) may give notice of the withdrawal of its case, or any part of it:

(a) at any time before a hearing to consider the disposal of the proceedings (or, if the Tribunal disposes of the proceedings without a hearing, before that disposal), by sending or delivering to the Tribunal a written notice of withdrawal; or

(b) orally at a hearing.

Rule 17(2) of the Tribunal Procedure Rules 2008 provides, however, that any notice of withdrawal 'will not take effect unless the tribunal consents to the withdrawal'.

The proposed withdrawal may be rather late in the day. In *MB v BEH MH NHS Trust* [2011] UKUT 328 (AAC), for example, the Upper Tribunal accepted that a patient should be able to withdraw his application mid-way through a hearing, at the conclusion of the RC's evidence.

It is not entirely clear what may prompt a tribunal to withhold its permission for the withdrawal of an application. In *R (on the application of O) v MHRT* [2006] EWHC 2659 (Admin), the High Court held that a tribunal may refuse to consent to withdrawal where the withdrawal was 'merely a tactical ploy and is not in the interests of the patient'. The phrase 'tactical ploy' has never, however, been defined satisfactorily, and in *KF, MO and FF v Birmingham & Solihull Mental Health NHS Foundation Trust* [2010] UKUT 185 (AAC), the Upper Tribunal warned of the 'danger of an unduly broad approach' to its definition, and doubted in fact whether it was helpful to use it at all. In his Practice Statement, 'Delegations of Functions to Staff on or after 2 November 2010' the Senior President of Tribunals implied that consent to withdrawal will often be a formality when he confirmed that consent to the withdrawal may be given by HMCTS administrative staff employed by HMCTS in cases where:

- the notice of withdrawal is received not less than 7 days before the listed hearing date;
- there is no concurrent application or reference;
- there is no reason to believe that the withdrawal is a tactical ploy.

15.3.8 Medical examination of the patient by the medical member

Until 2014, rule 34 of the Tribunal Procedure Rules 2008 required 'an appropriate member of the panel' (the medical member), so far as practicable, to conduct a preliminary examination of the patient and take such other steps as necessary to form an opinion of the patient's mental condition before any hearing took place. This general rule applied without exception to all tribunal hearings. As a result of changes to rule 34 which took effect in April 2014, however, there is no longer a presumption that a preliminary medical examination will take place in all cases. Different rules now apply, depending on whether or not the patient is detained under section 2 of the MHA 1983.

Cases under section 2 of the Mental Health Act 1983

Rule 34(1) of the Tribunal Procedure Rules 2008 provides that in cases under section 2 of the MHA 1983, the medical member must, so far as practicable, conduct a preliminary medical examination of the patient in order to form an opinion of the patient's mental condition, unless the tribunal is satisfied that the patient does not want such an examination.

All other cases

Rule 34(1) of the Tribunal Procedure Rules 2008 also provides that in all cases where the patient is not detained under section 2 of the MHA 1983, there will be *no* preliminary medical examination of the patient by the medical member unless:

- not less than 14 days before the hearing, the patient or his representative informs the tribunal in writing that the patient wishes there to be a preliminary medical examination; or
- in cases where the patient lacks the capacity to make a decision about the preliminary medical examination, not less than 14 days before the hearing, the patient's representative informs the tribunal in writing that he wishes there to be a preliminary medical examination; or
- the tribunal directs that there should be a preliminary medical examination.

Guidance from the Health, Education and Social Care Chamber (*Amendments to the Tribunal Procedure (First-tier Tribunal) (Health, Education and Social Care Chamber) Rules 2008*, 11 March 2014) indicates that a direction from the tribunal that there should be a preliminary examination may be made in advance of the hearing as part of the general case management powers, or on the day of the hearing itself. A direction on the day of the hearing itself will be appropriate where the patient completely fails to attend the hearing, in which case the panel itself should direct the medical member to conduct a preliminary examination on the ward before proceeding with the hearing 'unless such an interview is impractical or unnecessary'.

Purpose of preliminary examination

Whenever a preliminary examination does take place, it will be, as before, in order for the medical member to 'form an opinion of the patient's mental condition' (rule 34(1)(b) of the Tribunal Procedure Rules 2008). Any such opinion may cover the question of his detainability, not just diagnosis (see *R (on the application of S) v MHRT* [2002] EWHC 2522 (Admin) and *R (on the application of RD) v MHRT* [2007] EWHC 781 (Admin)). Such opinion as is formed, however, must be provisional. It should also be communicated to the other members of the tribunal and to the parties at the outset of the hearing.

Medical member's review of medical records

A medical member would normally be expected to review a patient's medical records as part of the preliminary examination. With this in mind, rule 32(9) of the Tribunal Procedure Rules 2008 (as amended by the Tribunal Procedure (Amendment) Rules 2014 (SI 2014/514) provides that:

(9)   the responsible authority must make records relating to the detention or treatment of the patient and any after-care services available to the Tribunal on request and the Tribunal or an appropriate member of the Tribunal may, before or at the hearing, examine and take notes and copies of such records for use in connection with the proceedings.

In light of the changes to rule 34 of the Tribunal Procedure Rules 2008, the guidance issued by the Health, Education and Social Care Chamber on 11 March 2014 (see above) confirms that the medical member continues to be expected to review the medical records as part of the preliminary examination where such an examination is required to take place, but that routine inspection of the records is not expected in cases where there is to be no preliminary examination or where the preliminary examination only arises because the patient fails to attend the hearing.

15.4   RULES AFFECTING CONDUCT OF HEARINGS

The following rules which apply to the conduct of MHT hearings are of particular note.

15.4.1   Requirement for a hearing

As a general rule, the tribunal must hold a hearing before making a decision which disposes of the proceedings (rule 35(1) of the Tribunal Procedure Rules 2008). The only exception is the case of a reference under section 68(2) of the MHA 1983 when the patient concerned is on a CTO. According to rule 35(3) (as amended by the Tribunal Procedure (Amendment) Rules 2012 (SI 2012/500)), no hearing need take place in such a case if:

(a)   the patient has stated in writing that he does not wish to attend or be represented at the hearing and the tribunal is satisfied that the patient has the capacity to decide whether or not to make that decision; or

(b)   the patient's representative has stated in writing that the patient does not wish to attend or be represented at the hearing.

15.4.2   Entitlement to attend and participate

Each *party* is entitled to attend the hearing (rule 36(1) of the Tribunal Procedure Rules 2008). This is subject, however, to rule 38(4), which allows the tribunal to direct the exclusion of any person from any hearing or part of it where:

(a)   the person's conduct is disrupting or likely to disrupt the hearing;

(b)   the person's presence is likely to prevent another person from giving evidence or making submissions freely;

(c)   the person needs to be excluded in order to give effect to a
        direction under rule 14(2);

(d)   the purpose of the hearing would be defeated by the attendance of
        that person.

Each *person notified of the proceedings* under rule 33 of the Tribunal Procedure
Rules 2008 is also entitled to attend and participate, to the extent that the
tribunal considers proper, or to provide written submissions (rule 36(2)).

15.4.3   Proceedings in absence

According to rule 39(1) of the Tribunal Procedure Rules 2008, the tribunal may
proceed in the absence of a *party* where it:

(a)   is satisfied that the party has been notified of the hearing or that
        reasonable steps have been taken to notify the party of the hearing; and

(b)   considers that it is in the interests of justice to proceed with the
        hearing.

According to rule 39(2) of the Tribunal Procedure Rules 2008, however, the
tribunal may not proceed in the absence of the *patient* unless also satisfied that:

(a)   the patient:

        (i)   has decided not to attend the hearing; or

        (ii)   is unable to attend the hearing for reasons of ill health; and

(b)   an examination under rule 34:

        (i)   has been carried out; or

        (ii)   is impractical or unnecessary.

15.4.4   Conduct of the hearing

The tribunal has considerable discretion as to how an individual hearing will be
conducted and may give directions under rule 15 of the Tribunal Procedure
Rules 2008 as to: the issues upon which it will require evidence and
submissions, the nature of the evidence or submissions it requires, the provision
of expert evidence, the number of witnesses that may be called, and the manner
in which evidence and submissions are provided. The tribunal may admit
evidence that would otherwise be inadmissible in civil proceedings
(rule 15(2)(a)). It may also exclude evidence on grounds, inter alia, that it would
be unfair to admit it (rule 15(2)(b)). Rule 15(3) allows for evidence to be taken
on oath, although this would only be in exceptional circumstances.

15.5   OTHER COMMON LAW AND STATUTORY PROVISIONS CONCERNING THE CONDUCT OF THE HEARING

15.5.1   Standard and burden of proof

The *standard of proof* in tribunal hearings is the normal civil one, the balance of probabilities (see *R (on the application of AN) v Mental Health Review Tribunal (Northern Region)* [2005] EWCA Civ 1605). The *burden of proof* varies according to the type of case:

- *Unrestricted detained patients*: the burden is on the detaining authority to show why the patient should not be discharged (section 72(1)(a) and (b) of the MHA 1983).
- *CTO patients*: the burden is on the responsible authority to show why the patient should not be discharged (section 72(1)(c)).
- *Guardianship patients*: the burden is on the patient to show why he should be discharged (section 72(4)).
- *Restricted detained patients*: the burden is on the detaining authority to show why the patient should not be discharged (section 73(1)(a)). The burden then shifts to the patient to show why discharge should not be conditional (section 73(1)(b)).
- *Conditionally discharged patients*: the decision whether to absolutely discharge a patient, or to remove or vary a condition, is a matter for the discretion of the MHT and there is no burden either way (section 75(3)) (however, see para 17.4.3).

15.5.2   An inquisitorial jurisdiction

The MHT is an inquisitorial jurisdiction. It is not, therefore, a passive arbiter which makes a decision simply on the basis of whatever evidence is presented to it and is instead entitled to play an active role in establishing the facts upon which its decision is made, and to form its own view on the evidence, regardless of the position taken by the respective parties.

In *R (on the application of X) v MHRT* [2003] EWHC 1272 (Admin), the High Court confirmed that the tribunal may initiate its own evidence-gathering exercise and is not restricted to basing its decision solely on the evidence put to it by the parties. The court noted that although the burden was on the detaining authority to establish to the tribunal's satisfaction that the conditions for detention existed, the tribunal will 'inevitably, and particularly in cases involving the release of someone who has committed a very serious offence ... be concerned that it has before it all relevant information which will enable it to reach the correct decision'.

In *R v London South and South West Region MHRT ex parte Moyle* [1999] MHLR 195, the High Court noted that it 'was clearly Parliament's intention that the tribunal should come to its own conclusion as to whether or not in the case of restricted patients the criteria for discharge had been met', and that, 'it is open to a tribunal provided they act rationally to disagree with the view of any psychiatrist whose evidence is put before it'.

In *R (on the application of MP) v First-tier Tribunal and West London Mental Health NHS Trust* [2012] UKUT 231 (AAC), the First-tier Tribunal stated that in view of the evidence from the RC that the patient's mental disorder was not of a nature or degree to warrant detention, it had no option but to discharge the patient from detention. The decision was successfully appealed on grounds, among others, that the tribunal had wrongly regarded itself as bound by the RC's view.

15.5.3   Bias

Proceedings in which there is bias on the part of the tribunal are objectionable as being in breach of the common law principle that any decision should be taken by an impartial body. As to what test for bias to apply, judgments from the House of Lords in *Magill v Porter* [2001] UKHL 67 and *Lawal v Northern Spirit Limited* [2003] UKHL 35 approved the common law test as being 'whether a fair minded and informed observer, having considered the given facts, would conclude that there was a real possibility that the tribunal was biased'.

Where there is the real possibility of bias, such proceedings would also be objectionable as being in breach of the right to a fair and public hearing from an 'independent and impartial tribunal' under Article 6 of the ECHR. The point may be taken on either basis and the same principles will apply to each.

The fact that the MHT's medical member is employed by the health authority which is detaining the patient would not, of itself, cause a fair minded observer to apprehend bias (*R on the application of PD) v West Midlands and North West MHRT* [2004] EWCA Civ 311).

Similarly, the mere fact that the MHT contains a member who has previously considered the patient's case does not give rise to a reasonable apprehension of bias. In *R (on the application of M) v MHRT* [2005] EWHC 2791 (Admin), the High Court decided that a 'fair minded and informed observer would not attribute to the judge an inability or reluctance to change his mind when faced with the rational basis for doing so'.

What then of the requirement under rule 34 of the Tribunal Procedure Rules 2008 that the medical member should see the patient before the hearing with a view to forming an opinion as to his mental condition, even his detainability? Does that not run the risk of creating a hearing which is biased from the outset? The answer given in *R (on the application of RD) v MHRT* [2007] EWHC 781 (Admin) was 'no', as long as any opinion formed by the medical member remains provisional. The same view was taken in *R (on the application of S) v MHRT* [2002] EWHC 2522 (Admin), where it was held that the 'forming of an opinion before the hearing is normally objectionable only if it is not provisional, liable to be changed by the evidence adduced and submissions of the parties, but is firm and concluded: in which case the hearing is an ineffective charade'.

In *GB v SW London and St George's MH NHS Trust and others* [2013] UKUT 58 (AAC), the Upper Tribunal took the view that a preliminary view expressed by the medical member during questioning of the RC ('I have no issue with the nature') had to be looked at in the context of the case as a whole, and could not, on the facts, be regarded as a concluded view. The case does illustrate, however, that tribunal members must exercise caution when commenting on the evidence, and should not give any indication of having formed a concluded view during the hearing. In *MB v BEH MH NHS Trust* [2011] UKUT 328 (AAC), for example, comments made by the judge at the conclusion of the RC's evidence, suggesting that the patient may wish to consider withdrawing his application given the strength of evidence against discharge, were evidence of a decision having been reached before the conclusion of the hearing, and were therefore objectionable, however well-intentioned.

Similarly, in *RN v Curo Care* [2011] UKUT 263 (AAC), a decision by the MHT to refuse to allow the legal representative to argue the case for a CTO indicated a concluded view from the outset of the hearing on an arguable point and was, therefore, found by the Upper Tribunal to amount to a breach of the right to a fair hearing.

In *Equilibrium Healthcare v AK* [2013] UKUT 543 (AAC), the Upper Tribunal considered an appeal from a hospital on the basis that the MHT's medical member was biased against the RC. Following a previous tribunal hearing in relation to a different patient approximately 3 years earlier, the medical member had questioned the fitness to practise of the RC and had reported him to both the CQC and the General Medical Council. Notwithstanding these actions, the Upper Tribunal concluded that there was insufficient evidence to suggest that the medical member was biased or, even if he had been previously, that the bias had continued for the 3-year period. The fair minded observer 'would know that tribunal members are selected for their ability to take a detached point of view'.

Chapter 16

Mental Health Tribunal Powers – Unrestricted Patients

16.1 INTRODUCTION

The powers of the MHT when considering the cases of unrestricted detained patients (section 2, 3, 37, 47 or 48 of the MHA 1983), patients subject to CTOs and those subject to guardianship are set out in section 72, and are considered in this chapter. Generally speaking, the primary question for any MHT exercising these powers is whether the relevant statutory criteria justifying the particular form of restriction (detention, CTO, guardianship) are in place, and whether or not, therefore, it is under a duty to discharge the patient. However, the MHT is also able to decide the timing of any discharge and, as an alternative to discharge from detention, to make recommendations with regard to transfer, leave and discharge onto a CTO.

The powers under section 72 of the MHA 1983 apply whether the MHT is considering the case as a result of an application or a reference. With applications, the powers are generally the same whether the applicant is the patient or the nearest relative, subject to the qualification set out at para 16.6.2.

16.2 DISCRETIONARY POWER OF DISCHARGE

Section 72 of the MHA 1983 provides the MHT with a general discretion to discharge any unrestricted patient. In the case of detained patients and CTO patients, the discretion comes from section 72(1), and in the case of guardianship, from section 72(4). Each subsection provides that the MHT 'may in any case direct that the patient be discharged'. In practice, the discretion is exercised very rarely, and, almost without exception, if the MHT discharges a patient, it will be because it is required to as a matter of law, not because it chooses to as a matter of discretion. Whether the MHT is required to discharge as a matter of law will be determined by the application of the relevant statutory discharge criteria.

16.3 DETAINED PATIENTS

16.3.1 Statutory criteria in cases under section 2 of the Mental Health Act 1983

According to section 72(1)(a) of the MHA 1983, the MHT which considers the case of a patient detained under section 2 must discharge if not satisfied:

(i) that he is then is suffering from mental disorder or mental disorder of a nature or degree which warrants detention in a hospital for assessment (or for assessment followed by medical treatment) for at least a limited period; or

(ii) that his detention as aforesaid is justified in the interests of his own health or safety or with a view to the protection of other persons.

Comparing these discharge criteria with the admission criteria under section 2 of the MHA 1983, the only difference is that whereas section 2(2)(b) requires an AMHP to be satisfied that a patient '*ought to be* ... detained in the interests of his own health or safety or with a view to the protection of other persons', section 72(1)(a)(ii) requires the MHT to be satisfied that, 'detention ... is *justified* in the interests of his own health or safety or with a view to the protection of other persons'.

16.3.2 Statutory discharge criteria in cases under sections 3, 37 and 47 of the Mental Health Act 1983

According to section 72(1)(b) of the MHA 1983, the MHT which considers the case of an unrestricted patient detained for treatment (sections 3, 37 and 47) must discharge if not satisfied:

(i) that he is then suffering from mental disorder or from mental disorder of a nature or degree which makes it appropriate for him to be liable to be detained in hospital for medical treatment; or

(ii) that it is necessary for the health or safety of the patient or for the protection of other persons that he should receive such treatment; or

(iia) that appropriate medical treatment is available for him; or

(iii) in the case of an application by virtue of paragraph (g) of section 66(1) above, that the patient, if released, would be likely to act in a manner dangerous to other persons or to himself.

The difference to the admission criteria under section 3 of the MHA 1983 is that whereas section 3(2)(a) requires an AMHP to be satisfied that the nature or degree of the disorder makes 'it appropriate for him to *receive medical treatment* in a hospital', section 72(1)(b)(i) requires the MHT to be satisfied that the nature or degree of the disorder makes it 'appropriate for him to *be liable to be detained* in a hospital for medical treatment'.

Unlike patients under section 2 of the MHA 1983, patients detained for treatment may only continue to be detained if the MHT is satisfied that appropriate treatment is available (see para 4.3.2).

16.3.3   Deferred or delayed discharge

If the MHT is required to discharge an unrestricted detained patient in accordance with either section 72(1)(a) or (b) of the MHA 1983, it may direct that discharge take effect 'on a future date' (section 72(3)). Such discharges are commonly referred to as 'deferred discharges', although the term 'delayed discharge' may be preferable since it avoids confusion with the slightly different power to 'defer' discharge in restricted cases under section 73(7) (see para 17.2.4). Whatever the terminology, the MHT is directing discharge, albeit delayed or deferred, and will have concluded that the criteria for detention no longer exist. The decision to discharge is not a provisional one and discharge will take effect on the date specified by the MHT.

The power will typically be used where the MHT is satisfied that the patient is ready for discharge but requires certain practical arrangements to be put in place before discharge can take effect. The MHA 1983 is silent on the period of the deferment, but in practice it will normally be for a matter of days or weeks. In *MP v Mersey Care NHS Trust* [2011] UKUT 107 (AAC), the MHT directed that discharge be delayed for a period of 6 weeks 'to enable the structured aftercare plan to be fully implemented'. That was not objectionable. What was, however, was an accompanying recommendation that the RC should implement a CTO at the point of discharge. As the Upper Tribunal noted, a finding by the MHT that the patient no longer met the criteria for detention prevented it from being able to then recommend a CTO.

16.3.4   Recommendation for leave or transfer

If the MHT decides not to discharge an unrestricted detained patient, it may, as an alternative, make a statutory recommendation under section 72(3) of the MHA 1983 that the patient is granted leave of absence (under section 17) or that he is transferred to another hospital or into guardianship (under section 19). The

Act is clear, however, that either recommendation may only be made 'with a view to facilitating his discharge on a future date' (section 72(3)(a)), and a recommendation for any other reason would have no statutory basis (see *R (on the application of LH) v MHRT and SSH* [2002] EWHC 1522 (Admin)).

Reconvening a hearing following a recommendation

A recommendation is, of course, only a recommendation, and the MHT cannot require the responsible authority to act in accordance with it. What the MHT can do, however, is to 'further consider [the patient's] case in the event of such recommendation not being complied with' (section 72(3)(b)). This will mean holding a further hearing and, possibly, re-visiting the original decision. In *R (on the application of O) v MHRT* [2006] EWHC 2659 (Admin), it was held that, 'it is open to the tribunal to consider the whole of the case (and) whether notwithstanding its previous decision, discharge has become appropriate'.

In practice, when making any statutory recommendation, the MHT will also set a review date, by which time a decision is expected to have been taken by the responsible authority on whether to comply with the recommendation. Once informed of the authority's response to the recommendation, the tribunal will decide whether to reconvene.

In *RB v Nottinghamshire Health Care NHS Trust* [2011] UKUT 73 (AAC), the Upper Tribunal urged caution on tribunals when considering both whether to make recommendations in the first place and whether to reconvene. Although, ultimately, the MHT can discharge where there has been no implementation of a recommendation, this is unlikely to occur, and, otherwise, there is no power to enforce recommendations, merely, as the Upper Tribunal noted, to 'embarrass the authority into explaining its thinking or, possibly, into compliance'. Tribunals should therefore guard against giving a patient 'false hope'.

16.3.5   Recommendation for a community treatment order

An alternative statutory recommendation that the MHT may make if it does not discharge a detained patient is that the RC should consider imposing a CTO. The power comes from section 72(3A) of the MHA 1983, which provides that if a tribunal feels that a CTO may be appropriate, it is not required to discharge the patient, but may instead:

(a)   recommend that the responsible clinician consider whether to make a community treatment order; and

(b)   may (but need not) further consider the patient's case if the responsible clinician does not make an order.

The recommendation in respect of a CTO is different to that in respect of either leave or transfer for three reasons. Firstly (and logically), it need not be with a view to facilitating discharge. Secondly, it is not a recommendation that the RC should pursue a particular course of action, merely a recommendation that he should consider doing so. Thirdly, the power to reconsider the patient's case is not triggered by non-compliance with the recommendation. The RC may consider the issue and decide not to discharge the patient onto a CTO. Although he will have complied with the recommendation, the MHT's power to reconsider is still available.

As with the other recommendations, all of the MHT's original powers are available in the event of a further hearing.

The power is of no relevance in cases under section 2 of the MHA 1983 since the RC has no power to impose a CTO on a patient detained under that section.

16.4   COMMUNITY TREATMENT ORDER PATIENTS

16.4.1   Statutory criteria

According to section 72(1)(c) of the MHA 1983, the MHT which considers the case of a patient who is already subject to a CTO must discharge if not satisfied:

> (i)   that he is then suffering from mental disorder or mental disorder of a nature or degree which makes it appropriate for him to receive medical treatment; or
> (ii)   that it is necessary for his health or safety or for the protection of other persons that he should receive such treatment; or
> (iii) that it is necessary that the responsible clinician should be able to exercise the power under section 17E(1) above to recall the patient to hospital; or
> (iv)   that appropriate medical treatment is available for him; or
> (v)   ...

The criteria are therefore almost identical to the CTO admission criteria set out in section 17A of the MHA 1983 (see para 20.3.1).

16.4.2   Power of recall

Invariably, the most contentious of the criteria in CTO cases will be whether it is necessary for the RC to be able to exercise the power of recall. In this regard, section 72(1A) of the MHA 1983 requires the MHT to pay particular attention to the risk of relapse associated with non-compliance with treatment and therefore the likelihood of the need for further in-patient treatment in the future. It provides that:

> (1A)   In determining whether the criterion in subsection (1)(c)(iii) above is met, the tribunal shall, in particular, consider, having regard to the patient's history of mental disorder and any other relevant factors, what risk there would be of a deterioration of the patient's condition if he were to continue not to be detained in a hospital (as a result, for example, of his refusing or neglecting to receive the medical treatment he requires for his mental disorder).

16.4.3   Deferred discharge from a community treatment order

In theory, the power under section 72(3) of the MHA 1983 to defer discharge applies to CTO patients as it does to detained patients, but the circumstances in which it would be necessary to defer the discharge of a CTO patient will be rare.

16.5   GUARDIANSHIP PATIENTS

According to section 72(4) of the MHA 1983, the MHT which considers the case of a patient subject to guardianship must discharge if satisfied:

> (a)   that he is not then suffering from mental disorder; or
> (b)   that it is not necessary in the interests of the welfare of the patient, or for the protection of other persons, that the patient should remain under such guardianship.

Unusually, therefore, the burden is on the patient to show why he should be discharged. That aside, the discharge criteria are in broadly similar terms to the admission criteria for guardianship set out in section 7 of the MHA 1983 (see para 21.4.2), the key difference being that the requirement for the mental disorder to be of a 'nature or degree which warrants reception into guardianship' is not included in the discharge criteria.

There is no power available under section 72 of the MHA 1983 for the MHT to defer or delay the discharge of a guardianship patient.

16.6   APPLICATIONS BY THE NEAREST RELATIVE

16.6.1   General considerations

The circumstances in which the nearest relative may apply to the MHT in respect of a patient are set out at para 14.4.3. Generally speaking, the powers available to the MHT in such cases are the same as they would be in the case of an application by the patient; the same discharge criteria will apply, the same discretionary power of discharge is available, as is the power to direct discharge on a later date, and the MHT has the power to make statutory recommendations as an alternative to discharge in the case of detained patients.

16.6.2 Additional statutory criterion in certain nearest relative applications

There is one type of nearest relative application, however, where the statutory criteria are different. In cases where the nearest relative's right to apply to the MHT has been triggered by the RC using his power to bar discharge of the patient under section 25 of the MHA 1983 (see para 18.2.2), an additional criterion is added to those which the MHT must already consider.

Where the nearest relative makes such an application (section 66(1)(g) of the MHA 1983), the patient will either be detained under section 3 or will be subject to a CTO. The MHT will, therefore, consider the application according to the normal statutory criteria, found in section 72(1)(b) in the case of patients under section 3 and section 72(1)(c) in the case of CTO patients. If it is not satisfied as to any of the usual statutory criteria, the MHT will discharge the patient. If, however, the MHT concludes that the statutory criteria for detention are met and if it would normally, therefore, uphold detention, it may not immediately do so. Instead, the MHT must ask itself the additional question of whether it is satisfied 'that the patient if released would be likely to act in a manner dangerous to other persons or himself'. It is only if it is able to answer 'yes' to this additional question that detention may be upheld by the MHT (section 72(1)(b)(iii) or section 72(1)(c)(v)).

The effect is that in the case of a nearest relative application under section 66(1)(g) of the MHA 1983 in respect of a patient under section 3, the MHT must discharge if not satisfied:

- that the patient is suffering from mental disorder or from mental disorder of a nature or degree which makes it appropriate for him to be liable to be detained in hospital for treatment; or
- that it is necessary for the health or safety of the patient or for the protection of others that he should receive such treatment; or
- that appropriate medical treatment is available; or
- that the patient if released would be likely to act in a manner dangerous to other persons or himself.

And in the case of a nearest relative application under section 66(1)(g) of the MHA 1983 in respect of a CTO patient, the MHT must discharge if not satisfied:

- that he is then suffering from mental disorder or mental disorder of a nature or degree which makes it appropriate for him to receive medical treatment; or
- that it is necessary for his health or safety or for the protection of others that he should receive such treatment; or
- that it is necessary that the RC should be able to exercise the power under section 17E(1) to recall the patient to hospital; or
- that appropriate medical treatment is available; or
- that the patient if discharged would be likely to act in a manner dangerous to other persons or himself.

The additional criterion will never apply in cases under section 2 of the MHA 1983 because the nearest relative does not have the right to apply to the MHT if discharge is barred.

When it is considering an application by a patient subsequent to the issuing of a barring report by the RC under section 25 of the MHA 1983, the MHT is not required to consider the additional dangerousness criterion. The patient should, nevertheless, invite the MHT to do so. In *R (on the application of W) v MHRT* [2005] 1 MHLR 134, it was held that the MHT would be entitled to consider the criterion when deciding whether to exercise its discretion to discharge under section 72(1).

Chapter 17

Mental Health Tribunal Powers – Restricted Patients

17.1 INTRODUCTION

The MHT may be asked to consider the cases of three different types of restricted patient under the MHA 1983: those detained under section 37/41, those subject to a restriction direction or limitation direction under section 47/49, section 48/49 or section 45A, or those who are already conditionally discharged. Different sections of the Act set out the various MHT's powers available in relation to each type of patient, and are considered in this chapter.

17.2 PATIENTS UNDER SECTION 37/41 OF THE MENTAL HEALTH ACT 1983

The MHT powers in relation to patients under section 37/41 of the MHA 1983 are set out in section 73. It provides no discretionary power to discharge, and the MHT may only therefore discharge a patient under section 37/41 if the detaining authority fails to satisfy it that the statutory criteria for detention are met.

17.2.1 Statutory criteria

Absolute discharge

According to section 73(1) of the MHA 1983, the MHT must direct the absolute discharge of a patient under section 37/41 if (emphasis added):

    (a)   *the tribunal is not satisfied* as to the matters mentioned in paragraph (b)(i), (ii) or (iia) of section 72(1) above; and

    (b)   *the tribunal is satisfied* that it is not appropriate for the patient to remain liable to be recalled to hospital for further treatment.

Conditional discharge

According to section 73(2) of the MHA 1983, the MHT must direct the conditional discharge of a patient under section 37/41 if:

(a)   paragraph (a) of section 73(1) applies; but
(b)   paragraph (b) of section 73(1) does not apply.

Applying these provisions, the MHT must first make a decision on whether the patient should be discharged, according to the criteria which would apply in respect of patients under section 3 of the MHA 1983 (section 73(1)(a)). If the criteria justifying detention remain in place, the patient will remain detained. If not, he will be discharged. If the patient is to be discharged, however, the additional question which the MHT must ask itself is whether discharge should be absolute or conditional. This calls for a judgement on whether the patient, when discharged, should be liable to recall to hospital (section 73(1)(b)). Where it is appropriate for the patient to be liable to recall to hospital, discharge will be conditional; where it is not appropriate, it will be absolute.

The burden is on the detaining authority to show why the patient should not be discharged, and is on the patient to show why discharge should not be conditional. In practice, if the patient is discharged, it will be almost always be conditional, and it would be highly unusual for the MHT to be satisfied that the patient did not need to be liable to recall.

17.2.2   Effect of an absolute discharge

If a patient is absolutely discharged, the hospital and restriction orders cease to have effect immediately and permanently (section 73(3) of the MHA 1983). The patient is no longer subject to the provisions of the Act, the SSJ has no further role to play, and any future engagement with mental health services by the patient will be on a purely voluntary basis.

17.2.3   Effect of a conditional discharge

If a patient is conditionally discharged, he is no longer subject to the hospital order. He does not lose his restricted status, however. Even though discharged from hospital, he remains a restricted patient for as long as the discharge remains conditional. The main consequences are that he must abide by any conditions imposed on him in respect of his care plan and he is liable to recall to hospital.

Duration of a conditional discharge

A conditional discharge is for an indefinite period and will last until a positive decision is taken to bring it to an end. The SSJ may bring the conditional discharge to an end by exercising his discretion to absolutely discharge the patient under section 42(2) of the MHA 1983. More commonly, however, a decision to absolutely discharge a conditionally discharged patient will be taken by the MHT using its powers under section 75(3) (see para 17.4).

Conditions attached to discharge

When conditionally discharging the patient, the MHT has a general discretion under section 73(4)(b) of the MHA 1983 as to the conditions it will impose. Somewhat counter-intuitively, there is, in fact, no requirement to impose conditions at all, but it would be unusual if there were none.

In *R (on the application of SH) v MHRT* [2007] EWHC 884 (Admin), Holman J suggested that, 'a condition could not lawfully be capricious and must be relevant and for a proper purpose within the scope of the statute'. In *SSJ v RB* [2011] EWCA Civ 1608, the Court of Appeal held that conditions cannot be imposed which would amount to a deprivation of liberty.

Whatever the condition, a patient is at liberty to choose not to comply with it. In relation to medical treatment, for example, a conditionally discharged patient is excluded from the provisions of Part IV of the MHA 1983 and cannot be treated without his consent. In *R (on the application of SH) v MHRT* 2007 [2007] EWHC 884 (Admin), therefore, Holman J suggested that a condition requiring compliance with medication is subject to the absolute right of the patient to choose whether to consent, and ought not to be imposed 'unless there is a proper basis for anticipating that the patient does, and will, consent to the treatment'.

What then will happen if a condition is breached? The MHA 1983 is silent. Section 73(4)(b) states that a patient 'shall comply' with any condition, but it does not stipulate what will happen in the event that a patient exercises his right not to, and the fact is that there is no automatic sanction. The greatest danger for the patient is that breach of a condition may lead to recall to hospital (see below), but the Act does not create an automatic link between breach of a condition and recall.

Liability to recall

The most important aspect of the conditional discharge is not the conditions, but the liability to recall to hospital that hangs over the patient until he is absolutely discharged. As long as the conditional discharge is in place, section 73(4)(a) of the MHA 1983 provides that the patient may be recalled by the SSJ using his discretionary power under section 42(3). Guidance from the MOJ on when the SSJ may exercise his discretion is considered at para 11.6.7.

17.2.4 Deferred conditional discharges

If it concludes that a patient should be conditionally discharged, the MHT need not direct discharge immediately. Section 73(7) of the MHA 1983 instead allows the MHT to 'defer a direction for the conditional discharge of a patient until such arrangements as appear to the tribunal are necessary for that purpose have been made to its satisfaction'. As was identified in *DC v Nottinghamshire Health Care NHS Trust and SSJ* [2012] UKUT 92 (AAC), the power is to *defer the direction* for the conditional discharge, 'which presupposes that there is a direction to discharge ready to take effect'. It follows, therefore, that the power may only be exercised once the tribunal has concluded that the patient no longer meets the criteria for detention. If the tribunal needs more information before deciding whether a conditional discharge is appropriate or, if so, what the conditions should be, the correct course is not to defer discharge but to adjourn the proceedings for the further information to be obtained.

A decision to defer may be appropriate where the MHT considers that the patient no longer needs to be detained, appropriate conditions have been identified, but a delay will occur while the authority under section 117 of the MHA 1983 puts the after-care arrangements in place.

In practical terms, where a conditional discharge is deferred, no date is set for the conditional discharge to take effect. Instead, the MHT will expect to be notified once the necessary arrangements are in place, at which point a conditional discharge will be directed without the need for a further hearing. When deferring discharge, however, the MHT is likely to set a further hearing date to review matters in case, by then, the conditional discharge has not yet been imposed for any reason.

The decision to grant a deferred conditional discharge should be regarded as provisional, and the MHT may re-visit its decision before discharge takes effect if there is a change in circumstances, for example a deterioration in the patient's mental health (see *R (on the application of IH) v Secretary of State for the Home Department and Secretary of State for Health* [2002] 1 MHLR 87).

17.2.5   Making recommendations

In contrast with its powers in respect of unrestricted patients, the MHT has no statutory power under section 73 of the MHA 1983 to make recommendations as an alternative to discharge. In cases under section 37/41, the decision is, essentially, discharge or not. The MHT may consider making an informal or extra-statutory recommendation, particularly in relation to issues such as leave or transfer. However, in *C and F v Birmingham and Solihull MH NHS Trust and another* [2013] EWCA Civ 701, the Court of Appeal found that there is no right to apply for such a recommendation and, therefore, the MHT does not err in law if it refuses to allow an argument in favour of one, nor if it refuses to provide reasons for this decision.

17.3   PATIENTS UNDER SECTION 47/49, SECTION 48/49 AND SECTION 45A OF THE MENTAL HEALTH ACT 1983

Chapter 12 considers the circumstances in which the SSJ may direct a transfer to hospital under section 47/49 of the MHA 1983, while Chapter 13 considers the circumstances in which the Crown Court may pass a sentence under section 45A. In the case of patients detained under either section, the decision-making powers of the MHT are contained in section 74, are identical, and are set out in para 17.3.1. These powers also apply to patients detained under section 48/49 (see para 17.3.2).

Any patient whose case falls to be considered by the MHT exercising its powers under section 74 of the MHA 1983 will be subject to an outstanding prison sentence (section 47/49 and section 45A) or will have been remanded in custody (section 48). The law, therefore, requires that ultimate decision-making authority rests with the SSJ, and there are significant limits on the MHT's powers. This should come as no surprise. Whereas the MHT may only consider risks associated with mental disorder when deciding whether to discharge, this category of patient will present risks which are unrelated to his mental disorder, something which requires separate consideration.

17.3.1   Cases under section 47/49 and section 45A of the Mental Health Act 1983

Mental health tribunal's duty of notification

The role of the MHT at the hearing of any application by, or reference of, a patient under section 47/49 or section 45A of the MHA 1983, is to 'notify the Secretary of State whether, in its opinion, the patient would, if subject to a restriction order, be entitled to be absolutely or conditionally discharged' (section 74(1)(a)). In other words, the MHT does not have the power to direct discharge itself and must, instead, carry out a hypothetical exercise to decide whether it would discharge if it could. The MHT must then notify the SSJ accordingly. Any decision regarding discharge is then for the SSJ. When carrying out its hypothetical exercise, the MHT will apply the section 73 discharge criteria (see para 17.2.1) in the normal way.

Mental health tribunal's power of recommendation

If the MHT decides that the patient would be entitled to be conditionally discharged and notifies the SSJ accordingly, it may also recommend to the SSJ that if he decides not to discharge the patient, he should nevertheless allow the patient to remain in hospital (section 74(1)(b) of the MHA 1983).

Response of the Secretary of State for Justice

If the MHT notifies the SSJ that the patient would be eligible for an absolute or conditional discharge, section 74(2) of the MHA 1983 provides that the SSJ may then, within the next 90 days, give notice to the MHT that the patient may be so discharged, and the MHT will direct the discharge of the patient accordingly. If the SSJ does not give notice within the 90-day period that the patient may be discharged by the MHT, the patient will be returned to prison, unless the MHT has made a recommendation under section 74(1)(b) that he should remain in hospital, in which case the SSJ may direct that he remain in hospital accordingly.

Practical application of section 74 of the Mental Health Act 1983 in cases where the Secretary of State for Justice is notified that the patient is ready for discharge

Whatever section 74 of the MHA 1983 may say, whenever the MHT notifies the SSJ in accordance with section 74(1)(a) that the patient is eligible for discharge, it is safe to assume that the SSJ will not respond by giving notice within the next 90 days that the patient may be discharged by the MHT. Instead, the patient will be returned to prison unless the MHT has also recommended that the patient remain in hospital. More likely than not, if the MHT has made the recommendation that he should remain in hospital, the SSJ will accede. What happens next depends upon the type of sentence being served by the patient:

- A patient serving an indeterminate or life sentence who has reached his tariff and is returned to prison may apply to the Parole Board for release.

- A patient serving an indeterminate or life sentence who has reached his tariff and who remains in hospital in accordance with an MHT recommendation will have his case referred automatically to the Parole Board.
- A patient serving an indeterminate or life sentence who has yet to reach his tariff and is returned to prison may apply to the Parole Board for release when his tariff is reached.
- A patient serving an indeterminate or life sentence who has yet to reach his tariff and who remains in hospital in accordance with an MHT recommendation may apply or will have his case referred to the Parole Board when his tariff is reached (section 74(5A)).
- A patient serving a determinate sentence yet to expire who is returned to prison will be released automatically at the end of his sentence.
- A patient serving a determinate sentence yet to expire who remains in hospital will not be released at the end of his sentence but will lose his restricted status. He will become a notional hospital order patient.

17.3.2   Cases under section 48/49 of the Mental Health Act 1983

The MHT's function at the hearing of an application or reference of a patient under section 48/49 of the MHA 1983 is exactly the same as it is for patients under section 47/49 and section 45A. It must notify the SSJ under section 74(1)(a) whether it would discharge the patient if it had the power to do so. In cases under section 48/49, however, if notified by the MHT that it would discharge the patient, the SSJ does not then have the power (however notional) under section 74(2) to direct the discharge of the patient. The patient must therefore be returned to prison, unless the MHT has also recommended that the patient should continue to remain in hospital (section 74(4)).

17.4   CONDITIONALLY DISCHARGED PATIENTS

The third type of restricted patient whose case may be considered by the MHT is the patient already subject to a conditional discharge, that is the patient who was previously detained under section 37/41 of the MHA 1983 but who has been conditionally discharged by the MHT under section 73 (see para 17.2), or, less commonly, discharged by the SSJ under section 42(2) (see para 11.7). Section 75 applies. Such patients have the right to apply to the MHT for the conditions attached to their discharge to be varied or, as is more often the case, for the conditions to be removed completely and for the restriction order to be brought to an end. If the restriction order is brought to an end, the effect is the same as an absolute discharge.

17.4.1   Powers under section 75 of the Mental Health Act 1983

According to section 75(3) of the MHA 1983, when the MHT considers the case of a patient who is already subject to a conditional discharge, it may:

(a)   vary any condition to which the patient is subject in connection with his discharge or impose any condition which might have been imposed in connection therewith; or

(b)   direct that the restriction order, limitation direction or restriction direction to which he is subject shall cease to have effect.

17.4.2   Limitation and restriction direction patients

In theory, the MHT powers apply equally to conditionally discharged patients who were previously subject to a limitation direction or a restriction direction (that is detained under section 45A or section 47/49 of the MHA 1983) as they do to patients who were previously detained under section 37/41. In practice, however, it is only the latter group of patients to whom section 75 will ever apply, and the reference to other types of restricted patients is purely notional. No one detained under section 45A or section 47/49 will be conditionally discharged (see para 17.3.1); they will, instead, be released on licence by the Parole Board.

17.4.3   Application of the powers under section 75 of the Mental Health Act 1983 to conditionally discharged patients

Whether considering an application from a conditionally discharged patient that the restriction order should cease to have effect (section 75(3)(b) of the MHA 1983) and that he should become absolutely discharged, or an application to vary or impose a condition (section 75(3)(a)), there are no statutory criteria for the MHT to apply and the decision is, in theory at least, a matter for its discretion. In practice, however, certainly at least when considering an application for an absolute discharge, there is clear guidance from case law that the MHT should act as though the burden of proof is on the patient (see *R (on the application of SC) v MHRT and SSH* [2005] EWHC 17 (Admin), and *RH v South London and Maudsley NHS Foundation Trust* [2010] EWCA Civ 1273).

Chapter 18

Discharge Powers Provided by Section 23 of the Mental Health Act 1983

18.1 INTRODUCTION

As far as most unrestricted detained patients are concerned, the decision to discharge from detention will not be made by an MHT following an application by the patient or a referral of his case. It will, instead, be made by the patient's RC, who will discharge the patient once satisfied that the statutory criteria justifying detention are no longer in place. The RC's power of discharge is created by section 23 of the MHA 1983, and is considered in this chapter, together with similar discharge powers available under section 23 to hospital managers and the patient's nearest relative.

As well as creating a power to discharge a patient from detention, section 23 of the MHA 1983 also creates the power to discharge a patient from a CTO or guardianship. These powers are considered separately, in Chapters 20 and 21, respectively.

18.2 PATIENTS UNDER PART II OF THE MENTAL HEALTH ACT 1983

18.2.1 Discharge by the responsible clinician

The RC is not bound by any procedural or statutory requirements when exercising the power of discharge. The question of when to discharge is simply a matter for his discretion. Acting as a public body, however, he must exercise the power reasonably and according to public law principles (see *R (on the application of Wirral Health Authority and Wirral Borough Council) v Dr Finnegan* [2001] EWHC 312 (Admin)).

The power should be kept under review at all times. In *Winterwerp v The Netherlands* (Application No 6301/73) [1979] ECHR 4, for example, it was held that for the purposes of Article 5(1) of the ECHR, the lawfulness of continued confinement depends upon the persistence of a true mental disorder. Similarly, in *R (on the application of C) v MHRT London South and South West Region* [2000] MHLR 220, Crane J noted that the RC 'has a continuing duty to consider whether the conditions (justifying detention) remain satisfied', and in *R v Drew* [2003] UKHL 25, the House of Lords observed that if the medical conditions justifying admission 'cease to be met at any time, the duty of the [RC], exercising a medical judgment, is to discharge the offender from hospital'.

Applying these principles, the 1983 Code advises (para 29.16) that the RC should make a positive decision to discharge as soon as he concludes that the criteria for detention are no longer met, and ought not to wait for authority for the patient's detention to lapse. It will, however, be virtually impossible to identify the precise point at which a patient stops meeting the criteria for detention, and the RC, like any detaining authority, is entitled therefore to exercise a 'measure of discretion' (see *Johnson v UK* (1999) 27 EHRR 296).

The RC's decision to discharge must be put in writing (section 23(1) of the MHA 1983). Regulation 18 of the Mental Health Regulations 2008 provides that the written notice of discharge 'shall be sent to the managers of the hospital in which the patient is liable to be detained ... as soon as practicable after it is made'.

18.2.2   Discharge by the nearest relative

The patient's nearest relative is also given a discretionary power of discharge by section 23 of the MHA 1983. As with the RC, discharge needs to be in writing (section 23(1)). The nearest relative has a complete discretion as to whether to exercise this power. He is under no obligation to consult with the RC or any other mental health professional before exercising it, and may choose to exercise it against professional advice. He would do well to exercise the discretion carefully, however, as there may be consequences if he does not. Firstly, in certain circumstances, the RC may bar discharge using section 25. Secondly, if the RC does bar discharge, the nearest relative will be prevented from exercising his power again for the next 6 months. Thirdly, the nearest relative may find himself the subject of a displacement application at the county court because he has exercised his power of discharge irresponsibly.

Notice of discharge

Unlike the power available to the RC or hospital managers (see para 18.2.3 in relation to the latter), the nearest relative's power under section 23 of the MHA

1983 is expressly subject to section 25, which requires 72 hours' notice in writing to be given to hospital managers of the intention to discharge the patient. The purpose is to give the patient's RC time to consider whether discharge should be barred. If before the expiry of the 72 hours, the RC serves a barring report, the discharge will be prevented. If he does not, then discharge will go ahead as intended.

The nearest relative's notice of discharge need be in no particular form, but the 1983 Code advises (para 29.23) that hospital managers should offer the nearest relative any help they require, such as providing them with a standard letter to complete.

Regulation 3(3) of the Mental Health Regulations 2008 requires that the notice of discharge (and the order itself) shall be served by:

- delivery of the order or notice at that hospital to an officer of the managers authorised by the managers to receive it, or
- sending it by prepaid post to those managers at that hospital, or
- delivering it using an internal mail system operated by the managers upon whom it is to be served, if those managers agree.

The *Reference guide to the Mental Health Act 1983* (para 12.106) provides that the 72 hours will run 'from the time when the notice is received by the authorised person, when it is received by post at the hospital to which it is addressed or when it is put in the internal mail system (as the case may be)'.

The MHA 1983 distinguishes the nearest relative's notice of intention to discharge (section 25(1)) from the written discharge order itself (section 23(1)), with the clear implication that discharge will not take effect automatically at the end of 72 hours, and that a written order is required at that point. The guidance from the 1983 Code, however, is that hospital managers should treat 'a discharge order given without prior notice as being both notice of intention to discharge the patient after 72 hours and the actual order to do so' (para 29.22).

Barring discharge

The RC may not bar discharge as a matter of course, not even if he is able to say that the patient continues to meet the criteria for detention under the MHA 1983. The RC may only bar discharge if he is of the opinion that the patient 'if discharged would be likely to act in a manner dangerous to other persons or himself' (section 25(1)). In such circumstances, the RC may, within 72 hours, furnish a report to hospital managers certifying this opinion, the effect of which will be to bar discharge. The report should be on Form M2 (regulation 25 of the Mental Health Regulations 2008).

The MHA 1983 does not define 'dangerous', but the 1983 Code suggests (para 29.21) that it 'focuses on the probability of dangerous acts, such as causing serious physical injury or lasting psychological harm, not merely on the patient's general need for safety and others' general need for protection'.

Section 25(2) of the MHA 1983 requires the hospital managers to inform the nearest relative if the RC does furnish a report.

The effect of barring discharge

The furnishing of Form M2 bars discharge. It also has the following consequences:

- No further order for the discharge of the patient may be made by that relative during the 6 months beginning with the date of the report (section 25(1)(b) of the MHA 1983). The 6 months runs irrespective of any subsequent change in the legal status of the patient.
- In cases under section 3 (not section 2), the furnishing of the RC's report triggers the right of the nearest relative to apply to the MHT for the patient's discharge (section 66(1)(g)). This is in addition to any right to make an application that the patient has. The nearest relative's right to make the application runs for 28 days from the day on which he is informed of the RC's report (section 66(2)(d)) (see para 16.6.2 for details of the criteria that the MHT will apply in such cases).
- Hospital managers should consider holding a review hearing (1983 Code, para 31.11).

Application to displace

The nearest relative may also be liable to become displaced in his role by the county court on the grounds that he has 'exercised without due regard to the welfare of the patient or the interests of the public his power to discharge the patient' (section 29(3)(d)). The county court's power exists irrespective of any barring report from the RC, but applications to the court for an order are more likely in such circumstances.

18.2.3 Discharge by hospital managers

Generally speaking, hospital managers will only consider exercising their power of discharge under section 23 of the MHA 1983 if called upon to review a patient's case. Any such review will almost certainly take the form of a hearing, which will be broadly imitative of an MHT hearing.

For the purpose of such hearings, the hospital managers will normally delegate their discharge powers to a panel comprising three or more people (section 23(4) and (6) of the MHA 1983). Whether the hospital is NHS or private, the panel should not contain employees or officers of the body. Additionally, in private hospitals, the panel should not include anyone who has a financial interest in the hospital. Usually, the panel will comprise people who are specifically appointed to the role of 'associate manager', and the hospital management will have pools of such associate managers from which to draw. By convention, the number of managers on the panel will be three, although there may be more.

There are no provisions dictating when a patient's case must be reviewed, but the 1983 Code advises (para 31.11) that managers:

- may undertake a review on whether or not a patient should be discharged at their discretion;
- must undertake a review if the RC submits to them a report under section 20 of the MHA 1983 renewing detention (or section 20A renewing a CTO);
- should consider holding a review when they receive a request from (or on behalf of) a patient;
- should consider holding a review when the RC furnishes a report to them under section 25 barring a nearest relative's discharge order.

In the second of these cases, it is desirable that managers conduct their review before the current period of detention (or CTO) ends (1983 Code, para 31.13). In the latter two cases, in deciding whether to hold a review at all, managers may take into account whether any MHT has recently considered the patient's case or is due to do so in the near future (1983 Code, para 31.12).

In preparation for the hearing, the 1983 Code advises, among other things, that:

- written reports should be obtained from the patient's clinical team including the RC and 'other key individuals involved in the patient's care' (para 31.25);
- copies of these reports should be provided to the patient and to his legal representative (para 31.26) in good time before the hearing so that the patient is able to consider them (para 31.27);
- subject to the views of the patient, the nearest relative should be informed of the hearing (para 31.28);
- relatives, carers and other relevant people may be invited to put their views to the managers' panel in person, again subject to the views of the patient (para 31.29).

Conduct of the hearing itself is a matter for the individual managers' panel but the procedure generally 'needs to balance informality against the rigours demanded by the importance of the task' (1983 Code, para 31.32). Whatever procedure is adopted, the patient should be given a full opportunity, and any necessary help, to explain why he should no longer be detained (or on a CTO). He should have the benefit of a representative if he chooses, and should also be allowed to have a relative, friend or advocate there to support him. During the hearing, the RC and other members of the clinical team will be asked to provide their views on whether the patient's detention or CTO is justified and to explain the grounds on which those views are based. It will be normal for the patient and/or his representative to be able to put questions to members of the clinical team.

As is the case with the RC and the nearest relative, hospital managers have a discretion as to whether to discharge, and are not bound by any statutory criteria. Guidance for managers on how to exercise the discretion is, however, provided in the 1983 Code (paras 31.14–31.22), and makes clear that they are expected to apply the same discharge criteria as would be applied by an MHT. As the 1983 Code puts it (para 31.14), '[t]he essential yardstick is whether the grounds for continued detention or continued SCT under the Act are satisfied'. Making a similar point in *R v Riverside Mental Health Trust ex parte Huzzey* (1998) 43 BMLR 167, Latham J noted 'if the criteria for admission no longer exists, I can't see how any decision by hospital managers not to discharge can be other than perverse'.

Managers must not forget, however, that they are exercising a discretion, and in *R (on the application of SR) v Huntercombe Maidenhead Hospital* [2005] 1 MHLR 379, it was held that the managers had erred in law in proceeding on the basis that if they disagreed with the RC's finding of dangerousness, then, as a matter of course, they must order discharge. They had failed to consider their residual discretion.

18.3   PATIENTS UNDER PART III OF THE MENTAL HEALTH ACT 1983

18.3.1   Hospital order patients under section 37 of the Mental Health Act 1983

Discharge powers available to the RC and hospital managers under section 23 of the MHA 1983 apply to unrestricted hospital order patients just as they do to patients under Part II (Schedule 1, Part I). The nearest relative, however, has no power of discharge under section 23 in respect of hospital order patients. The nearest relative does, however, have a compensatory right to apply to the MHT for the discharge of a hospital patient (see Chapter 14 for details), a right not available to the nearest relative of a patient under Part II.

18.3.2   Other unrestricted detained patients under Part III of the Mental Health Act 1983

Discharge powers under section 23 of the MHA 1983 do not apply to patients detained under section 35, 36 or 38.

18.3.3   CTO patients under Part III of the Mental Health Act 1983

Discharge powers in respect of CTO patients under Part II of the MHA 1983 are considered at para 20.9.

A patient who is on a CTO under Part III of the MHA 1983, that is a CTO following a period of detention under Part III, may be discharged from the CTO by his RC and by hospital managers, but not by his nearest relative (Schedule 1, Part I). The nearest relative does, however, have the right to apply to the MHT for the patient's discharge (see Chapter 14).

18.3.4   Guardianship patients under Part III of the Mental Health Act 1983

Discharge powers in respect of guardianship patients under Part II of the MHA 1983 are considered at para 21.8.

A patient who is subject to guardianship under Part III of the MHA 1983, that is a guardianship order made by a court under section 37, may be discharged by his RC and by the LSSA, but not by his nearest relative (Schedule 1, Part I). The nearest relative does have the right to apply to the MHT for the patient's discharge (see Chapter 14).

18.4   PATIENTS UNDER PART III OF THE MENTAL HEALTH ACT 1983 – RESTRICTED

The discharge powers under section 23 of the MHA 1983 available to the RC and hospital managers also apply to restricted patients under Schedule 1, Part II. These are, however, essentially notional powers since section 41(3)(c)(iii) provides that they may only be exercised with the consent of the SSJ.

The nearest relative's power of discharge under section 23 of the MHA 1983 is irrelevant to a restricted patient as he has no nearest relative for the purposes of the Act.

Although the RC and hospital managers can each technically discharge restricted patients with the consent of the SSJ, this would be exceptionally rare. Where the RC thinks that a restricted patient should be discharged, he will either encourage the patient to apply for discharge to the MHT, or will recommend that the SSJ exercise his power of discharge under section 42(2) of the MHA 1983. Hospital managers could also invite the SSJ to exercise this power, but, in fact, managers' hearings are rarely convened in respect of restricted patients because they serve such little purpose.

Part Six

After-care

Chapter 19

After-care under Section 117 of the Mental Health Act 1983

19.1 INTRODUCTION

A patient who leaves hospital following detention for treatment under the MHA 1983 has the advantage of a statutory entitlement, free of charge, to certain health and social care services in the community, something which distinguishes him from other mental health service users. The entitlement is created by section 117 and is referred to as 'after-care'. The extent of this entitlement is considered in this chapter.

19.2 ELIGIBLE PATIENTS

After-care is available for any patient who has been detained for treatment under the MHA 1983 (section 117(1)), that is anyone:

> (1)   ... detained under section 3 above, or admitted to a hospital in pursuance of a hospital order under section 37 above, or transferred to a hospital in pursuance of a hospital direction under section 45A above or a transfer direction made under section 47 or 48 above ....

The entitlement arises whether or not the patient is restricted.

The patients for whom an entitlement to after-care will *not* arise are those detained under sections 2, 4, 5, 35, 36, 38, 135 and 136 of the MHA 1983.

19.3 HEALTH AND SOCIAL CARE

After-care covers both health and social care needs, and the duty to arrange its provision therefore falls on local health *and* local social services authorities (section 117(2) of the MHA 1983), who should have jointly agreed protocols in place identifying which authority will have responsibility for funding which services (Health Service Circular and Local Authority Circular (HSC 2000/003: LAC (2000) 3)).

While the burden to provide after-care under section 117(2) of the MHA 1983 falls on both CCGs and LSSAs, the burden on LSSAs also comes from an additional statutory source, section 47(1) of the National Health Service and Community Care Act 1990 (NHSCCA 1990), which requires a local authority to carry out an assessment of the need for 'community care services' of any person who it appears may be in need of such services. For these purposes, 'community care services' is defined to include after-care services provided under section 117 of the MHA 1983.

19.4   DECIDING WHAT CONSTITUTES AN AFTER-CARE SERVICE (SEE ALSO APPENDIX 12)

There remains no statutory definition of the term 'after-care', and uncertainty continues as to the extent of its scope. Which services fall within its definition and which do not? What are its limits? Guidance is neither extensive, nor particularly helpful. What seems relatively clear, however, is that an after-care service is one which meets a health care or social care need, aims to keep the patient well, and is designed to help a patient avoid re-admission to hospital in the future.

The 1983 Code (para 27.5) is particularly vague and offers little assistance other than to confirm that, 'as well as meeting [a patient's] immediate needs for health and social care, after-care should aim to support them in regaining or enhancing their skills, or learning new skills, in order to cope with life outside hospital'.

Courts, too, have generally avoided being prescriptive about how the term is defined. In *R v London Borough of Richmond ex parte W* [1999] 1 MHLR 149, for example, Sullivan J suggested that, 'it would seem sensible to confer a considerable degree of discretion upon health authorities and local authorities having to provide after-care services in situations that are bound to be particularly problematic and demanding'. He did suggest, however, that the precise extent of the duty in any particular case 'will be defined by the local authority's assessment of a person's needs under Section 47(1)(a) of the 1990 Act' (see para 19.11.2).

In *Clunis v Camden & Islington Health Authority* [1998] 3 All ER 180, Beldon LJ said that, 'social work, support in helping the patient with problems of employment, accommodation or family relationships, the provision of domiciliary services and the use of day centre and residential facilities' were the type of services that would fall within the definition.

In *R v Manchester City Council ex parte Stennett and Others* [2002] UKHL 34, the House of Lords provided a little more clarity by confirming that, 'caring residential accommodation' also came within after-care's scope.

Although the aim is to keep the patient's mental health stable so as to avoid the need for re-admission to hospital, it seems increasingly clear that the term cannot be defined so as to create a right to *any* service which may prevent a deterioration in a person's mental health, and is instead restricted to those services which address a need deriving from, or related to, a person's mental disorder. This was confirmed in *R (on the application of Mwanza) v London Boroughs of Greenwich and Bromley* [2010] EWHC 1462 (Admin), where it was held that although homelessness might provoke a deterioration in a patient's mental health, that would not be enough to bring the provision of accommodation within the scope of after-care services. The need for accommodation is a common one and does not arise from mental disorder. It would be different, of course, if the accommodation in question was specifically designed to meet needs arising from mental disorder.

In the same spirit, Mostyn J, in *R (on the application of Afework) v London Borough of Camden* [2013] EWHC 1637 (Admin), suggested that, 'the services must relate to the reason and only to the reason for the detention in hospital'. He found, therefore, that, 'basic or pure or ordinary accommodation does not come within the concept of aftercare services'.

19.5 WHEN DOES THE ENTITLEMENT TO AFTER-CARE ARISE?

According to section 117(1) of the MHA 1983, the duty arises in relation to patients who 'cease to be detained and, whether or not immediately after so ceasing, leave hospital'. The trigger is, therefore, the patient's departure from hospital. A patient may remain in hospital on a voluntary basis following discharge from his section, but this has no bearing on his entitlement to after-care, which has already arisen as a consequence of the original decision to detain for treatment.

19.5.1 Leave under section 17 of the Mental Health Act 1983

The MHA 1983 is silent on whether a patient who is on extended leave under section 17 as a prelude to discharge has an entitlement to after-care while he is on leave, but it is commonly accepted that he does (see, e.g. *R v London Borough of Richmond ex parte W* [1999] 1 MHLR 149, in which Sullivan J confirmed that, 'a person on leave under section 17 is in just as much, if not more, need of care when he leaves hospital as a person who leaves hospital subject to guardianship or supervision' and so 'for the purposes of section 117, he has ceased to be detained and left hospital').

19.5.2   Duty in respect of discharge planning

While the MHA 1983 creates no duty to plan any after-care in advance of discharge, it is generally accepted that there is a responsibility on the authorities under section 117 to plan appropriately. The 1983 Code, for example, notes (para 27.8) that:

> Although the duty to provide after-care services begins when the patient leaves hospital, the planning of after-care needs to start as soon as the patient is admitted to hospital. PCTs [now CCGs] and LSSAs should take reasonable steps to identify appropriate after-care services for patients before their actual discharge from hospital.

The 1983 Code specifically refers (para 27.9) to the need for after-care planning in preparation for MHTs. In advance of tribunal hearings, therefore, CCGs/ LSSAs should:

- consider putting practical preparations in hand for after-care in every case;
- in particular consider doing so where there is a strong possibility that the patient will be discharged if appropriate after-care can be arranged;
- where a tribunal has provisionally decided to give a restricted patient a conditional discharge, do their best to put after-care in place which would allow that discharge to take place.

The point is a simple one. Where a patient is deemed ready for discharge by a tribunal as long as there are arrangements in place for treatment in the community, there is a danger of delay if the authorities are under no obligation before discharge to actually make those arrangements. This was considered in *R (on the application of B) v Camden London Borough Council & Others* [2005] EWHC 1366 (Admin), where it was suggested that although the duty to provide after-care only arises at the point of discharge, 'practicality requires section 117 authorities to be under a duty before discharge, at least in cases where a tribunal has provisionally decided that a conditional discharge is appropriate'.

In *R v Camden & Islington Health Authority ex parte K* [2001] EWCA Civ 240, it was suggested that the duty arises in the following way (at [20]):

> (a) A Health Authority has the power to take preparatory steps before discharge of a patient;
> (b) It will normally be the case that, in the exercise of its discretionary power, an authority should give way to a Tribunal decision, and should use reasonable

endeavours to fulfil the conditions imposed by such a decision, insofar as they relate to medical care;

(c) Failure to use such endeavours, in the absence of strong reasons, would be likely to be an unlawful exercise in discretion.

In whatever way the duty is said to exist, it is clear that it applies only in cases where discharge is a realistic possibility, and care teams need not spend too long putting together elaborate discharge packages in advance of tribunal hearings where, on any reasonable view, the prospects of the patient's discharge are remote. In *AM v West London MH NHS Trust and SSJ* [2012] UKUT 382 (AAC), the Upper Tribunal held that the MHT had been entitled to refuse an adjournment application on behalf of the patient and to continue with a hearing, even though the social work evidence was 'incomplete, even inadequate', and no realistic plans for discharge had been constructed by the care team. Where the patient was not yet receiving unescorted leave, the case had not progressed to the point 'where the issue of after-care that was actually available would arise'.

19.6 IDENTIFYING THE RELEVANT CLINICAL COMMISSIONING GROUP OR LOCAL SOCIAL SERVICES AUTHORITY (SEE ALSO APPENDIX 12)

According to section 117(3) of the MHA 1983, the CCG and LSSA responsible for providing the services will be the ones for the area 'in which the person concerned is resident or to which he is sent on discharge by the hospital in which he was detained'. Although on the face of it, this provision creates the potential for conflict between the authorities for the area in which the person was resident before admission and those for the area to which he is sent afterwards (if different), the correct interpretation is settled and the responsibility for providing after-care falls on the authorities for the area in which the patient is resident prior to detention. This was confirmed in *R v MHRT ex parte Hall* [1999] EWHC 351 (Admin), where Scott Baker J held that the words 'or to which he is sent on discharge by the hospital' are designed simply to cater for the situation where a patient does not have a current place of residence at the time of his admission to hospital. This interpretation was then adopted in *R (on the application of Hertfordshire County Council) v London Borough of Hammersmith and Fulham* [2011] EWCA Civ 77 and *R (on the application of Sunderland City Council) v South Tyneside Council* [2011] EWHC 2355 (Admin).

Questions will undoubtedly still arise, however, as to the meaning of the term 'is resident'. To what extent, for example, is someone who is staying temporarily in a particular area 'resident' there for the purposes of section 117 of the MHA 1983 if he is then detained under section 3? Advice from the Department of Health (*Ordinary Residence: Guidance on the identification of the ordinary residence of people in need of community care services, England*, October 2013 (effective from October 2013)) is that the term 'resident' 'should be given its ordinary and natural meaning subject to any interpretation by the courts'. What then of any interpretation by the courts? Certain points are clear. In *R (on the application of Hertfordshire County Council) v London Borough of Hammersmith and Fulham* [2011] EWCA Civ 77, it was confirmed that a person is not to be regarded as resident in any particular area if he is required to be there by virtue of his detention under the MHA 1983. That case also confirmed that the 'deeming provisions' from the National Assistance Act 1948 do not apply in relation to responsibility under section 117, so that where a person is placed by one LSSA in accommodation which is in an area run by another LSSA, it is the latter LSSA which will be the responsible LSSA for the purposes of section 117 if the person has become ordinarily resident in the latter area and is then detained under section 3.

In *R (on the application of Sunderland City Council) v South Tyneside Council* [2012] EWCA Civ 1232, Lloyd LJ suggested that in seeking to understand the term 'resident' for the purposes of section 117(3) of the MHA 1983, it was unhelpful to consider cases (in particular, *Barnet v Shah* [1983] 2 AC 309) which had attempted to define the term 'ordinary residence' for the purposes of different legislation. He also agreed (at [31]):

> with the comment made in other cases that, in general, when considering any case in which there is doubt as to the place of a person's residence, the question is not only that of physical presence, and that it may be relevant to consider why the person is where he or she is, and to what extent his or her presence there is voluntary. Thus, if a person has a home, the fact that he or she is not there on a given date or for a particular period does not mean that he or she is not still resident there, if the absence is accounted for by, for example, a holiday, a business trip, or having to spend time in hospital, whether following an injury, an operation or some other form of treatment, possibly over a prolonged period, or, for that matter, a period of imprisonment following a criminal conviction.

According to Lloyd LJ's judgment, however, even though a prolonged stay in hospital as an informal patient does not mean that a person's home stops being his residence for the purposes of section 117 of the MHA 1983, the situation changes if the home becomes no longer available to return to. If, for example, the person chooses to terminate the tenancy while in hospital, or if the accommodation stops being available as a result of the actions of the landlord, the patient either becomes resident at the hospital or is not resident anywhere.

19.7   DURATION OF ENTITLEMENT TO AFTER-CARE

The duty to provide after-care continues until the CCG and LSSA (which must decide jointly) 'are satisfied that the person concerned is no longer in need of such services' (section 117(2) of the MHA 1983).

The 1983 Code advises (para 27.19) that, 'the most clear cut circumstances in which after-care will end is where the person's mental health has improved to a point where they no longer need services because of their mental disorder'. Authorities must not assume, however, that a community patient who is stable no longer requires services, as very often it will only be the continuing provision of after-care services that secures the stability. The point was taken in Local Government Ombudsman complaint number 06/B/16774 (regarding Bath & North East Somerset Council, 12 December 2008), where the Ombudsman adjudicated on a complaint that the council had unreasonably discontinued funding of after-care. Having been detained in hospital under section 3 of the MHA 1983, the complainant was discharged to a residential home specialising in dementia care. Three years later, a decision was taken that the patient should be discharged from after-care under section 117 on the basis that her mental health was stable, she was not at risk of re-admission and that she was accepting of the placement. She, therefore, became liable for the care home fees. Her complaint was upheld by the Ombudsman. The council had misapplied the law. Whether or not the patient was stable was an 'irrelevant consideration', and in deciding whether she was at risk of re-admission the council had failed to take into account 'the vital contribution of the residential home'.

In the case of a CTO, the CCG and LSSA have no discretion and may not withdraw after-care services while the patient remains subject to the CTO (section 117(2) of the MHA 1983).

19.8   EFFECT OF RE-ADMISSION TO HOSPITAL ON THE DUTY TO PROVIDE AFTER-CARE

Re-admission to hospital on a voluntary basis, under section 2 of the MHA 1983 or under the MCA 2005, is unlikely to have any bearing on the ongoing need for after-care. The right to after-care is triggered by an initial admission under the MHA 1983 for treatment and will continue until there is no longer any perceived need, regardless of any hospital admissions during that period.

The same point might be made in respect of a new admission under section 3 of the MHA 1983, although such an admission would, of course, trigger a fresh right to after-care at the point of discharge, and may therefore mean that responsibility for providing after-care changes from one authority to another, depending on where the patient was resident prior to admission.

19.9   CHARGING FOR AFTER-CARE SERVICES

A patient cannot be charged for the provision of any after-care services, a point confirmed in *R v Manchester City Council ex parte Stennett and Others* [2002]

UKHL 34, where the contention that section 117 of the MHA 1983 was merely a gateway requiring the health or social services authority to provide services under other Acts was rejected. On the contrary, it was held that the duty to provide services arises under section 117 itself, and on the basis that section 117 contains no charging provisions, there is no right to charge for the services.

The financial implications can be significant. A patient who moves into a residential or nursing care home following a hospital admission, for example, may expect his care home fees to be covered by section 117 of the MHA 1983 if he has been detained under section 3 (assuming the move into the home has been identified as an after-care need), but not if he was in hospital voluntarily, detained under section 2 or detained under the DOLS provisions (see *DM v Doncaster Metropolitan Borough Council* [2011] EWHC 3652 (Admin)).

19.10   AFTER-CARE AND PRISON

The after-care provisions apply at the point at which a patient 'leaves hospital' (section 117(1) of the MHA 1983). In the context of cases under section 3, this will invariably be when the patient returns to live in the community. For patients detained for treatment under section 47, 48 or 45A, however, leaving hospital may well mean a return to prison, in which case the after-care provisions apply, not just for the return to prison, but also to subsequent release into the community.

Department of Health guidance (*Good Practice Procedure Guide. The transfer and remission of adult prisoners under s47 and s48 of the Mental Health Act* (DOH, 2011), see Chapter 12) recommends that any prisoner transferred to hospital for treatment should only be returned to prison after there has been a full multi-agency section 117 meeting which should 'agree after-care arrangements including a care plan to accompany the prisoner on their return to custody'.

19.11   HEALTH CARE AND SOCIAL CARE
PROVISION GENERALLY

It is instructive to compare the situation of those who have a statutory entitlement to after-care with those who do not.

19.11.1   Health care

Mental health patients in England to whom section 117 of the MHA 1983 does not apply are in the same position as any other member of society and have no *particular* right to have any health care needs assessed or met.

In its first report, the Joint House of Commons/House of Lords Committee on the Draft Mental Health Bill (Session 2004/2005) questioned whether the commonly acknowledged importance of preventative mental health care was reflected in the actual provision of services on the ground. It noted evidence to suggest that many of those made subject to the compulsory powers of the MHA 1983 had not previously had access to appropriate mental health services and that had they done so, detention would have been avoidable. Citing evidence of 'people seeking help voluntarily, only to be turned away and then committing an offence and ending up detained under the MHA', the Committee was driven to recommend 'that service users have the right to ask for an assessment of their need for mental health care as a resident or non-resident patient, and that authorities be required to justify in writing any decision to decline such a voluntary assessment'. It also recommended that the Mental Health Bill should 'include a duty on public services to assess and to seek to meet the mental health needs of people with mental health problems'.

These recommendations were rejected and, section 117 of the MHA 1983 aside, there remains an absence of any entitlement to an assessment of need or the provision of services.

Patients in Wales are in a different position as a result of the Mental Health (Wales) Measure 2010 (2010 nawm 7) (see Appendix 1).

19.11.2   Community or social care (see also Appendix 12)

For anyone who needs community care services but to whom section 117 of the MHA 1983 does not apply, the best that can be said is that he has an entitlement to an assessment of his needs, but no entitlement to the provision of services to meet those needs.

Section 47 of the NHSCCA 1990 establishes the right to the assessment of needs. According to section 47(1), where it appears to a local authority that any person for whom they may provide or arrange for the provision of community care services may be in need of such services, the authority:

(a)   shall carry out an assessment of his needs for those services, and
(b)   having regard to the result of that assessment, shall then decide whether his needs call for the provision by them of any such services.

The community care services in respect of which an assessment must be carried out are defined by section 46(3) of the NHSCCA 1990 as being services which the local authority provides under:

(a)   Part III of the National Assistance Act 1948;

(b)   section 45 of the Health Services and Public Health Act 1968;

(c)   section 254 of, and Schedule 20 to, the National Health Service Act 2006, and section 192 of, and Schedule 15 to, the National Health Service (Wales) Act 2006;

(d)   section 117 of the Mental Health Act 1983; ...

Services provided under section 2 of the Chronically Sick and Disabled Persons Act 1970 are also treated as community care services for the purposes of the Act.

Generally speaking, the services covered by these provisions and in respect of which an assessment must be carried out are: residential accommodation, domiciliary services and community-based support services.

Determining eligibility for community care services

Section 47 of the NHSCCA 1990 creates no more than the right to an assessment of entitlement to community care services. Whether an individual is actually provided with a service is left to the discretion of the relevant local authority.

Guidance on how local authorities should exercise their discretion was issued by the Department of Health in its 2003 publication, *Fair access to care services – guidance on eligibility criteria for adult social care* (FACS), and eligibility is now commonly referred to as being measured against the FACS criteria, although the FACS guidance was in fact superseded by further guidance from the Department of Health in February 2010, *Prioritising need in the context of Putting People First: a whole system approach to eligibility for social care – guidance on eligibility criteria for adult social care, England 2010.*

According to the current guidance, cases should be divided up into four bands reflecting the seriousness of needs: critical, substantial, moderate and low. Generally speaking, the greater the risk to independence and to the health and well-being of the individual, and the greater the danger of abuse or neglect if the services in question are not provided, the more likely his needs are to be considered critical. It is for the local authority to determine the band into which each case will fall, and also to determine the bands in respect of which it will provide services. Most local authorities provide services only in respect of cases which fall into the substantial or critical need band.

Chapter 20

Community Treatment Orders

20.1   INTRODUCTION

CTOs were, perhaps, the most significant change in mental health law brought about by the MHA 2007, and were intended as a solution to the longstanding problem of providing effective community-based treatment for certain patients with chronic, relapsing mental disorders who were reluctant to accept help. The widespread perception was that many such patients (colloquially known as 'revolving door patients') faced a destructive pattern of repeated admissions to hospital caused by non-compliance with community treatment plans, in particular an unwillingness or inability to take prescribed medication. Something, it was felt, needed to change.

In order to prevent such non-compliance therefore and, hopefully, repeated admissions to hospital, the MHA 2007 amendments to the MHA 1983 effected changes which mean that certain patients can now be put on a CTO at the point at which they are discharged from hospital. The effect is that they are made subject to a set of conditions designed to regulate their behaviour, and are also liable to recall to hospital without the need for a formal assessment under the MHA. This regime (very similar to the conditional discharge regime in respect of restricted patients) is meant to provide a coercive framework within which a patient's co-operation with treatment is more likely to be achieved, and further hospital admissions avoided.

The provisions concerning CTOs (also referred to as supervised community treatment or SCT) are set out in sections 17A–17G of the MHA 1983, as amended by the MHA 2007, and are considered in this chapter.

20.2   ELIGIBLE PATIENTS

Any unrestricted patient who has been detained in hospital for treatment under section 3, 37 or 47 of the MHA 1983 (section 17A, Schedule 1, Part I, and section 47(3)) is eligible for the imposition of a CTO. A CTO may not, therefore, be imposed on a patient who has been detained only for assessment under section 2. Nor may it be imposed on a restricted patient (section 41(3)(aa)).

20.3   DECISION TO IMPOSE A COMMUNITY TREATMENT ORDER

If there is to be one, a CTO will be imposed at the point at which the patient is discharged from liability to detention in hospital. Whether to impose one is a decision for the patient's RC, who must, firstly, satisfy himself that the relevant statutory criteria are met.

20.3.1   Criteria

According to section 17A(5) of the MHA 1983, the criteria which must be met before a CTO can be imposed on a patient are:

(a)   the patient is suffering from a mental disorder of a nature or degree which makes it appropriate for him to receive medical treatment;

(b)   it is necessary for his health or safety or for the protection of other persons that he should receive such treatment;

(c)   subject to his being liable to be recalled as mentioned in paragraph (d) below, such treatment can be provided without his continuing to be detained in a hospital;

(d)   it is necessary that the responsible clinician should be able to exercise the power under section 17E(1) below to recall the patient to hospital; and

(e)   appropriate medical treatment is available for him.

In other words, the RC must conclude that the patient still needs treatment for his mental disorder, that this no longer needs to be as an in-patient, that the patient can therefore be discharged, but that he needs to be subject to the power of recall to hospital.

20.3.2   Power of recall

Very often, discussions around the need for a CTO will focus on the central issue of whether the RC needs the power of recall (section 17A(5)(d) of the

MHA 1983). When deciding on the need for this power, section 17A(6) requires that the RC shall:

> (6)   ... in particular, consider, having regard to the patient's history of mental disorder and any other relevant factors, what risk there would be of a deterioration of the patient's condition if he were not detained in a hospital (as a result, for example, of his refusing or neglecting to receive the medical treatment he requires for his mental disorder).

The point is clear. The power of recall hanging over the patient is designed to persuade him to comply with the treatment that is offered. The greater the risk therefore of non-compliance with treatment, and the greater the risk of a deterioration in his mental health as a result, the greater the case is for the power of recall as part of the CTO.

The RC would, however, ordinarily need to point to a patient's history of non-compliance (and consequent deterioration) before he could say that other options had been exhausted and that the power of recall had therefore become necessary. As the 1983 Code points out (para 25.7), the 'key factor in the decision is whether the patient can safely be treated for mental disorder in the community *only* if the responsible clinician can exercise the power to recall the patient to hospital for treatment if that becomes necessary'.

20.3.3   Agreement of the approved mental health professional

The only significant procedural safeguard at the outset is that the RC must obtain the agreement of an AMHP, both that the criteria are met *and* that the CTO is appropriate (section 17A(4) of the MHA 1983). In this respect, the role of the AMHP is to 'consider the wider social context for the patient' (1983 Code, para 25.24). Somewhat surprisingly, therefore, the AMHP need not have had any previous involvement in the patient's care, nor even have met the patient.

20.3.4   The patient

In theory, a CTO may be imposed without the consent of the patient. However, it may not be used to force a patient to do something against his will (see para 20.4) and in practice is only likely to work, therefore, if there is a degree of consensus from the outset. Although reluctant, many patients will agree to the CTO because it signals their discharge from hospital.

A CTO may be imposed on a patient who lacks the capacity to agree to it.

20.3.5   Leave under section 17 of the Mental Health Act 1983

The RC is expected to consider the possibility of a CTO whenever a patient is granted long-term leave under section 17 of the MHA 1983. Indefinite leave or leave for a specified period of more than 7 days may not, therefore, be granted unless the RC has first considered whether to put the patient onto a CTO (section 17(2A)).

20.4   EFFECT OF A COMMUNITY TREATMENT ORDER

Once the CTO is made (in writing, Form CTO1, regulation 6(1)(a) of the Mental Health Regulations 2008), the patient becomes a 'community patient' (section 17A(7) of the MHA 1983). Significantly, however, the original authority for detention (the application under section 3 or the order under section 37) does not then cease to have effect (section 17D(1)); it is simply 'suspended' (section 17D(2)(a)).

Although authority to detain is suspended rather than extinguished completely, section 17D(2)(b) of the MHA 1983 makes clear that any references in the Act, or other Acts or subordinate legislation, to patients who are detained or liable to be detained are not to be regarded as references to community patients.

A CTO will then last initially for a period of up to 6 months, and is renewable for a further 6 months, followed by periods of 12 months at a time (section 20A(1) of the MHA 1983). The renewal procedure is set out in section 20A and is essentially the same as that for the extension of detention under section 3 (see para 8.5).

Generally speaking, the CTO carries with it no compulsory powers in respect of care or treatment. A patient may not, therefore, be given any form of treatment against his will (subject to rare exceptions involving a CTO imposed on someone who lacks the capacity to consent to treatment; see paras 20.11.3 and 20.11.5). Instead, the CTO creates a more subtle coercive framework which is designed to foster a patient's compliance with treatment. The framework comprises two main elements: firstly, a series of conditions with which the patient is expected to comply; secondly, a liability to recall to hospital if it is felt that further treatment as an in-patient is required.

20.5 CONDITIONS ATTACHED TO A COMMUNITY TREATMENT ORDER

20.5.1 Mandatory conditions

Two conditions must be attached to any CTO. The first is a condition that the patient makes himself available for examination by the RC when he is considering whether to extend the CTO (section 17B(3)(a) of the MHA 1983). The second is that the patient should make himself available for examination by a SOAD when the examination is for the purpose of authorising treatment under the CTO (section 17B(3)(b); see 20.11).

20.5.2 Discretionary conditions

Section 17B(1) of the MHA 1983 allows for additional conditions to be attached to the CTO at the discretion of the RC. According to section 17B(2), however, the RC may only specify conditions which both he and the AMHP agree are 'necessary or appropriate' for:

(a) ensuring that the patient receives medical treatment;
(b) preventing risk of harm to the patient's health or safety;
(c) protecting other persons.

The patient should be consulted before any conditions are imposed, and no CTO should be imposed with conditions with which the patient is never likely to comply. The 1983 Code suggests (para 25.33) that conditions should:

- be kept to a minimum number consistent with achieving their purpose;
- restrict the patient's liberty as little as possible while being consistent with achieving their purpose;
- have a clear rationale, linked to one or more of the purposes set out in paragraph 25.30; and
- be clearly and precisely expressed, so that the patient can readily understand what is expected.

CTOs may not have conditions attached which would individually or collectively amount to a deprivation of a patient's liberty, a point expressly confirmed by the Minister of State at the Health Department at the time of the introduction of the MHA 1983 (Appendix 3 to *Joint Committee on Human Rights Report on Mental Health Bill*, February 2007).

20.5.3   Varying discretionary conditions

Section 17B(4) and (5) of the MHA 1983 provide the RC with the power to vary or suspend any of the discretionary conditions. Agreement of the AMHP to any variation is not required, but the 1983 Code suggests (para 25.41) that, 'it would not be good practice to vary conditions which had recently been agreed with an AMHP without discussion with that AMHP'. Similarly, although the patient's consent to any change of conditions is not required, it ought to be obtained if the CTO is to work.

20.5.4   Breach of conditions

Breach of one of the two mandatory conditions carries with it an automatic power to recall to hospital (section 17E(2) of the MHA 1983), although recall in such circumstances is likely only to be so that the purpose of the condition can be achieved. No automatic sanction attaches to breach of any discretionary condition, but section 17B(6) provides that the RC may take into account any breach when deciding whether to exercise the power of recall (see para 20.6).

20.6   LIABILITY TO RECALL

The essential feature of the CTO is that for its duration, a patient remains liable to recall to hospital (section 17E of the MHA 1983). As with a conditional discharge for a restricted patient, while conditions may be imposed to regulate a patient's behaviour following discharge, it is, in the main, the liability to recall to hospital that makes the order effective; indeed, whether the patient needs to be liable to recall is the question the answer to which will determine whether a CTO is imposed in the first place.

The power of recall is created by section 17E(1) of the MHA 1983. It provides that the RC may recall a community patient to hospital if he is of the opinion that:

>   (a)   the patient requires medical treatment in hospital for his mental disorder; and
>   (b)   there would be a risk of harm to the health or safety of the patient or to other persons if the patient were not recalled to hospital for that purpose.

Breach by the patient of a discretionary condition may be relevant in deciding whether he should be recalled (section 17B(6) of the MHA 1983), but recall may be justified whether or not there is a breach of a condition.

As an alternative to recall, a community patient may agree to return to hospital on a voluntary basis with the CTO remaining in place.

20.7   RECALL PROCEDURE

Recall is exercised by giving notice in writing to the patient (section 17E(5) of the MHA 1983). The written notice will be in the form set out in Form CTO3 (regulation 6(3)(a) of the Mental Health Regulations 2008), and should be either given to the patient directly or delivered (by hand or first class post) to his usual or last known address (regulation 6(5)). Once served, written notice provides authority to detain the patient.

A patient who is in hospital on a voluntary basis at the time of the proposed recall from the CTO may be served with notice of recall by hand while in hospital, but section 5(6) of the MHA 1983 prevents the RC or nurses from using their holding power under section 5(2) or (4) to prevent the patient from leaving the ward while the notice is being served.

Recall to hospital does not necessarily bring the CTO to an end. Instead, it allows detention for a period of 72 hours, during which a decision can be taken on the viability of continuing with the order. During those 72 hours, the RC may revoke the CTO (section 17F(4) of the MHA 1983; see para 20.8), or release the patient (section 17F(5)). If the RC has done neither by the end of the 72-hour period, the patient must be released back on to a CTO (section 17F(6)).

20.8   REVOCATION OF A COMMUNITY
TREATMENT ORDER

Revocation of a CTO may only take place if a patient has first been recalled (section 17F(1) of the MHA 1983). To then revoke, the RC must be satisfied that the criteria justifying detention for treatment under section 3 are met (section 17F(4)(a)). Revocation will be in writing. The RC must have the agreement of an AMHP that the detention criteria under section 3 are met and that it is 'appropriate to revoke the order' (section 17F(4)(b)). Once a CTO is revoked, the patient reverts to his earlier status as a detained patient under section 3 (section 17G(2)) or under section 37 (Schedule 1, Part I, para 2B). For the purpose of calculating future renewal periods and eligibility for tribunal applications, however, the patient is treated as if admitted to hospital on the day on which the order is actually revoked (section 17G(5)).

Revocation automatically triggers a referral of a patient's case to the MHT (section 68(7) of the MHA 1983).

20.9 DISCHARGE FROM A COMMUNITY TREATMENT ORDER

Section 23(2)(c) of the MHA 1983 provides the RC and hospital managers with the power to discharge the patient from the CTO. The general principles governing the exercise of this discretion are the same as those governing the exercise of the similar discretion in respect of detained patients, and are considered in Chapter 18.

As they are with detained patients, *hospital managers* are provided with specific guidance by the 1983 Code (para 31.17) on what criteria to apply when reviewing the case of a CTO patient. The expectation is that they will discharge if the statutory criteria for detention (section 72(1)(c) of the MHA 1983; see para 16.4.1) are no longer met.

The *nearest relative* may discharge a patient from a CTO using section 23(2)(c) of the MHA 1983, but only one who was previously subject to detention under section 3, not section 37. As with detained patients, the nearest relative's power is qualified to the extent that it requires 72 hours' notice and may be barred by the RC on the grounds that the patient if discharged 'would be likely to act in manner dangerous to other persons or to himself' (section 25(1A)). This is considered further at para 18.2.2.

A patient may also be discharged by the *MHT*. Rules governing entitlement to applications and references are considered in Chapter 14, and the criteria to be applied by the MHT in respect of CTO cases are considered at para 16.4.

20.10 ALTERNATIVE WAYS FOR A COMMUNITY TREATMENT ORDER TO END

Apart from discharge, a CTO may come to an end in one of the following ways:

- The underlying basis for detention comes to an end (e.g. the hospital order is overturned on appeal or the basis of the detention under section 3 of the MHA 1983 is found to be invalid).
- It is revoked following recall (section 17G) (in which case, the underlying basis for detention is revived).
- It expires at the end of its current period unless it is extended in accordance with the provisions of section 20A. (The expiry of the CTO in this way will bring to an end both the CTO and the underlying basis for detention (section 20(B)(1).)
- The patient is detained in custody for a period which lasts longer than 6 months (section 22(1)).

What happens if a patient who is already on a CTO is detained under a new section 2 or section 3 of the MHA 1983 during the currency of his CTO, or a court imposes a hospital order under section 37 on a patient who is already subject to a CTO? The following rules will apply:

- the new section or court order is not invalidated by the existing CTO;
- if a patient is assessed and detained under section 2 (or section 4) while already subject to a CTO, the new detention will have no effect on the existing CTO;
- if a patient is assessed and detained under section 3 while already subject to a CTO *which was imposed following a previous period of detention under section 3*, the new detention will mean that the CTO automatically comes to an end (section 6(4));
- if a patient is assessed and detained under section 3 while already subject to a CTO *which was imposed following a hospital order under section 37*, the new detention will have no effect on the existing CTO;
- If a patient is given a hospital order under section 37 by a court while already subject to a CTO, the new detention will mean that the CTO automatically comes to an end, whatever the type of detention that originally preceded the CTO (section 40(5)).

20.11 TREATMENT PROVISIONS – PART 4A OF THE MENTAL HEALTH ACT 1983

The provisions concerning treatment of community patients are set out in Part 4A of the MHA 1983. Sections 64A–64D apply to adults, sections 64E–64F apply to children (for these purposes, anyone under the age of 16) and sections 64FA–64H apply to both.

20.11.1 Decision-making framework regarding treatment on a community treatment order

There is a standard approach to decision-making concerning treatment under a CTO which is set out below. In summary, there must be authority for the treatment in the first place, there is then an additional 'certificate requirement' to be met in the case of treatment under section 58 of the MHA 1983 (medicine after 3 months) and section 58A (ECT) and, lastly, there are certain circumstances when the additional certificate requirement for section 58 and section 58A treatment can be overlooked. The application of this decision-making framework varies according to whether the patient has capacity (in the case of adults) or competence (in the case of children). For adults, capacity is to be determined according to the MCA 2005 (section 64K(2)). For children, competence is decided according to the common law principles considered at para 24.3.1.

20.11.2   Adults with capacity

Authority for treatment

An adult with capacity may only be treated under a CTO if he consents to the treatment (section 64C(2)(a) of the MHA 1983).

Certificate requirement in cases under section 58 and section 58A of the Mental Health Act 1983

Even with the patient's consent, the administration of medicine beyond the date 3 months from when it was originally given (whether in hospital or the community) or ECT treatment may only continue if:

- a SOAD has certified in writing that it is appropriate for the treatment to be given or for the treatment to be given subject to such conditions as may be specified in the certificate and where those conditions are satisfied (sections 64B(2)(b) and 64C(4)(a) and (b) of the MHA 1983); or
- an approved clinician in charge of the patient's treatment has certified in writing that the patient has capacity to consent to the treatment and has consented to it (section 64C(4A)) (except where treatment is ECT in respect of under 18 year olds; section 64C(4B)).

Cases where the certificate requirement does not apply

The certificate is not required, however, where:

- the treatment is 'immediately necessary' (see section 64C(5) and (6) of the MHA 1983) and the patient consents (section 64B(3)(b)(i)); or
- the treatment is the administration of medicine and is during the first month of the CTO (section 64B(4)).

20.11.3   Adults who lack capacity

Authority for treatment

An adult who lacks the necessary capacity cannot lawfully consent to treatment. Authority must, therefore, come from one of the following three alternative sources:

- a donee of a lasting power of attorney (LPA) or deputy appointed by the Court of Protection may consent on the patient's behalf (section 64C(2)(b) of the MHA 1983);
- the approved clinician in charge of treatment, having taken steps to establish whether the patient lacks capacity to consent, reasonably

believes that the patient lacks capacity, has no reason to believe that the patient objects to the treatment or if he does, it is not necessary to use force to give the treatment, and is satisfied that the treatment does not conflict with an advance decision or the decision of a donee or deputy appointed by the Court of Protection (section 64D);

- in an emergency, the approved clinician in charge of treatment reasonably believes that the patient lacks capacity to consent, that the treatment is 'immediately necessary' and, if it is necessary to use force to give the treatment, the treatment needs to be given in order to prevent harm, and the use of force is proportionate (section 64G(2)–(4)).

Certificate requirement in cases under section 58 and section 58A of the Mental Health Act 1983

Even with authority from a lawful source, medicine beyond 3 months or ECT may only be given if a SOAD certifies in writing that it is appropriate for the treatment to be given or for the treatment to be given subject to such conditions as may be specified in the certificate and where those conditions are satisfied (section 64C(4)(a) and (b) of the MHA 1983).

Cases where the certificate requirement does not apply

The certificate is not required, however, where:

- the treatment is 'emergency treatment' and is authorised in accordance with section 64G of the MHA 1983 (emergency treatment for patients who lack capacity or competence); or
- the treatment is 'immediately necessary' (section 64C(5) and (6)) and has been consented to by a donee or deputy (section 64(B)(3)(b)(ii)); or
- the treatment is the administration of medicine during the first month of the CTO (section 64B(4)).

20.11.4   Competent children

Authority for treatment

A competent child may only be treated under a CTO if he consents to the treatment (section 64E(6)(a) of the MHA 1983).

Certificate requirement in cases under section 58 and section 58A of the Mental Health Act 1983

Even with the consent of the competent child, the administration of medicine beyond the date 3 months from when it was originally given may only continue if:

- a SOAD certifies in writing that it is appropriate for the treatment to be given or for the treatment to be given subject to such conditions as may be specified in the certificate and where those conditions are satisfied (section 64E(7) of the MHA 1983); or
- the approved clinician in charge of the treatment has certified in writing that the patient has the competence to consent and has consented (section 64E(7)).

Even with the consent of the competent child, ECT treatment may only be given if:

- a SOAD certifies in writing that it is appropriate for the treatment to be given or for the treatment to be given subject to such conditions as may be specified in the certificate and where those conditions are satisfied (section 64E(7)(a) of the MHA 1983).

Cases where the certificate requirement does not apply

The certificate is not required, however, where:

- treatment is 'immediately necessary' and the patient consents (section 64E(3)(b) of the MHA 1983); or
- the treatment is the administration of medicine within the first month of the CTO (section 64E(4)).

20.11.5   Children who lack competence

Authority for treatment

A child who lacks the relevant competence cannot lawfully consent to treatment. Authority for treatment must, therefore, come from one of the following two sources:

- the approved clinician in charge of treatment takes reasonable steps to establish the patient's competence, has a reasonable belief that the patient lacks competence, has no reason to believe that the patient objects or, if he does object, it is not necessary to use force against the patient in order to give the treatment (section 64F(2)–(5) of the MHA 1983);
- in an emergency, the approved clinician reasonably believes that the patient lacks competence to consent, treatment is immediately necessary and if it is necessary to use force, the treatment needs to be given in order to prevent harm to the patient and the use of such force is proportionate (section 64G(2)–(4)).

The certificate requirement

Even with authority from a lawful source, medicine beyond 3 months or ECT, may only be given if a SOAD certifies in writing that it is appropriate for the treatment to be given, or given subject to such conditions as may be specified and those conditions are satisfied (section 64E(7) of the MHA 1983).

Cases where the certificate requirement does not apply

The certificate is not required, however, where:

- treatment is emergency treatment in accordance with section 64G of the MHA 1983 (section 64E(3)(a));
- treatment is the administration of medicine and is within the first month of the CTO (section 64E(4)).

20.12   TREATMENT PROVISIONS FOLLOWING RECALL OR REVOCATION

The treatment of patients who are recalled from a CTO or whose CTO is revoked is covered by Part IV of the Act (not Part 4A), specifically section 62A. In general terms, in the period following recall or revocation, the rules governing treatment of patients are as they would be for any other detained patient (see Chapter 9), subject to the following:

- Authority for the *administration of medicine* under section 58 is not required if the treatment is still within three months from the point at which the patient was first administered medicine as a detained patient (section 62A(2)).
- Authority for the *administration of medicine* under section 58 is not required if the treatment is still within one month from the point at which the patient was put onto a CTO (section 62A(3)(b)).
- Authority for the *administration of medicine* under section 58 is not required if a certificate under Part 4A is already in place expressly authorising such treatment in the event of recall (section 62A(3)(a) and (5)). However, where the CTO is actually revoked, treatment under the authority of the Part 4A certificate only applies pending compliance with section 58 (section 62A(7)).
- Authority for the *administration of ECT* under section 58A is not required if there is authority to treat the patient (a patient with capacity consents or, for a patient without capacity, there is a SOAD certificate in place) and there is a certificate under Part 4A in place expressly authorising such treatment in the event of recall (section 62A(4) and (5));

- *Medicine or ECT* which was being administered under a Part 4A certificate while the patient was on a CTO may continue following recall, even though not expressly authorised in the event of recall, if the approved clinician in charge of treatment considers that the discontinuance of treatment would cause serious suffering to the patient (section 62A(6)). Such treatment may only continue pending compliance with section 58 or section 58A.
- In cases where the certificate requirement is no longer met, the administration of *medicine or ECT* is not precluded following recall (pending compliance with section 58 or section 58A) where discontinuance would cause serious suffering to the patient (section 62A(6A)).

Chapter 21

Guardianship

21.1   INTRODUCTION

Guardianship is another example of supervised care in the community provided under the MHA 1983. Whereas, however, a CTO addresses the patient's health and his need for treatment, guardianship addresses the patient's welfare and his need for protection.

Put very simply, guardianship involves the appointment of a guardian who is given certain powers to help a patient manage his own welfare. The idea is not a new one. Under section 34 of the Mental Health Act 1959, a guardian had 'all such powers as would be exercisable by him ... if he were the father of the patient and the patient were under the age of 14 years'. Times change, however, and since the MHA 1983, a guardian's powers have been much more circumscribed, to the extent that they are almost notional. Its continuing value as a tool for the care of the mentally disordered is, therefore, now much more questionable, something which is perhaps reflected by the declining frequency of its use. It remains of potential use where there are concerns that mental disorder affects a patient's ability to look after his own affairs, and may typically be used, therefore, in respect of the elderly or those with learning disabilities. Many that are subject to guardianship will lack capacity and may, therefore, also be subject to decision-making under the MCA 2005.

There are various routes by which a patient may end up subject to guardianship but by far the majority will arrive there as a result of a civil application under section 7 of the MHA 1983. Apart from a brief consideration of the alternative routes, therefore, this chapter focusses on such applications.

21.2   ALTERNATIVE ROUTES INTO GUARDIANSHIP

The alternative routes to an application under section 7 of the MHA 1983 are as follows.

21.2.1   Court orders under section 37 of the Mental Health Act 1983

A guardianship order under section 37 of the MHA 1983 may be imposed as a sentence in criminal proceedings, although this court power is used sparingly. The criteria for the imposition of the order, and its effect, are considered at para 10.5.1.

21.2.2   Transfer under section 19 of the Mental Health Act 1983

A patient already liable to detention in hospital (including a patient under section 2 of the MHA 1983) may be transferred into the guardianship of the LSSA or any other person approved by such an authority (section 19(1)(a)). The procedure is covered by regulation 7 of the Mental Health Regulations 2008.

21.3   GUARDIANSHIP APPLICATIONS UNDER SECTION 7 OF THE MENTAL HEALTH ACT 1983 – THE PROCEDURE FOR MAKING AN APPLICATION

Essentially, the procedure for making an application for guardianship under section 7 of the MHA 1983 mirrors the procedure for making an application for the admission of a patient to hospital under section 3.

21.3.1   Considering the case

Section 13(1) of the MHA 1983 requires an LSSA to make arrangements for an AMHP to consider the patient's case whenever the authority has reason to think that an application for guardianship may need to be made.

21.3.2   The applicant

Section 11(1) of the MHA 1983 provides that an application for admission into guardianship may be made either by an AMHP or by the patient's nearest relative. As with applications for hospital admissions, however, the vast majority of applications will be made by the AMHP. Unlike applications for admission to hospital, an AMHP need not have interviewed the patient before making an application for guardianship (section 13(2)).

The application must be made within 14 days of the applicant having personally seen (although not necessarily having interviewed) the patient (section 11(5) of the MHA 1983).

21.3.3   Consulting the nearest relative

According to section 11(4) of the MHA 1983, an AMHP may not make an application for guardianship where the nearest relative has notified the AMHP or the LSSA of his objection to the application being made. The AMHP is also prevented from making an application if he has not consulted the person (if any) appearing to be the nearest relative of the patient, although this requirement to consult does not arise if it appears to the AMHP that in the circumstances such consultation is not reasonably practicable or would involve unreasonable delay.

An AMHP may apply to the county court for an order displacing the nearest relative under section 29(3)(c) of the MHA 1983 if the nearest relative 'unreasonably objects to the making of a guardianship application in respect of the patient'.

21.3.4   Medical recommendations

Any guardianship application must be based on written recommendations from two RMPs, one of whom needs to be approved under section 12(2) of the MHA 1983 as having special experience in the diagnosis or treatment of a mental disorder (section 7(3)).

21.3.5   Submitting the application

The application will need to name the proposed guardian, who 'may be either a local social services authority or any other person' (section 7(5)). The vast majority of guardians will be the LSSA. If the person named is not the LSSA, the application shall have no effect 'unless it is accepted on behalf of the person concerned by the local social services authority for the area in which he resides' and it must be 'accompanied by a statement in writing by that person that he is willing to act as guardian' (section 7(5)). In these (rare) cases, section 34(3) provides that the LSSA for the area in which the person who is the guardian resides will be the 'responsible local social services authority' for the purposes of the application (see para 21.6.3).

The application for guardianship should be forwarded to the LSSA named in the application as guardian, or, in the case of a private guardian, to the LSSA for the area in which the private guardian resides (section 11(2) of the MHA 1983). It should be submitted within 14 days of the last examination by an RMP (section 8(2)). Once accepted by the LSSA, the application confers on the guardian the powers set out in section 8 (see para 21.5).

Where the LSSA is named as guardian, it may delegate its functions (regulation 21(1) of the Mental Health Regulations 2008), the only exception to this rule being that the LSSA may not delegate its power of discharge under section 23 of the MHA 1983 (see para 21.8.1). Functions will normally be delegated to an AMHP.

Section 10(3) of the MHA 1983 allows a county court, upon application, to order guardianship of a patient to be transferred to the LSSA 'or to any other person approved for the purpose by that authority' if the existing guardian has performed his or her functions 'negligently or in a manner contrary to the interests of the welfare of the patient'.

21.4   CRITERIA FOR GUARDIANSHIP

The application may only be accepted if the patient meets the criteria for admission to guardianship as set out in section 7 of the MHA 1983.

21.4.1   Age limit

According to section 7(1) of the MHA 1983, the application may not be made unless the patient has 'attained the age of 16 years'.

21.4.2   Statutory criteria

According to section 7(2) of the MHA 1983, the application may be made on the grounds that:

(a)   he is suffering from mental disorder, of a nature or degree which warrants his reception into guardianship under this section; and

(b)   it is necessary in the interests of the welfare of the patient or for the protection of other persons that the patient should be so received.

21.4.3 Learning disability

A person with learning disability may not be regarded as having a mental disorder for these purposes, and may not, therefore, be the subject of a guardianship application, unless the learning disability is associated with 'abnormally aggressive or seriously irresponsible conduct' (section 1(2A) of the MHA 1983).

21.5 GUARDIAN'S POWERS

21.5.1 Section 8 of the Mental Health Act 1983

The powers available to a guardian are set out in section 8(1) of the MHA 1983. There are, in fact, only three:

(a) the power to require the patient to reside at a place specified by the authority or person named as guardian;

(b) the power to require the patient to attend at places and times so specified for the purpose of medical treatment, occupation, education or training;

(c) the power to require access to the patient to be given, at any place where the patient is residing, to any registered medical practitioner, approved mental health professional or other person so specified.

The last two are hardly powers at all, given that there is no sanction in the event that the patient decides not to comply with them, and while there is slightly more substance to the power to require residence at a specified place (see para 21.5.2), the overall impression is not one of a particularly powerful statutory weapon. If guardianship is to prove useful, therefore, it is likely to be for reasons other than reliance on the powers available under section 8 of the MHA 1983.

The *Reference guide to the Mental Health Act 1983* (para 19.9) suggests that, 'in large part, the effectiveness of guardianship relies on the moral (rather than legal) authority of guardians and the quality of their relationship with the patient', and, in a similar vein, the 1983 Code suggests (para 26.8) that guardianship is most likely to be appropriate where 'the patient is thought to be likely to respond well to the authority and attention of a guardian and so be more willing to comply with necessary treatment and care for their mental disorder'.

21.5.2   Power to require residence at a specified place

There is at least a sanction attached to the power to require residence at a specified place, with section 18(3) of the MHA 1983 authorising:

> (3)   … any officer on the staff of a local social services authority, by any constable or by any other person authorised in writing by the guardian or the LSSA to take into custody and return to the place of residence any guardianship patient who has absented himself without leave from the place of residence.

Even here, however, while there is a power to return the patient to the place of residence, there is no power to prevent him from leaving in the first place, since guardianship may not be used as a legal framework to justify the deprivation of a patient's liberty.

The limitations of this power are, therefore, readily apparent and the advice from the 1983 Code (para 26.35) is that, '[i]f a patient consistently resists exercise by the guardian of any of their powers, it can normally be concluded that guardianship is not the most appropriate form of care for that person, and the guardianship should be discharged'.

21.6   GUARDIAN'S RESPONSIBILITIES

21.6.1   The need for a comprehensive care plan

Guardianship is as much about responsibility as it is about power. Any application for guardianship should, therefore, be accompanied by a comprehensive care plan, identifying which services the patient will need and who will provide them. The 1983 Code identifies (para 26.21) that the key elements of any plan should be:

- suitable accommodation to help meet the patient's needs;
- access to day care, education and training facilities, as appropriate;
- effective co-operation and communication between all those concerned in implementing the plan; and
- (if there is to be a private guardian) support from the LSSA for the guardian.

21.6.2   Responsibilities of private guardians

A private guardian has additional responsibilities which are set out in regulation 22 of the Mental Health Regulations 2008. They include the requirement to appoint an RMP to act as the nominated medical attendant of the patient, and an ongoing requirement to keep the LSSA notified of all matters relevant to the operation of the guardian's role.

21.6.3   Duty to visit

Regulation 23 of the Mental Health Regulations 2008 requires that the responsible LSSA (either the LSSA which is the guardian or, in the case of a private guardian, the LSSA for the area in which he resides) should arrange for the patient to be visited at least once every 3 months and for one of those visits to be conducted by an approved clinician or RMP approved under section 12(2) of the MHA 1983.

21.7   DURATION OF GUARDIANSHIP

Guardianship will run for an initial period of 6 months beginning with the date upon which the application was accepted, and may be renewed, initially, for a further period of 6 months and, subsequently, for further periods of one year at a time (section 20(1) and (2) of the MHA 1983).

The procedure for renewal is set out in section 20 of the MHA 1983 and mirrors the procedure for renewal of detention under section 3 (see para 8.5). The patient's 'appropriate practitioner' must examine the patient within the 2-month period ending when guardianship would otherwise cease, and furnish a report if he is satisfied that the criteria for guardianship remain in place (section 20(7)). The report must be furnished to the guardian and, where this is a person other than a LSSA, to the responsible LSSA (section 20(6)). Where a report is furnished in this way, authority for guardianship will be renewed (section 20(8)). Section 34(1) defines 'appropriate practitioner' as the patient's RC if the guardian is the LSSA, and the 'nominated medical attendant' if the guardian is a person other than the LSSA.

21.8   DISCHARGE FROM GUARDIANSHIP

21.8.1   Discharge powers under section 23 of the Mental Health Act 1983

A patient subject to guardianship may be discharged by his RC, by the LSSA (as opposed to hospital managers) or by his nearest relative. As with detained and CTO patients, these powers derive from section 23 of the MHA 1983. The general principles governing the exercise of discharge powers are considered in Chapter 18, but the following points are of specific application to guardianship patients.

Private guardians

A private guardian does not have the power to discharge a patient from guardianship.

Local social services authorities

An equivalent to the hospital managers' power of discharge under section 23 of the MHA 1983 is invested in the 'responsible LSSA'. Where the LSSA is the guardian, that authority will also be the 'responsible LSSA', but in the case of a private guardian, the responsible authority will be the LSSA for the area in which the guardian resides (section 34(3)).
The 1983 Code provides (para 26.18) that:

> LSSAs may consider discharging patients from guardianship at any time, but must consider doing so when they receive a report from the patient's nominated medical attendant or responsible clinician renewing their guardianship under section 20 of the Act.

Any decision by the responsible LSSA to discharge is exercisable by three or more members of that authority or by any committee set up by it to make the decision (section 23(4) of the MHA 1983). Regulation 21(2) of the Mental Health Regulations 2008 provides that the LSSA may not delegate the power of discharge to an officer.

Unlike hospital managers, LSSAs do not have the benefit of extensive advice from the 1983 Code on when hearings should be held, how they should be conducted or what criteria should apply. However, the general principles which govern the conduct of hospital managers' hearings (1983 Code, Chapter 31) should apply equally to LSSAs.

Nearest relative

Except in cases where guardianship has been imposed under section 37 of the MHA 1983, the nearest relative may discharge the patient. Unlike detained or CTO patients, the power is not subject to the power of the RC to bar discharge under section 25, and there is, therefore, no requirement to provide 72 hours' notice.

21.8.2 Mental health tribunal power of discharge

A patient may also be discharged by the MHT using its powers under section 72(4) of the MHA 1983 (see para 16.5).

21.9 EFFECT OF A HOSPITAL ADMISSION ON GUARDIANSHIP

Guardianship is unaffected by a voluntary admission to hospital or by an admission under section 2 of the MHA 1983, but admission to hospital under section 3 will bring to an end any guardianship imposed under section 7 (section 6(4)), and an admission under section 37 will bring to an end *any* previously imposed guardianship (section 40(5)).

21.10 TRANSFER OF A PATIENT FROM GUARDIANSHIP TO HOSPITAL

A patient who is subject to guardianship may be transferred to hospital under section 19(1)(b) of the MHA 1983. The effect of the transfer is that the patient is then treated as though detained under section 3. This provides an alternative to carrying out a formal assessment under the MHA. The procedure to be adopted is set out in regulation 8 of the Mental Health Regulations 2008.

21.11 GUARDIANSHIP AND THE MENTAL CAPACITY ACT 2005

There will be a significant number of patients in respect of whom decision-making could take place under guardianship or the MCA 2005, or both, and there is nothing wrong in principle with a patient being subject to the two regimes at the same time. Use of the MCA 2005 may be appropriate, in particular, in cases where a patient's freedom of movement needs to be significantly inhibited at any place of residence. Guardianship may not be used to authorise a deprivation of liberty, but the MCA 2005 might, if in accordance with the provisions under Schedule A1, Hospital and Care Home Residents: Deprivation of Liberty (see Chapter 23). It was noted in *C v Blackburn & Darwen Borough Council* [2011] EWHC 3321 (COP), however, that the combination of guardianship and DOLS should be 'an alerting factor as to the appropriateness of guardianship'. It was also suggested that when there is a dispute about the place of residence of a resisting incapacitated person, then neither guardianship nor DOLS was necessarily appropriate and that 'substantial decisions of that kind ought properly to be made by the Court of Protection, using its power to make welfare decisions under section 16 of the MCA'.

Part Seven

Mental Capacity Act 2005

Chapter 22

Mental Capacity Act 2005 – Overview

22.1   INTRODUCTION

The MCA 2005 stands apart from the MHA 1983 as a completely separate statutory framework. Whereas the MHA 1983 is concerned with mental disorder, the MCA 2005 is concerned with mental capacity. More specifically, it is concerned with decision-making in relation to those who lack the capacity to make decisions for themselves, those who are unable to make a decision because of 'an impairment of, or a disturbance in the functioning of, the mind or brain' (section 2(1) of the MCA 2005).

Decision-making is central to the MCA 2005. Although the Act may apply whenever there is a malfunctioning of the mind or brain, this is only to the extent that this affects a person's capacity to make a decision. Where there is no decision to make, the Act serves no purpose.

Anyone caring for, or dealing with, a person aged 16 or older who lacks, or may lack the capacity to make any decision should comply with the MCA 2005. In those cases to which it applies, the Act sets out the key principles which govern decision-making, provides a statutory test for determining whether someone does, in fact, have the capacity to make a decision, and provides guidance for use in deciding how to act in their best interests if they do not. It also provides statutory protection for those making decisions in good faith on behalf of the incapacitated person, and, in cases where difficult or contentious issues need resolving, the Act provides that the Court of Protection may assist.

The scope of the MCA 2005 is considered in this chapter. Reference is made to the relationship that the Act has with the MHA 1983, since there will inevitably be circumstances to which both Acts could apply. This issue is also considered in Chapter 9 as part of a review of treatment for mental disorder under the MHA 1983, and in Chapter 23 as part of a review of DOLS.

As with the MCA 2005, the person on behalf of whom a decision falls to be made is referred to as 'P'.

22.2   CODE OF PRACTICE OF THE MENTAL CAPACITY ACT 2005

Although comprehensive, one of the most significant features of the MCA 2005 is that it is anything but prescriptive about day-to-day decision-making concerning those without capacity. Guidance from its accompanying Code of Practice (2005 Code) is, therefore, particularly important.

Section 42(4) of the MCA 2005 places a legal duty to have regard to the 2005 Code on anyone acting in relation to a person who lacks capacity in one or more of the following ways:

> (a)   as the donee of a lasting power of attorney,
> (b)   as a deputy appointed by the court,
> (c)   as a person carrying out research in reliance on any provision made by or under this Act (see sections 30 to 34),
> (d)   as an independent mental capacity advocate,
> (da)   in the exercise of functions under Schedule A1 [see Chapter 23],
> (db)   as a representative appointed under Part 10 of Schedule A1 [see Chapter 23],
> (e)   in a professional capacity,
> (f)   for remuneration.

The vast majority of decision-makers, unpaid carers, family and friends are under no such legal obligation, but the reasonableness of any decision they take, and possibly, therefore, whether they are protected from liability for any acts that they carry out (see para 22.10) will be assessed according to their compliance with the 2005 Code's guidance.

22.3   KEY PRINCIPLES OF THE MENTAL CAPACITY ACT 2005

The MCA 2005 begins (section 1) by setting out five key principles which should govern all decision-making. These are:

- A person must be assumed to have capacity unless it is established otherwise (section 1(2)).
- A person is not to be treated as unable to make a decision unless all practicable steps to help him to do so have been taken without success (section 1(3)).

- A person is not to be treated as unable to make a decision merely because he makes an unwise decision (section 1(4)).
- An act done, or decision made, under the Act for or on behalf of the person who lacks capacity must be done, or made, in his best interests (section 1(5)).
- Before the act is done, or the decision is made, regard must be had to whether the purpose for which it is needed can be as effectively achieved in a way that is less restrictive of the person's rights and freedom of action (section 1(6)).

22.4 DECISIONS EXCLUDED FROM THE SCOPE OF THE MENTAL CAPACITY ACT 2005

The MCA 2005 also makes clear that certain areas of decision-making are specifically excluded from its scope.

22.4.1 Children and young people

Children (under 16)

As a rule, the MCA 2005 does *not* apply to anyone under the age of 16 (section 2(5)). The only two exceptions to this are:

- the Court of Protection's power under section 16 to make decisions relating to P's property and affairs (see para 22.12) will extend to under 16 year olds 'if the court considers it likely that P will still lack capacity to make decisions in respect of that matter when he reaches 18' (section 18(3));
- the offence under section 44 of the MCA 2005 of ill-treating or wilfully neglecting a person who lacks capacity applies where the victim is under the age of 16.

Young people (16 and 17 year olds)

The MCA 2005 applies to 16 and 17 year olds as it does to adults, subject to the following exceptions:

- a lasting power of attorney may not be validly created by anyone below the age of 18 (section 9(2)(c));
- an advance decision to refuse treatment may not be validly made by anyone below the age of 18 (section 24(1));

- the power of the Court of Protection to execute a will on behalf of P under section 18(1)(i) may not be exercised for anyone below the age of 18 (section 18(2));
- the DOLS provisions (Schedule A1) (see Chapter 23) may not be used as authorisation for the deprivation of the liberty of anyone below the age of 18 (Schedule A1, para 13).

22.4.2   Treatment regulated by the Mental Health Act 1983

The MCA 2005 may not be used to authorise medical treatment for mental disorder, or consent to a patient being given medical treatment for mental disorder, if at the time when it is proposed to treat the patient, his treatment is regulated by Part IV of the MHA 1983 (section 28(1) of the MCA 2005). In other words, if a patient is being treated for mental disorder under the MHA 1983, authority for that treatment must come from that Act and not from the MCA 2005.

ECT treatment for 16 and 17 year olds who are in hospital informally and who do not have the capacity to consent is specifically authorised under section 28(1A) of the MCA 2005. Although ECT is generally regulated by the MHA 1983, that Act does not provide authority for treatment for this particular category of patient, and the MCA 2005 therefore fills the gap.

The treatment of patients subject to a CTO (section 17A of the MHA 1983) is regulated by Part 4A of the MHA 1983, not Part IV. A CTO patient without capacity may, therefore, be treated for mental disorder under the MCA 2005 as he is not subject to the exclusion under section 28(1) of that Act. Statutory protection for decision-makers (see para 23.10) does not, however, apply in respect of patients aged 16 or over who are subject to a CTO (section 28(1B) of the MCA 2005).

22.4.3   Family relationships and similar matters

According to section 27(1) of the MCA 2005, nothing in the Act permits a decision on any of the following matters to be made on behalf of a person:

(a)   consenting to marriage or a civil partnership,
(b)   consenting to have sexual relations,
(c)   consenting to a decree of divorce being granted on the basis of two years' separation,
(d)   consenting to a dissolution order being made in relation to a civil partnership on the basis of two years' separation,

(e)   consenting to a child's being placed for adoption by an adoption agency,

(f)   consenting to the making of an adoption order,

(g)   discharging parental responsibilities in matters not relating to a child's property,

(h)   giving a consent under the Human Fertilisation and Embryology Act 1990 (c. 37),

(i)   giving a consent under the Human Fertilisation and Embryology Act 2008.

22.4.4 Voting rights

According to section 29 of the MCA 2005, the Act may not be used as authorisation for voting on behalf of someone without capacity at an election for any public office or any referendum.

22.4.5 Assisted suicide

According to section 62 of the MCA 2005, the Act has no effect on the existing law relating to unlawful killing or assisting suicide.

22.5 RELEVANCE OF THE COMMON LAW TESTS FOR CAPACITY

The areas of decision-making to which the MCA 2005 will not apply are, therefore, relatively narrow, and most decisions concerning most people who lack capacity will come within its scope. Assuming this to be so, the first issue to be addressed in any case is whether the person concerned does, in fact, lack the capacity to make a particular decision, and in this respect, one of the Act's most important features is that it now provides a statutory test for deciding capacity (see para 22.6) which may be applied in respect of any decision that needs to be made. Even so, there remain certain common law capacity tests in a variety of different areas of law which, in theory at least, may still also be applied. Examples are provided in the 2005 Code (para 4.32):

- the capacity to make a will (*Banks v Goodfellow* (1870) LR 5 QB 549);
- the capacity to make a gift (*Re Beaney (deceased)* [1978] 2 All ER 595);
- the capacity to enter a contract (*Boughton v Knight* (1873) LR 3 PD 64);
- the capacity to litigate (*Masterman-Lister v Brutton & Co and Jewell & Home Counties Dairies* [2003] 3 All ER 162, CA);
- the capacity to enter into a marriage (*Sheffield City Council v E & S* [2005] 1 FLR 965).

Faced then in certain circumstances with either a common law or the statutory test to apply, the suggestion proposed by the 2005 Code (para 4.33) is that, 'judges can adopt the new definition if they think it appropriate'. The expectation is, however, that the use of common law tests will become increasingly rare. The statutory test is, after all, based on the existing common law principles.

22.6   STATUTORY TEST FOR CAPACITY

In the vast majority of cases, decisions regarding a person's capacity should now, therefore, be taken by applying the statutory test. This is set out in section 2(1) of the MCA 2005, according to which a person 'lacks capacity in relation to a matter if at the material time he is unable to make a decision for himself in relation to the matter because of an impairment of, or a disturbance in the functioning of, the mind or brain'.

Certain points of significance arise from this definition. Firstly, the test is *decision-specific*. It refers to whether a person has capacity 'in relation to a matter'. The MCA 2005 does not recognise the concept of a person having a *general* lack of capacity, and capacity must be assessed in relation to whatever decision has to be made. It follows that a person may have the capacity to make some decisions but not others, and each time a decision is called for, therefore, there must be an assessment of capacity. Secondly, the test is also *time-specific*. The question is whether the person lacks capacity 'at the material time', that is the time at which he is called upon to make the decision. Implicit, therefore, is a recognition that a person's capacity to make a particular decision may fluctuate, and, in fact, section 2(2) emphasises that, 'it does not matter whether the impairment of disturbance is permanent or temporary'. Thirdly, and most significantly, the test is broken down into *two distinct parts*:

- *The diagnostic test*: Is there an impairment of, or a disturbance in the functioning of, mind or brain?
- *The functional test*: Does the impairment or disturbance in the functioning of the mind or brain mean that the person is unable to make a decision for himself in relation to the matter in question?

22.6.1   Diagnostic test

It will usually be relatively easy to determine whether, as a matter of fact, there is an impairment of or disturbance in the functioning of the mind or brain. Any mental or physical state which has the required effect will do, and there may be a variety of causes, ranging from mental disorder, learning disability or brain damage, to lack of consciousness or drunkenness.

22.6.2   Functional test

It is not enough for there to simply be an impairment of or disturbance in the mind or brain, however. The person must also be 'unable to make a decision for himself in relation to the matter' (section 2(1) of the MCA 2005). It is after all the ability to make a decision which is the central feature of the Act. How then does one make this critical assessment? The answer is supplied by section 3(1), according to which a person is to be regarded as being unable to make a decision for himself if he is unable:

    (a)   to understand the information relevant to the decision;

    (b)   to retain that information;

    (c)   to use or weigh that information as part of the process of making the decision; or

    (d)   to communicate his decision (whether by talking, using sign language or any other means).

Understanding information relevant to the decision

A person is not to be regarded as unable to understand the information relevant to the decision if he is able to understand an explanation of it given to him in a way that is appropriate in the circumstances (using simple language, visual aids or any other means) (section 3(2) of the MCA 2005).

The information 'relevant to the decision' will include the nature of the decision, the reason why the decision is needed and the likely effects of deciding one way or the other, or making no decision at all (section 3(4) of the MCA 2005).

Retaining information

Retention of information for the purposes of making the decision need only be temporary (section 3(3) of the MCA 2005).

Using or weighing the information

This is perhaps the most contentious aspect of the four parts of the functional test in that it calls for an evaluation of the quality of the person's decision-making. In *A Primary Care Trust v P and Others* [2009] EW Misc 10 (EWCOP), concerning a young man with a severe form of uncontrolled epilepsy and mild learning disability, the test was described by Hedley J as being whether he was able to 'engage in the decision-making process itself and be able to see the various points of the argument and to relate one to the other'. In that case, the cumulative effect of a variety of factors, including the young man's 'inability to ... visualise any prospect of having a different view to his mother on any subject that matters', meant that he did not.

In *R v Dr Collins & Ashworth Hospital Authority ex parte Brady* [2000] 1 MHLR 17, Ian Brady, on hunger strike, was found (applying a similar common law test) to lack capacity to make a decision regarding food refusal and forcible feeding. His severe personality disorder, it was concluded, fuelled a hostility to authority which undermined his otherwise undoubted ability to appreciate the risk of food refusal and meant an impaired ability to weigh the information relevant to the decision.

Similarly, in *Re E (Medical Treatment: Anorexia)* [2012] EWHC 1639 (COP), a 32-year-old woman suffering from severe anorexia nervosa who refused to eat was found by Peter Jackson J to lack the capacity to make a decision about forcible feeding because her anorexia meant an obsessive fear of weight gain rendering her 'incapable of weighing the advantages and disadvantages of eating in any meaningful way'. Without reaching a conclusion on the point, Peter Jackson J did not dissent from the view expressed during expert medical evidence that, 'anyone with severe anorexia would lack capacity to make such a decision'.

In *KK v STCC* [2012] EWHC 2136 (COP), Baker J, adopting the approach previously taken in *LBJ v RYJ* [2010] EWHC 2664 (Fam), found that it is 'not necessary for a person to demonstrate a capacity to understand and weigh up every detail of the respective options, but merely the salient ones'.

Communicating the decision

This aspect of the test is likely to be of very limited application. The Explanatory Note to the MCA 2005 suggests that it will apply only to a small number of people, in particular, those suffering from 'locked-in syndrome'.

22.7   APPLYING THE STATUTORY TEST

Having the benefit of a statutory test is one thing. Applying it is quite another. Who then is responsible for conducting a capacity assessment and how should they do it?

22.7.1   Who will decide whether someone has capacity?

The MCA 2005 does not dictate *who* should conduct the test for capacity in any given case, but the 2005 Code points out (para 4.38) that the person assessing capacity will normally be 'the person who is directly concerned with the individual at the time the decision needs to be made'. For the vast majority of day-to-day decisions (e.g. washing, dressing, personal hygiene, eating, drinking, communication, mobility and purchases), the assessment will normally, therefore, fall to a family member or carer, while in respect of other decisions, responsibility will fall to whichever professional is concerned, a doctor or health care professional when the assessment is regarding a health care decision, for example, or a solicitor with regard to a legal transaction.

More complex decisions may require professional advice on the issue, but 'the final decision about a person's capacity must be made by the person intending to make the decision or carry out the action' (2005 Code, para 4.42).

In particularly difficult or contentious cases, the Court of Protection can be asked to make a decision (see para 22.12).

22.7.2   What method should be used to assess capacity?

The MCA 2005 does not dictate *how* capacity should be assessed in any given case, but in the absence of any prescribed procedure, the person responsible for making an assessment should, in general terms, do what is reasonable in the circumstances to establish P's capacity. Anyone who carries out any act in relation to P will have a statutory defence against liability for the act if he is able to show that he took reasonable steps and had a reasonable belief that P lacked capacity (assuming he also has a reasonable belief that the decision is in P's best interests) (see para 22.10).

What steps are reasonable to establish whether P lacks capacity will depend on the nature of the matter, and the more serious or significant it is, the more formal the assessment should be.

The 2005 Code notes (para 4.44) that, 'carers and care workers do not have to be experts in assessing capacity' and they will 'not usually need to follow formal processes, such as involving a professional to make an assessment'. It would be absurd, for example, if a formal capacity assessment were required each time a carer was deciding whether the person in their care should have a bath or watch TV. If challenged, however, a carer or care worker will need to be able to show that there is an objective reason for believing that the person lacks capacity in relation to whichever decision is being questioned. It may be reasonable to expect a carer to involve a professional in the assessment of P's capacity where the decision that needs to be made is complicated or has serious consequences, or family members, carers and/or professionals disagree about a person's capacity.

Where the decision on capacity is to be made by a professional (e.g. a health care professional or a lawyer), the expectation is that there should be a fuller assessment, reflecting that professional's higher degree of knowledge and experience (2005 Code, para 4.45).

22.7.3   Principles to apply in a capacity assessment

However, formal the procedure, the person assessing capacity should always apply the relevant principles from section 1 of the MCA 2005, namely:

- a person is presumed to have capacity unless it is established otherwise (section 1(2));
- a person should not be treated as lacking capacity unless all practicable steps to help him make the decision have been taken without success (section 1(3));
- an unwise decision does not necessarily mean that a person lacks capacity (section 1(4)).

Considering the last of these points in particular, professionals conducting assessments should guard against the danger, identified by Baker J in *KK v STCC* [2012] EWHC 2136 (COP), that they 'may objectively conflate a capacity assessment with a best interests analysis', and 'consciously or subconsciously attach excessive weight to their own views'.

22.8   IDENTIFYING THE DECISION-MAKER

In the event that P is assessed as lacking the capacity to make a particular decision, responsibility for making the decision will, therefore, fall to someone else. The question then is who that person should be. As usual, however, the MCA 2005 does not provide the answer. Guidance instead comes from the 2005 Code, and is found at para 5.8:

- For most day-to-day actions or decisions, the decision-maker will be the carer most directly involved with the person at the time.
- Where the decision involves the provision of medical treatment, the doctor or other member of healthcare staff responsible for carrying out the particular treatment or procedure is the decision-maker.

- Where nursing or paid care is provided, the nurse or paid carer will be the decision-maker.
- If a Lasting Power of Attorney (or Enduring Power of Attorney) has been made and registered, or a deputy has been appointed under a court order, the attorney or deputy will be the decision-maker, for decisions within the scope of their authority.

It is, of course, also envisaged that there will be circumstances, particularly in relation to the compilation of a health or social care plan, where there will be joint responsibility for decision-making (2005 Code, para 5.11).

22.9   BEST INTERESTS

Whoever makes the decision on behalf of P is required to ensure that it is made in his best interests (section 1(5) of the MCA 2005). This may be easier said than done, but useful guidance comes from section 4, which sets out certain key principles that must inform the decision-making process. In effect, it provides a checklist with which any decision-maker on behalf of P should be familiar.

Section 4(1) of the Mental Capacity Act 2005 – unjustified assumptions

No determination of best interests may be made merely on the basis of (section 4(1) of the MCA 2005):

    (a)   the person's age or appearance; or

    (b)   a condition of his, or an aspect of his behaviour, which might lead others to make unjustified assumptions about what might be in his best interests.

Section 4(2) of the Mental Capacity Act 2005 – all relevant circumstances

The decision-maker 'must consider all the relevant circumstances', defined by section 4(11) of the MCA 2005 as being those circumstances of which the person making the determination is aware, and which it would be reasonable to regard as relevant. Section 4(2) also requires the decision-maker to have particular regard to the matters set out in section 4(3)–(7) (below).

Section 4(3) of the Mental Capacity Act 2005 – likelihood of P regaining capacity

The decision-maker must consider (section 4(3) of the MCA 2005):

(a)   whether it is likely that the person will at some time have capacity in relation to the matter in question, and

(b)   if it appears likely that he will, when that is likely to be.

Section 4(4) of the Mental Capacity Act 2005 – encouraging P's participation

The decision-maker must, so far as is reasonably practicable, permit and encourage P to participate or to improve his ability to participate as fully as possible in any act done for him and any decision affecting him.

Section 4(5) of the Mental Capacity Act 2005 – life-sustaining treatment

Where the determination relates to life-sustaining treatment, the decision-maker must not be motivated by a desire to bring about P's death. Being motivated by a desire to bring about someone's death is one thing; concluding that it is in someone's best interests that he be allowed to die is another. The 2005 Code therefore confirms (para 5.33) that section 4(5) 'cannot be interpreted to mean that doctors are under an obligation to provide, or to continue to provide, life-sustaining treatment where that treatment is not in the best interests of the person, even where that person's death is foreseen' (see also *W & M v S & an NHS Primary Care Trust* [2011] EWHC 2443 (Fam)).

Section 4(6) of the Mental Capacity Act 2005 – P's wishes and feelings

The decision-maker must consider, so far as is reasonably ascertainable (section 4(6) of the MCA 2005):

(a)   the person's past and present wishes and feelings (and, in particular, any written statement made by him when he had capacity),

(b)   the beliefs and values that would be likely to influence his decision if he had capacity, and

(c)   the other factors that he would be likely to consider if he were able to do so.

The decision-maker is not bound by P's wishes and feelings or beliefs and values. The test is what is in P's best interests, which calls for consideration of a number of other factors (see *In the matter of P* [2009] EWHC 163 (Ch)). The closer that P is to having capacity, however, the greater is the weight that should be attached to his wishes and feelings (see *Re M, ITW v Z and others* [2009] EWHC 2525 (Fam)).

Section 4(7) of the Mental Capacity Act 2005 – views of others

The decision-maker must take into account, if it is practicable and appropriate to consult them, the views of (section 4(7) of the MCA 2005):

(a)   anyone named by the person as someone to be consulted on the matter in question or on matters of that kind,

(b)   anyone engaged in caring for the person or interested in his welfare,

(c)   any donee of a lasting power of attorney granted by the person, and

(d)   any deputy appointed for the person by the court …

22.10   PROTECTION FOR DECISION-MAKERS

22.10.1   Section 5 of the Mental Capacity Act 2005

Although the main purpose of the MCA 2005 is to provide a legal framework within which decisions can be made on behalf of the incapacitated, there is, generally, no mechanism for obtaining authorisation in advance for the vast majority of decisions that need to be made. Applications can be made to the Court of Protection for authorisation to carry out specific acts, but this will be only for the very serious or very contentious cases.

Without a mechanism for authorisation in advance, protection for the decision-maker comes instead, after the event, in the form of protection from liability if he is able to show that he has acted reasonably. More specifically, protection is provided for those acts to which section 5 of the MCA 2005 applies.

An act is one to which section 5 of the MCA 2005 applies if:

- *before doing the act*, the person takes reasonable steps to establish whether P lacks capacity in relation to the matter in question (section 5(1)(a)); *and*
- *when doing the act*, the person reasonably believes that P lacks capacity in relation to the matter and that it will be in P's best interests for the act to be done (section 5(1)(b)).

Protection then comes from section 5(2) of the MCA 2005, which provides that the decision-maker who has complied with these requirements will thereby avoid any liability that he would have avoided if P had had the capacity to consent to the act and had consented. This is subject, however, to section 5(3), which provides that the decision-maker cannot use section 5 to escape liability for acts of negligence in carrying out the act.

22.10.2   Limitations on protection for decision-makers

Acts of restraint

Where the act in question involves *restraint* of P, the protection offered by section 5 of the MCA 2005 is only available if two further conditions are satisfied (section 6(1)):

- the person reasonably believes that it is necessary to do the act in order to prevent harm to P (section 6(2));
- the act is a proportionate response to the likelihood of P suffering harm and the seriousness of that harm (section 6(3)).

Restraint is defined by section 6(4) of the MCA 2005 to mean the use of or threat of use of force to secure the doing of an act which P resists, or the restriction of P's liberty of movement whether or not P resists.

Advance decisions

Protection from liability under section 5 of the MCA 2005 does not extend to cover decisions concerning treatment of P where the person who carries out treatment is satisfied that a valid and applicable advance decision (see para 22.11.2) to the contrary exists (sections 5(4) and 26(2)).

Decisions made by the donee of a lasting power of attorney or by court appointed deputy

Similarly, section 5 of the MCA 2005 provides no authorisation for any decisions made in respect of P which conflict with any decision made within the scope of his authority by the donee of an LPA or a court appointed deputy (section 6(6)). However, section 6(6) does not prevent a person providing life-sustaining treatment or doing any act which he reasonably believes to be necessary to prevent a serious deterioration in P's health while a decision on the issue is sought from the Court of Protection.

22.11   ADVANCE PLANNING UNDER THE MENTAL CAPACITY ACT 2005

As well as dealing with decision-making in the present, the MCA 2005 provides ways in which an individual may plan for his loss of capacity in the future by authorising the creation of powers of attorney, which enable an individual to appoint someone else to make decisions on his behalf, and by authorising the creation of advance decisions, which enable an individual to refuse in advance specified medical treatment offered after he has lost capacity.

22.11.1 Lasting power of attorney

According to section 9(1) of the MCA 2005, an individual may create an LPA which authorises another individual(s) to make decisions on his behalf about all or any of the following:

(a)   P's personal welfare or specified matters concerning P's personal welfare, and

(b)   P's property and affairs or specified matters concerning P's property and affairs.

Unless stipulated to the contrary, a *personal welfare* LPA will be regarded as authority for decision-making on behalf of the donor in areas such as where and with whom the donor should live, day-to-day care, including diet and dress, who the donor may have contact with, and consent to or refusing medical examination and treatment on the donor's behalf (2005 Code, para 7.21). Unless stipulated to the contrary, a *property and affairs* LPA will confer authority on the donee to make decisions which will include, for example, the buying or selling of property, the opening, closing or operating any bank, building society or other account, giving access to the donor's financial information, and claiming, receiving and using benefits, pensions, allowances and rebates (2005 Code, para 7.36).

Detailed rules governing the creation, registration and scope of an LPA, the appointment of donees, and revocation of LPAs are set out in sections 9–14 of the MCA 2005, and the powers of the Court of Protection in relation to LPAs are set out in sections 22 and 23.

22.11.2 Advance decisions

According to section 24(1) of the MCA 2005, anyone who is at least 18 years old and has the capacity to do so is entitled to make an advance decision specifying health care treatment which is not to be carried out in the future if it is proposed at a time when he lacks capacity.

This is merely an extension of the common law principle (e.g. see *Airedale NHS Trust v Bland* [1993] 2 WLR 316) that a patient with capacity is at liberty to decide whether or not to accept medical treatment which is offered to him. Section 26(1) of the MCA 2005, therefore, provides that as long as the advance decision is valid and applicable to the treatment contemplated, it will take effect as if it was being made at the time the treatment is being offered.

Rules concerning the creation, validity, applicability and effect of advance decisions are set out in sections 24–26 of the MCA 2005. Generally speaking, the formal requirements are minimal, and, for example, except in the case of a decision concerning life-sustaining treatment, it need not even be in writing. The Court of Protection powers in relation to advance decisions are set out in section 26.

The MHA 1983 enables a patient to be treated for mental disorder without consent, and an advance decision cannot be relied upon to prevent future treatment that would otherwise be authorised under that Act. Advance decisions are not, however, without value to the patient in such circumstances.

The Participation Principle (1983 Code, para 1.5) requires the patient to be given the opportunity to be involved as far as practicable in the planning of his own treatment, and both the 1983 Code and the 2005 Code advise clinicians to take account of views expressed in an advance decision and to consider, for example, whether treatment which the patient has not ruled out may be possible as an alternative to the one to which he objects. Any decision not to comply with an advance decision should be justified in writing in the patient's notes (2005 Code, para 13.36).

22.12   COURT OF PROTECTION

The vast majority of decisions taken in relation to those who lack capacity will be relatively straightforward, without controversy and, hopefully, in accordance with the provisions of the 2005 Code. Ultimately, however, any decisions which are particularly difficult or contentious may be referred for resolution to the Court of Protection, the specialist court created by the MCA 2005.

In contrast to the previous Court of Protection, which existed prior to 2005 and which only had the power to deal with the property and affairs of those without capacity, the new Court of Protection has extensive powers to deal with personal welfare *and* property and affairs issues, and in this regard, has 'the same powers, rights, privileges and authority as the High Court' (section 47(1) of the MCA 2005). The court also has its own rules (the Court of Protection Rules 2007 (SI 2007/1744)) and makes its own Practice Directions.

22.12.1 Powers available to the Court of Protection

Essentially, the court is able to make *declarations* on issues such as whether an individual has capacity, and the lawfulness of proposed actions if he does not, to make *decisions* in relation to the affairs of a person that lacks capacity, and to appoint *deputies* to make decisions on an ongoing basis in relation to the affairs of a person that lacks capacity.

As well as being able to make final decisions in relation to these matters, section 48 of the MCA 2005 gives the court the power to make *interim* orders and directions in respect of any matter if:

(a)   there is reason to believe that P lacks capacity in relation to the matter,

(b)   the matter is one to which its powers under this Act extend, and

(c)   it is in P's best interests to make the order, or give the directions, without delay.

Making declarations

Section 15(1) of the MCA 2005 entitles the court to make declarations as to:

(a)   whether a person has or lacks capacity to make a decision specified in the declaration;

(b)   whether a person has or lacks capacity to make decisions on such matters as are described in the declaration;

(c)   the lawfulness or otherwise of any act done, or yet to be done, in relation to that person.

A decision under section 15(1)(c) of the MCA 2005 as to the lawfulness of a proposed act would include a decision as to whether it is in P's best interests.

Making decisions

Section 16(2)(a) of the MCA 2005 gives the court its own power to make a decision in relation to P's personal welfare or his property and affairs. The range of matters that may be covered by a decision in relation to P's personal welfare is extensive and is set out in section 17(1):

(a)   deciding where P is to live;

(b)   deciding what contact, if any, P is to have with any specified persons;

(c)   making an order prohibiting a named person from having contact with P;

(d)   giving or refusing consent to the carrying out or continuation of a treatment by a person providing health care for P;

(e)   giving a direction that a person responsible for P's health care allow a different person to take over that responsibility.

The equally extensive range of matters that may be covered by a decision in relation to P's property and affairs is set out in section 18(1) of the MCA 2005:

(a)   the control or management of P's property;

(b)   the sale, exchange, charging, gift or other disposition of P's property;

(c)   the acquisition of property in P's name or on P's behalf;

(d)   the carrying on, on P's behalf, of any profession, trade or business;

(e)   the taking of a decision which will have the effect of dissolving a partnership of which P is a member;

(f)   the carrying out of any contract entered into by P;

(g)   the discharge of P's debts and of any of P's obligations, whether legally enforceable or not;

(h)   the settlement of any of P's property whether for P's benefit or for the benefit of others;

(i)   the execution for P of a will;

(j)   the exercise of any power (including a power to consent) vested in P whether beneficially or as a trustee or otherwise;

(k)   the conduct of legal proceedings in P's name or on P's behalf.

Appointing deputies

As an alternative to making a one-off decision under section 16(2)(a) of the MCA 2005, the court may utilise its power under section 16(2)(b) to appoint a deputy to make future decisions on P's behalf in relation to his personal welfare and/or his property and affairs. Section 16(3) notes, however, that the powers of the court under section 16 are subject to the overriding duty to have regard to the Act's principles and to act in P's best interests, and section 16(4) requires that, when deciding whether it should make a decision itself in relation to a matter or appoint a deputy to make the decision, the court must have regard to the principles that:

(a)   a decision by the court is to be preferred to the appointment of a deputy to make a decision, and

(b)   the powers conferred on a deputy should be as limited in scope and duration as is reasonably practicable in the circumstances.

The appointment of a deputy for personal welfare decisions tends to be rare. In property and affairs cases, however, the court is much more likely to take the view that it is in P's best interests to have a deputy, rather than have P's financial affairs continually referred back to court.

The rules concerning the appointment of deputies, and restrictions on their powers, are set out in sections 19 and 20 of the MCA 2005.

22.12.2 When should applications to the Court of Protection be made?

The 2005 Code makes clear (para 8.16) that, '[a]pplications concerning a person's *capacity* are likely to be rare – people can usually settle doubts and disagreements informally' (emphasis added).

Similarly, the expectation is that most decisions concerning P's *personal welfare* can be made without reference to the court, and applications should be contemplated only in those cases where a decision is particularly difficult, where there are disagreements which cannot be resolved by any other means or where there is a series of ongoing decisions which will need to be made. The 2005 Code suggests (para 8.18), however, that certain types of health care treatment should always be referred to the court for a decision:

- decisions about the proposed withholding or withdrawal of artificial nutrition and hydration (ANH) from patients in a permanent vegetative state (PVS)
- cases involving organ or bone marrow donation by a person who lacks capacity to consent
- cases involving the proposed non-therapeutic sterilisation of a person who lacks capacity to consent to this (e.g. for contraceptive purposes) and
- all other cases where there is a doubt or dispute about whether a particular treatment will be in a person's best interests.

Conversely, the expectation is that most matters relating to the *property and affairs* of P will require intervention by the court. The 2005 Code suggests, therefore (para 8.4), that an order of the court will usually be necessary for matters relating to P's property and affairs unless the only income is state benefits or there is a previously made LPA (or, under the old law, enduring power of attorney) in place.

22.12.3 Who will make an application to the Court of Protection?

In order to filter the deserving from the non-deserving applications, section 50(2) of the MCA 2005 provides that, generally speaking, permission is required from the Court before any application may be made. According to section 50(1), however, the requirement to obtain permission from the Court does not apply where the application is made:

(a) by a person who lacks, or is alleged to lack, capacity,
(b) if such a person has not reached 18, by anyone with parental responsibility for him,

(c)   by the donor or donee of a lasting power of attorney to which the application relates,

(d)   by a deputy appointed by the court for a person to whom the application relates, or

(e)   by a person named in an existing order of the court, if the application relates to the order.

Chapter 23

Deprivation of Liberty Safeguards

23.1 INTRODUCTION

Anyone deprived of his liberty is entitled to expect that his detention is in accordance with a procedure prescribed by law (Article 5(1) of the ECHR) and that he may take proceedings to decide upon its lawfulness (Article 5(4)).

For those mental health patients detained under the MHA 1983, the Act itself provides a prescribed procedure and a means by which detention can be challenged. Article 5 of the ECHR is satisfied. Consider, however, those mental health patients who lack the capacity to make a decision on admission to a hospital or care home, who are passively compliant, and who end up being admitted without resisting and without the use of the MHA 1983. While there is nothing wrong in principle with a person who lacks capacity being admitted informally to a hospital or care home for treatment or care which is in his best interests, the admission becomes problematic if, when looked at objectively, even though the patient is not resisting, the circumstances of the admission amount to a deprivation of liberty. Without a legal framework in place to authorise that deprivation of liberty, the admission will be in breach of the patient's rights under Article 5.

Historically, the problem has been one of relatively large numbers of patients in hospitals or care homes who lacked the capacity to agree to be there, who were not actively resisting and who were not, therefore, subject to the MHA 1983, but who were, nevertheless, adjudged to be deprived of their liberty with no legal framework to protect them. The landmark case of *HL v UK* (Application No 45508/99) [2004] ECHR 471 vividly illustrated this significant gap in the law (see para 23.2). The result of the case was to provoke the UK government into creating the DOLS as an entirely new framework, compliant with Article 5 of the ECHR, authorising the admission to hospitals and care homes of incapacitated patients, for use when the MHA 1983 was deemed inappropriate.

DOLS were introduced by amending the MCA 2005, with the addition of a new Schedule A1 to that Act (see para 23.3). This chapter considers the background to this change in the law, the key principles of the new framework and the procedure which must now be followed whenever a deprivation of liberty occurs in a hospital or care home setting. When reviewing these changes, however, it may be worth considering how long they will remain in place, since the new framework has been the subject of serious and sustained criticism. In its report on the implementation of the MCA 2005 generally (*Mental Capacity Act 2005: post-legislative scrutiny*, The Stationery Office, 13 March 2014), the House of Lords Select Committee on the MCA 2005 singled out the DOLS provisions for particular criticism. The provisions, it noted, are 'poorly drafted, overly complex and bear no relationship to the language and ethos of the Mental Capacity Act'. The report expressed concern that the provisions were also poorly implemented, which meant that, 'thousands, if not tens of thousands, of individuals are being deprived of their liberty without the protection of the law'. The committee's conclusion was that the DOLS provisions are not fit for purpose, and the only appropriate recommendation is 'to start again'. The recommendation was for a 'comprehensive review of the Deprivation of Liberty Safeguards with a view to replacing them with provisions that are compatible in style and ethos to the rest of the Mental Capacity Act'.

23.2   *HL v UK*

HL was a man in his late 40s who suffered from severe autism. He was cared for in Bournewood Hospital on an informal basis for many years. In 1994, he was discharged into the care of Mr and Mrs E. In 1997, following an incident of self-harm, HL was taken back to Bournewood Hospital and remained there. He lacked the capacity to consent to his admission to hospital or to the treatment that he then received, but he did not resist his admission and nor did he seek to leave hospital. The clinical team were clear, however, that if HL did try to leave hospital then the MHA 1983 would have been employed to prevent him from doing so. He was under their continuous supervision and control.

Mr and Mrs E attempted to secure HL's discharge from hospital but were refused permission. They were told that HL would only be released when the professionals considered it appropriate. Through his litigation friend, HL challenged the hospital's refusal to discharge him. His case eventually went to the ECtHR where it was argued by the UK government that HL was not, as a matter of fact, detained but, even if he was, his detention was lawful, according to the common law doctrine of necessity. The ECtHR concluded that, notwithstanding HL's lack of resistance to being in hospital, there was a deprivation of his liberty and, therefore, a breach of both Articles 5(1) and 5(4) of the ECHR in the absence of any procedure prescribed by law governing the deprivation of liberty or of any procedure available for HL to challenge the lawfulness of his detention.

23.3 CHANGE IN THE LAW

Following *HL v UK* (Application No 45508/99) [2004] ECHR 471, new legislation, or at least an amendment to existing legislation, was necessary. Although the MHA 1983 was of course available as a statutory framework for detention, it was felt not to meet the needs of the case in point, or of many cases like it. The starting-point for detention under that Act is resistance to admission or treatment. The Act is used when the patient is non-compliant, whether or not he has capacity. Following *HL v UK*, however, it was clear that a deprivation of liberty might be adjudged to exist in the case of a patient without capacity who is passively compliant, where there is no non-compliance or resistance, but where there is, nevertheless, continuous supervision and control. It was also clear that the existing framework of the MHA 1983 would not be appropriate for such cases. The UK government's response to *HL v UK* was, therefore, to use the MHA 2007 to introduce amendments to the MCA 2005 in order to create a new, additional statutory framework for authorising the detention of patients.

Section 4A(5) of the MCA 2005 now provides that a person 'may deprive P of his liberty if the deprivation is authorised by Schedule A1' to that Act, and Schedule A1, entitled 'Hospital and Care Home Residents: Deprivation of Liberty', now sets out the procedure for authorising deprivations of liberty in *HL v UK* type cases.

The amendments to the MCA 2005 also resulted in a new Code of Practice, specific to DOLS provisions, the Deprivation of Liberty Safeguards Code, published in 2008 (DOLS Code).

The DOLS provisions were introduced to supplement the existing legal framework under the MHA 1983, not to replace it. In *GJ v The Foundation Trust and Others* [2009] EWHC 2972 (Fam), Charles J suggested that (at [60]):

> the underlying purpose of the amendments to the MCA 2005 [was] to fill a gap, namely the '*Bournewood Gap*'. This shows that the purpose was not to provide alternative regimes but to leave the existing regime under the MHA 1983 in place with primacy and to fill a gap left by it and the common law.

More recent cases have suggested, however, that the DOLS provisions are there not just to fill a gap, but can, in fact, be seen as an alternative to the MHA 1983 in appropriate cases (see *DN v Northumberland Tyne and Wear NHS Foundation Trust* [2011] UKUT 327 (AAC) and *AM v South London and*

Maudsley NHS Foundation Trust and SSH [2013] UKUT 365 (AAC); see also para 23.8).

23.4   HOSPITALS AND CARE HOMES

The official title of Schedule A1 to the MCA 2005 is 'Hospital and Care Home Residents: Deprivation of Liberty', and its provisions only apply to deprivations of liberty that occur within the setting of a hospital or care home. Schedule A1 cannot be used as a procedure to justify deprivation of liberty in any other setting; specific authority would need to come instead from the Court of Protection, using its power to make decisions regarding P's welfare under section 16(2)(a) of the MCA 2005 (see para 22.12.1).

23.5   DEPRIVATION OF LIBERTY

The first task in applying the DOLS provisions is to decide whether a deprivation of liberty exists. In practice, this presents undoubted difficulties, and quite what restriction or series of restrictions will constitute a deprivation of someone's liberty, particularly in the case of a person in a care home without capacity who is passively compliant, may provide a source of endless debate. There is no definitive answer. The MCA 2005 deliberately provides no definition of the term and notes instead (section 64) that, 'references to deprivation of a person's liberty have the same meaning as in Article 5(1) of the ECHR'. Somewhat unhelpfully, Article 5(1) also fails to provide its own definition of the term. Practitioners must, therefore, rely on guidance from case law and other sources.

23.5.1   Case law

Courts have had to wrestle with the meaning of the term 'deprivation of liberty' for many years, not just in the context of DOLS.

In *Guzzardi v Italy* (Application No 7367/76) [1980] ECHR 5, the ECtHR drew the important distinction between a deprivation of liberty and a restriction on liberty. Article 5 of the ECHR would be engaged for one, but not the other. Unsurprisingly, the difference between a deprivation and a restriction is not necessarily easy to establish, and is 'merely one of degree or intensity'.

Any assessment must involve a comprehensive review of the facts of the particular case. For example, 'The starting point must be the concrete situation of the individual concerned and account must be taken of a whole range of criteria such as the type, duration, effects and manner of implementation of the measure in question' (*Ashingdane v UK* (Application No 8225/78) [1985] ECHR 8).

In *Stanev v Bulgaria* (Application No 36760/06) [2012] ECHR 46, the ECtHR identified the *Ashingdane* case as also establishing the principle that in the context of deprivation of liberty on mental health grounds, 'a person could be regarded as having been "detained" even during a period when he was in an open hospital ward with regular unescorted access to the unsecured hospital grounds and the possibility of unescorted leave outside the hospital'.

These principles were applied to the case of a mental health patient without capacity in hospital in *HL v UK* (Application No 45508/99) [2004] ECHR 471, as a result of which the ECtHR held that the 'key factor' in determining that there was a deprivation of liberty was that the health care professionals had 'exercised complete and effective control' over the patient's care and movements. The case also confirmed that there does not need to be actual restraint for there to be a deprivation of liberty.

Looking at the definition in a broader context, in *Storck v Germany* (Application No 61603/00) [2005] ECHR 406, the ECtHR identified its own three key features of a deprivation of liberty:

- *an objective element*, namely a person's confinement in a particular restricted space for a not negligible time;
- *a subjective element*, namely that a person has not validly consented to the confinement in question;
- the deprivation of liberty must be one for which the *state is responsible*.

In her lead judgement in *P v Cheshire West and Chester City Council and another, and P and Q v Surrey County Council* [2014] UKSC 19, Lady Hale provided guidance on what the 'acid test' should be for identifying a deprivation of liberty in the case of a mental health patient in a community placement. Asking herself 'what are the particular features of their "concrete situation" on which we need to focus', Lady Hale concluded (at [49]):

> The answer, as it seems to me, lies in those features which have consistently been regarded as 'key' in the jurisprudence which started with *HL v United Kingdom* 40 EHRR 761: that the person concerned 'was under continuous supervision and control and was not free to leave'.

Significantly, she also identified factors which are not relevant to the test as being 'the person's compliance or lack of objection … the relative normality of the placement (whatever the comparison made) ... and the reason or purpose behind a particular placement'.

23.5.2   Deprivation of Liberty Safeguards Code of Practice

Aside from case law, useful practical guidance on identifying a deprivation of liberty is to be found in the DOLS Code (para 2.5). Factors which may suggest one are:

- Restraint is used, including sedation, to admit a person to an institution where that person is resisting admission.
- Staff exercise complete and effective control over the care and movement of a person for a significant period.
- Staff exercise control over assessments, treatment, contacts and residence.
- A decision has been taken by the institution that the person will not be released into the care of others, or remitted to live elsewhere, unless the staff in the institution consider it appropriate.
- A request by carers for a person to be discharged to their care is refused.
- The person is unable to maintain social contacts because of restrictions placed on their access to other people.
- The person loses autonomy because they are under continuous supervision and control.

23.6   APPLYING FOR AUTHORISATION FOR A DEPRIVATION OF LIBERTY

Assuming the difficulties in identifying a deprivation of liberty can be overcome, attention then turns to the procedure to be adopted in a hospital or care home setting when a deprivation of liberty exists for which no existing lawful authority is in place. In theory, the DOLS procedure, as set out in Schedule A1 to the MCA 2005, is a simple one. The *managing authority* of a hospital or care home is responsible for monitoring all of its patients or residents. Whenever a deprivation of liberty is identified in respect of any one of them (the 'relevant person'), the managing authority must apply for authorisation for the deprivation of liberty to its relevant *supervisory body*. If such authorisation (known as a 'standard authorisation') is obtained, the deprivation of liberty will be lawful.

23.6.1   Managing authority

In the case of an NHS hospital, the managing authority is the NHS trust or authority responsible for managing the hospital in which the relevant person is or is to be resident (Schedule A1, para 176).

In the case of a private hospital, it is the person registered or required to be registered under Part 1, Chapter 2 of the Health and Social Care Act 2008 in respect of regulated activities carried on in the hospital (Schedule A1, para 177 to the MCA 2005).

In the case of a care home, it is the person registered or required to be registered under Part 1, Chapter 2 of the Health and Social Care Act 2008 in respect of the provision of residential accommodation, together with nursing or personal care, in the care home (Schedule A1, para 179 to the MCA 2005).

23.6.2 Supervisory body

In the case of both hospitals and care homes, the supervisory body will be the local authority for the area in which the person is ordinarily resident, and if the person is not ordinarily resident anywhere, it will be the local authority for the area in which the hospital or care home is situated (Schedule A1, paras 180 and 182 to the MCA 2005).

23.6.3 Duty to make the application

Whether or not a deprivation of liberty already exists, whether or not the relevant person is already a resident of the relevant hospital or care home, an application for a standard authorisation in respect of the relevant person must be made by the managing authority to the relevant supervisory body whenever it appears that at some stage within the next 28 days (Schedule A1, para 24 to the MCA 2005):

- the relevant person is going to be accommodated in the relevant hospital or care home in circumstances which amount to a deprivation of liberty; and
- it is likely that all of the qualifying requirements (see para 23.7) will be met.

Requirements as to the form and content of an application are set out in regulation 16 of the Mental Capacity Act (Deprivation of Liberty: Standard Authorisations, Assessments and Ordinary Residence) Regulations 2008 (SI 2008/1858).

23.7 QUALIFYING REQUIREMENTS

The response of the supervisory body to an application for authorisation must be to conduct an assessment in order to decide whether the qualifying requirements for an authorisation to be granted are met. There are six qualifying requirements. If any is not met, the authorisation may not be granted and any deprivation of liberty will be unlawful unless authorisation comes from another source. Separate assessments must be conducted in respect of each of the six qualifying requirements (Schedule A1, para 33(2) to the MCA 2005). The qualifying requirements to assess are:

- *Age requirement*: the relevant person *must be 18 years* or older (Schedule A1, para 13).
- *Mental health requirement*: the relevant person *must have a mental disorder* within the meaning of the MHA 1983 but disregarding any exclusion for persons with learning disability (Schedule A1, para 14).
- *Mental capacity requirement*: the relevant person *must lack capacity* in relation to the question of whether or not he should be accommodated in the relevant hospital or care home for the purpose of being given the relevant care or treatment (Schedule A1, para 15).
- *Best interests requirement*: there are four conditions which must be met (Schedule A1, para 16). These are:

  - the relevant person is, or is to be, a detained resident (that is, detained in a hospital or care home in circumstances which amount to a *deprivation of liberty*);
  - it is in the *best interests* of the relevant person for him to be a detained resident;
  - in order to prevent harm to the relevant person, it is *necessary* for him to be a detained resident;
  - detention is a *proportionate* response to:

    — the likelihood of the relevant person suffering harm, and
    — the seriousness of the harm.

- *Eligibility requirement*: this is considered separately at para 23.8.
- *No refusals requirement*: a person meets this requirement unless:

  - he has made a valid advance decision which is applicable to some or all of the relevant treatment; or
  - accommodation in the relevant hospital or care home for the purpose of receiving some or all of the relevant care or treatment is in conflict with a valid decision of the donee of an LPA or deputy appointed by the Court of Protection (Schedule A1, para 18).

23.8   ELIGIBILITY REQUIREMENT – DEPRIVATION OF LIBERTY SAFEGUARDS AND THE MENTAL HEALTH ACT 1983

The eligibility requirement deserves particular consideration since it focusses attention on the relationship between DOLS and the MHA 1983.

The relevant person must be eligible for DOLS authorisation. He will be eligible unless Schedule 1A says that he is not (para 17 of Schedule A1). Schedule 1A, para 2 sets out the circumstances in which a person will not be eligible for DOLS. In essence, it provides that eligibility for DOLS will be decided according to whether the MHA 1983 already applies, or should already apply to that person. If the MHA 1983 does or should already apply, the person will be ineligible. The particular types of cases in which, according to Schedule 1A, a person will be ineligible for DOLS can be summarised as follows:

- when he is already detained under the MHA 1983;
- when he is already subject to leave under section 17, guardianship under section 7, a CTO or a conditional discharge and the authorisation would place the patient in conflict with an obligation under the MHA 1983 regime;
- when he is not detained under the MHA 1983 but is within its scope, that is, he requires treatment for mental disorder, could be treated under the Act and is objecting to the detention.

In *AM v South London and Maudsley NHS Foundation Trust and SSH* [2013] UKUT 365 (AAC), Charles J noted the 'complicated legislative provisions' created by DOLS. He also noted that the difficulties in applying them are only 'compounded when (decision-makers) have to consider the relationship between the MHA and the MCA', and most would agree that the relationship between DOLS and the MHA 1983, as encapsulated by the eligibility requirement, is a challenging one. The nature of the relationship was reviewed in *DN v Northumberland Tyne and Wear NHS Foundation Trust* [2011] UKUT 327 (AAC), from which two particular points emerge:

- The fact that a person is already detained under the MHA 1983 does not mean that he cannot be discharged directly from that regime to a DOLS regime. Although on the face of it, applying Schedule 1A, para 2, detention under the MHA 1983 renders a person ineligible for DOLS, it is the circumstances which will apply at the time the authorisation for DOLS comes into effect which are relevant. If, by then, detention under the MHA 1983 is no longer in place, the person will be eligible for DOLS. In a written submission to the Upper Tribunal in *DN v Northumberland Tyne and Wear NHS Foundation Trust* [2011] UKUT 327 (AAC), the Head of Mental Health Act Policy at the Department of Health confirmed his view that, 'there is nothing to prevent a prospective application for an MCA DOLS authorisation in anticipation of, or the expectation that, the person concerned will be discharged from detention under MHA'. This approach was adopted by the Upper Tribunal.

- In deciding whether a person could be detained under the MHA 1983, and is therefore ineligible for DOLS because he is within the scope of the Act, account should be taken of whether use of the Act is necessary, and in deciding whether use of the Act is necessary, a decision-maker is entitled to take into account whether a 'suitable and less restrictive alternative under DOLS' is available.

Each of these points serves to emphasise that, contrary to any sense that DOLS is only there to fill a gap left by the MHA 1983, the two frameworks can and should be seen in certain circumstances as alternative sources of authorisation for detention between which a decision-maker may need to choose. This was confirmed in *AM v South London and Maudsley NHS Foundation Trust and SSH* [2013] UKUT 365 (AAC), where it was noted that the availability of the DOLS regime is (at [75]):

> one of the factors that needs to be considered by the MHA decision maker in carrying out that search, as [is its] overall impact in best achieving the desired objective when compared with other available choices and so detention under ss. 2 and 3 MHA.

The eligibility requirement assessment should be conducted accordingly.

In *AM v South London and Maudsley NHS Foundation Trust and SSH* [2013] UKUT 365 (AAC), Charles J suggested that the following three-stage approach should be adopted by decision-makers when considering which legal framework to choose:

- Ask whether the relevant person has the capacity to consent to hospital admission under section 131 of the MHA 1983. If he does have capacity, the MCA 2005 is irrelevant, and the only issue is whether the person should be admitted on a voluntary basis or detained under the MHA 1983. If he does not have capacity, the MCA 2005 may be relevant and stage two should be considered.
- Next, consider whether the hospital can rely on the provisions of the MCA 2005 to assess or treat the person. Here, there are two issues to consider. Firstly, will the person be eligible for DOLS? If the person is objecting to hospital admission ('non-compliant incapacitated'), he will be ineligible. Secondly, will DOLS be required? DOLS will be required when 'it appears that judged objectively there is a risk that cannot sensibly be ignored that the relevant circumstances amount to a deprivation of liberty'. If the hospital can rely on DOLS, because the person is eligible and DOLS would be required, consider stage three.
- Lastly, choose between the MHA 1983 and DOLS. Having reached stage three, the decision-maker is faced with a genuine choice between two

legal frameworks for the deprivation of liberty, and is entitled to take into account the availability of DOLS when deciding whether detention under the MHA 1983 for either assessment or treatment can be said to be necessary. The decision-maker will need to take account of the actual availability of a DOLS regime and should then consider the merits of each regime on the facts. Relevant factors will be: what is in the person's best interests (as per a DOLS best interests assessment), what conditions can be imposed under DOLS, whether the person has fluctuating capacity, and the 'comparative impact of both the independent scrutiny and review and the enforcement provisions relating to the MHA scheme on the one hand and MCA scheme and its DOLS on the other'. The search should also be for the least restrictive way of achieving the proposed assessment or treatment, and, in this respect, Charles J accepted the proposition that, 'it will *generally but not always* be more appropriate to rely on DOLS' when it is the less restrictive of the two options.

23.9   ASSESSORS

The supervisory body will appoint assessors to decide whether each of the requirements is met. Appointment of the assessors will be according to rules set out in the Mental Capacity (Deprivation of Liberty: Standard Authorisations, Assessments and Ordinary Residence) Regulations 2008 (SI 2008/1858). These provide that:

- there must be at least two assessors overall;
- the mental health assessor must be an approved doctor under section 12(2) of the MHA 1983 or a doctor with a minimum of 3 years' post-registration experience in the diagnosis or treatment of mental disorder;
- the best interests assessor (BIA) may be an AMHP, a social worker, a nurse, an occupational therapist or a psychologist, any of which will need to have 2 years' post-qualification experience and to have completed best interest assessment training;
- the age and no refusal assessor may be anyone who is eligible to be a BIA;
- the mental capacity assessor may be anyone who is eligible to be the mental health assessor or anyone who is eligible to be the BIA;
- the eligibility assessor may be anyone who is eligible to be the BIA and is also an AMHP;
- the assessments will be carried out within 21 days of receipt by the supervisory body of the request for authorisation from the managing authority.

23.10   BEST INTERESTS ASSESSOR'S REPORT

The BIA will provide a report following his assessment. In the event that it supports a standard authorisation, the report should state the maximum period for which the authorisation may be granted (Schedule A1, para 42 to the MCA 2005). This should be the maximum period for which it would be appropriate for the relevant person to be detained, or one year, whichever is the shorter. The BIA may also make recommendations about conditions to which the standard authorisation should be subject (Schedule A1, para 43) and recommend anyone suitable to be appointed as the relevant person's representative (Schedule A1, para 143).

23.11   DECISION OF THE SUPERVISORY BODY

Where the qualifying requirements are met, the supervisory body has no discretion. It must grant a standard authorisation (Schedule A1, para 50(1) to the MCA 2005). If the result of the assessment is that one of the qualifying requirements is not met, however, the assessment process must stop. The DOLS Code (para 5.20) advises that the managing authority must then 'review the relevant person's actual or proposed care arrangements to ensure that a deprivation of liberty is not allowed to either continue or commence'.

23.11.1   Terms and effect of a standard authorisation

Whenever a standard authorisation is granted, it must be in writing (Schedule A1, para 54 to the MCA 2005) and state (Schedule A1, para 55(1)):

(a)   the name of the relevant person;
(b)   the name of the relevant hospital or care home;
(c)   the period during which the authorisation is to be in force;
(d)   the purpose for which the authorisation is given;
(e)   any conditions subject to which the authorisation is given;
(f)   the reason why each qualifying requirement is met.

The authorisation may not exceed the period recommended by the BIA, nor 12 months in any event (Schedule A1, para 51 to the MCA 2005). Authorisation may be subject to conditions recommended by the BIA (Schedule A1, para 53). The supervisory body is not bound to impose recommended conditions (Schedule A1, para 53), but where one is not accepted, it should consult with the BIA first to check that this does not alter the BIA's recommendation generally.

23.12 URGENT AUTHORISATION

The managing authority may be required to grant itself an urgent authorisation for a deprivation of liberty in circumstances where a standard authorisation will not be obtained in time (Schedule A1, para 74 to the MCA 2005). An urgent authorisation for a deprivation of liberty must be granted:

- when the managing authority is required to make a request for standard authorisation and believes that the need for the relevant person to be a detained resident is so urgent that it is appropriate for the detention to begin before it makes the request (Schedule A1, para 76(2));
- when the managing authority has made a request for standard authorisation and believes that the need for the relevant person to be a detained resident is so urgent that it is appropriate for the detention to begin before the request is disposed of (Schedule A1, para 76(3)).

An urgent authorisation can never be granted, therefore, without a request for a standard authorisation being made at the same time.

It is for the managing authority to decide the duration of the urgent authorisation, but it may not exceed 7 days (Schedule A1, para 78 to the MCA 2005). In exceptional cases, where a request for standard authorisation has been made and where it is essential that the existing deprivation of liberty continue until the request has been considered, the supervisory body may extend the urgent authorisation upon application by the managing authority (Schedule A1, para 84). The extension, if agreed, may not exceed 7 days (Schedule A1, para 85) and the managing authority may only apply for one such extension (Schedule A1, para 77).

23.13 CHALLENGING A MANAGING AUTHORITY'S FAILURE TO SEEK AUTHORISATION

The DOLS provisions also supply a form of protection for those who may be deprived of their liberty but in respect of whom no application for authorisation has been made. In such cases, any person other than the managing authority of the relevant hospital or care home (Schedule A1, para 68(5) to the MCA 2005) is entitled to apply to a supervisory body for a decision on whether there is an unauthorised deprivation of liberty. In order for such an application to be valid, however, the following conditions must apply:

- the person has notified the managing authority that it appears to them that there is an unauthorised deprivation of liberty (Schedule A1, para 68(2));
- the managing authority has been asked by the person to obtain a standard authorisation (Schedule A1, para 68(3));
- the managing authority has not requested a standard authorisation within a reasonable period after being asked to do so (Schedule A1, para 68(4)).

Where the supervisory body receives an application, it must arrange for a BIA to carry out within 7 days an assessment of whether there is a deprivation of liberty (Schedule A1, para 69(2) to the MCA 2005 and regulation 14 of the Mental Capacity (Deprivation of Liberty: Standard Authorisations, Assessments and Ordinary Residence) Regulations 2008 (SI 2008/1858)). The requirement on the supervisory body to arrange an assessment would not apply, however, where:

- the request appears to be frivolous or vexatious (Schedule A1, para 69(4));
- the question of whether there is an unauthorised deprivation of liberty has already been decided, and, since the decision, there has been no change of circumstances which would merit the question being decided again (Schedule A1, para 69(5)).

Where the outcome of the assessment is that there is an unauthorised deprivation of liberty, a full assessment as per the standard authorisation process must then take place (Schedule A1, para 71 to the MCA 2005). If the managing authority concludes that there is no option but to continue with the deprivation of liberty while the full assessment is carried out, it should grant itself an urgent authorisation and seek the standard authorisation within 7 days.

23.14   RELEVANT PERSON'S REPRESENTATIVE

One of the most important safeguards created by DOLS for the person for whom a deprivation of liberty is authorised is the requirement on the supervisory body to appoint a person to be the relevant person's representative as soon as practicable after a standard authorisation is given (Schedule A1, para 139(1) to the MCA 2005). The selection must be of someone who is expected to:

- maintain contact with the relevant person;
- represent the relevant person in matters relating to or connected with the deprivation of liberty;
- support the relevant person in matters relating to or connected with the deprivation of liberty.

Guidance on the appointment and role of the relevant person's representative is contained in DOLS Code, Chapter 7.

23.15 ROLE OF THE COURT OF PROTECTION IN DEPRIVATION OF LIBERTY SAFEGUARDS CASES

The Court of Protection also plays a safeguarding role in DOLS cases:

- In *standard authorisation cases*, the court may determine any question relating to whether the relevant person meets one or more of the qualifying requirements, the period during which the standard authorisation is to be in force, the purpose for which the standard authorisation is given and the conditions to which the standard authorisation is subject (section 21A(2) of the MCA 2005). It may also vary or terminate the standard authorisation, or direct the supervisory body to do the same (section 21A(3)).
- In *urgent authorisation cases*, the court may determine any question relating to whether the urgent authorisation should have been given, the period during which the authorisation is to be in force, and the purpose for which the urgent authorisation is given (section 21A(4)). It may also vary or terminate the urgent authorisation, or direct the managing authority to do the same (section 21A(5)).

Part Eight

Other Aspects of Mental Health Law

Chapter 24

Children and Young People

24.1   INTRODUCTION

This chapter focusses on the special considerations which apply in respect of children or young people who may require treatment for mental disorder. In this respect, 'children' means those who are under the age of 16, and young people means those who are either 16 or 17 years old. Attention is paid in particular to the various legal frameworks within which decision-making around hospital admission and treatment must take place.

24.2   CHILDREN AND ADOLESCENT MENTAL HEALTH SERVICES

Mental health service provision for the under 18s is a specialist area and the 1983 Code, therefore, suggests (para 36.75) that, 'those responsible for the care and treatment of children and young people should be child specialists'. This invariably means health professionals from Child and Adolescent Mental Health Services (CAMHS), the multi-disciplinary service common to all localities which organises and provides the full range of mental health services for children and young people, from primary care, to specialist community-based care, through to specialist in-patient units.

Where any assessment is being carried out with a view to detaining a child or young person under the MHA 1983, the AMHP or one of the two RMPs involved should be a CAMHS specialist. If none is available, one should be consulted as soon as possible after the assessment (1983 Code, para 36.20).

One particular area of CAMHS provision is that of specialist in-patient units for children and young people, an aspect of the service which caters for a need recognised by the MHA 1983. Section 131A(2) stipulates that for any under 18 year old admitted to hospital, whether or not detained, 'the managers of the hospital shall ensure that the patient's environment in the hospital is suitable having regard to his age (subject to his needs)'. According to the 1983 Code (para 36.68), being cared for in an age suitable environment in accordance with section 131A means:

- appropriate physical facilities;
- staff with the right training, skills and knowledge to understand and address their specific needs as children and young people;
- a hospital routine that will allow their personal, social and educational development to continue as normally as possible; and
- equal access to educational opportunities as their peers, in so far as that is consistent with their ability to make use of them, considering their mental state.

In practice, this should mean being looked after on a dedicated children or young persons' ward, and it will only be in exceptional circumstances that a child or young person should be accommodated on an adult ward. Exceptional circumstances might include, for example, a short-term emergency measure where safety considerations take precedence, a patient expressing a reasonable preference for being nursed on an adult ward, or a patient being just short of his 18th birthday and it being thought disruptive to the patient's care to have a short-term placement on a CAMHS unit before transfer to an adult unit.

The 1983 Code suggests (para 36.70) that in the exceptional circumstances where a young patient is not accommodated in a CAMHS unit 'then discrete accommodation in an adult ward, with facilities, security and staffing appropriate to the needs of the child, might provide the most satisfactory solution'.

24.3   LEGAL AUTHORITY TO ADMIT AND/OR TREAT A CHILD OR YOUNG PERSON

There are a variety of possible sources of authority for admitting to hospital and treating a child or young person. In the first instance, authority may of course come from the child or young person himself. Otherwise, in certain circumstances, it may come from the person with parental responsibility for the child or young person. Alternatively, use may be made of the MHA 1983 or of the MCA 2005, and even, occasionally, the authority of the High Court under its inherent jurisdiction. Each is considered in turn.

24.3.1   Admission and treatment with the consent of the child or young person

Children

A child below the age of 16 will be able to lawfully consent to hospital admission and treatment if he has the *competence* to consent, applying the common law test for competence set out by Lord Scarman in *Gillick v West Norfolk and Wisbech Area Health Authority* [1985] UKHL 7. According to this test, the child's competence to make his own decisions arises 'when he reaches sufficient understanding and intelligence to be capable of making his own mind up on the matter requiring decision'.

If a child is '*Gillick*-competent' and, therefore, has 'sufficient understanding and intelligence' to make the decision, he may consent to admission or treatment, and such consent may not then be overridden by anyone with parental responsibility for the child.

As with any assessment of capacity in adults, an assessment of competence needs to be undertaken each time there is a new decision to be made.

Young people

With young people, the issue is capacity, not competence, but the same principle (that a young person with capacity may agree to his own admission or treatment) applies, albeit on a statutory footing. There are in fact two relevant statutes, one covering admission and one covering treatment:

- Section 131(3) of the MHA 1983 provides that if a 16 or 17 year old has capacity (applying the test for capacity from the MCA 2005 – section 131(5)(a)), he may consent to his own hospital *admission*. This consent may not then be overridden by anyone with parental responsibility for him.
- Section 131 of the MHA 1983 makes no reference to a young person's ability to consent to *treatment*, but section 8 of the Family Law Reform Act 1969 deals with the point. It provides that a 16 or 17 year old with capacity may validly consent 'to any surgical, medical or dental treatment which, in the absence of consent, would constitute a trespass to his person'. This consent, too, may not be overridden.

24.3.2   Decisions authorised by person with parental responsibility

In certain circumstances, authority for admission or treatment may, instead, come from a person with parental responsibility for the child or young person. The rules governing who may have parental responsibility are set out in the Children Act 1989. Before looking at when such a person may be entitled to make a decision, it is important to clarify when they will not be so entitled.

Circumstances when parental responsibility may not be relied upon

As already noted, the wishes of a person with parental responsibility may not override the decision of a *Gillick*-competent child or a young person with capacity who *agrees* to hospital admission or treatment.

In addition to this, the wishes of a person with parent responsibility should not override those of a *Gillick*-competent child or young person with capacity who *refuses* admission or treatment. Instead, the MHA 1983 should be used (see para 24.3.3). With *children*, this is a development of the common law principle and the application of Article 5 of the ECHR. The 1983 Code notes (para 36.43) that, 'the trend in recent cases is to reflect greater autonomy for competent under 18s, so it may be unwise to rely on the consent of a person with parental responsibility'. In *RK v BCC* [2011] EWCA Civ 1305, the Court of Appeal was less uncertain. It accepted the proposition that, 'an adult in the exercise of parental responsibility may impose, or may authorise others to impose, restrictions on the liberty of the child', but made clear that, 'restrictions so imposed must not in their totality amount to a deprivation of liberty. Deprivation of liberty engages the Article 5 rights of the child and a parent may not lawfully detain or authorise the deprivation of liberty of a child'. For *young people*, as far as admission is concerned at least, there is a clear statutory footing. Section 131(4) provides that a 16 or 17 year old with capacity who does not consent to hospital admission may not be admitted to hospital informally on the authority of someone with parental responsibility. As for treatment, the same principle should apply even though there is no statutory provision (section 8 of the Family Law Reform Act 1969 dealing only with the young person's right to agree to treatment).

Circumstances when parental responsibility may be relied upon

Parental responsibility may, however, provide lawful authority for the admission to hospital and treatment of a *child who lacks Gillick-competence or a young person who lacks capacity*. This is only likely to apply, however, where the decision in question is within what is known as the 'zone of parental control'.

It should be noted that the zone of parental control is not a firm legal concept, and is simply an attempt by the 1983 Code to provide guidance on the extent to which someone with parental responsibility may make decisions in relation to a child or young person. The 1983 Code advises (para 36.9) that the concept of the zone 'derives largely from case law from the European Court of Human Rights'.

Reaching a conclusion on whether a decision in any given case falls within the zone may be difficult, but the key issues will be whether the decision is one that a parent would normally be expected to make, and whether there are any indications that the parent might not act in the best interests of the child or young person. The more contentious the decision, the less likely it is to fall within the zone.

The 1983 Code advises (para 36.12) that mental health professionals should consider the following factors when deciding whether a decision to be made falls within the zone:

- the nature and invasiveness of what is to be done to the patient (including the extent to which their liberty will be curtailed) – the more extreme the intervention, the more likely it will be that it falls outside the zone;
- whether the patient is resisting – treating a child or young person who is resisting needs more justification;
- the general social standards in force at the time concerning the sorts of decisions it is acceptable for parents to make – anything that goes beyond the kind of decisions parents routinely make will be more suspect;
- the age, maturity and understanding of the child or young person – the greater these are, the more likely it will be that it should be the child or young person who takes the decision; and
- the extent to which a parent's interests may conflict with those of the child or young person – this may suggest that the parent will not act in the child or young person's best interests.

Further to the guidance from the 1983 Code, it is clear from *RK v BCC* [2011] EWCA Civ 1305 that a decision which involves the deprivation of the liberty of the child or young person would not fall within the zone.

24.3.3 Use of the Mental Health Act 1983

There is no lower age limit on detention under the MHA 1983, and any child or young person may be detained if the relevant statutory criteria are met. The Act is always, therefore, a potential source of authority for admission in appropriate cases, and will generally be relied on where the child or young person has the competence or capacity to agree to hospital admission, but declines to do so. Once admitted under its provisions, a child or young person may then be treated under the Act in the normal way.

24.3.4 Use of the Mental Capacity Act 2005

Children

The MCA 2005 has no application to anyone under the age of 16. A child may, therefore, neither be admitted to hospital nor treated under its provisions.

Young people

For the most part, the MCA 2005 applies to 16 and 17 year olds as it would to adults. A young person who lacks capacity may, therefore, be admitted to hospital and/or treated under the Act in appropriate cases (see Chapter 22 for a summary of the principles which will then apply).

The DOLS provisions under Schedule A1 to the MCA 2005 (see Chapter 23) do not apply to 16 and 17 year olds, however, and where admission to hospital involves a deprivation of liberty, DOLS may not, therefore, be relied upon as authorisation for it. Also, unlike their adult counterparts, 16 and 17 year olds may not make use of the Act to make an advance decision to refuse medical treatment (section 24(1)).

24.3.5   Inherent jurisdiction of the High Court

The High Court retains an inherent jurisdiction to make decisions regarding the admission to hospital and treatment of children and young people. It, therefore, provides another possible source of authority for admission or treatment, but is likely to be the authority of last resort. The remaining extent of this jurisdiction is uncertain, but it is unlikely that applications to the High Court will be appropriate in cases where a competent child or a young person with capacity is required to make a decision, where a decision regarding admission or treatment can properly be made under the MHA 1983 or the MCA 2005, or where the authority of a parent can be relied on. The 1983 Code suggests (para 36.66) that the High Court's jurisdiction may be called upon where the child:

- is not Gillick competent and where the person with parental responsibility cannot be identified or is incapacitated;
- is not Gillick competent and where one person with parental responsibility consents but another strongly disagrees and is likely to take the matter to court themselves;
- is not Gillick competent and where there is concern that the person with parental responsibility may not be acting in the best interests of the child in making treatment decisions on behalf of the child, eg where hostility between parents is a factor in any decision making or where there are concerns as to whether a person with parental responsibility is capable of making a decision in the best interests of the child;
- is not Gillick competent and where a person with parental responsibility consents but the decision is not within the zone of parental control, eg where the treatment in question is ECT; or
- is Gillick competent or is a young person who is capable of making a decision on their treatment and is refusing treatment.

It is only the last of these which suggests that there is still a decision-making role for the High Court in the case of a young person (as opposed to a child) at all, and in most such cases the MHA 1983 is likely to be the most appropriate source of authority.

Taking account of the principles in paras 24.3.1–24.3.5, Table 24.1 summarises the likely source of authority for decision-making in various scenarios.

Table 24.1   Authority to admit and/or treat a child or young person

Scenario	*Source of authority*
Competent child agrees to admission	Child
Competent child refuses admission	MHA 1983
Non-competent child needs admission	Parent (if zone of parental control) or MHA 1983
Competent child agrees to treatment	Child
Competent child refuses treatment	MHA 1983 or High Court
Non-competent child needs treatment	Parent (if zone of parental control)/MHA 1983/High Court
Young person with capacity agrees to admission	Young person
Young person with capacity refuses admission	MHA 1983
Young person without capacity needs admission	MCA 2005 (no DOLS)/parent (if zone of parental control)/MHA 1983
Young person with capacity agrees to treatment	Young person
Young person with capacity refuses treatment	MHA 1983/High Court
Young person without capacity needs treatment	Parent (if zone of parental control)/MHA 1983/MCA 2005/High Court

24.4   SECURE ACCOMMODATION ORDERS

Where the main objective in relation to a child or young person with mental disorder is to control behaviour rather than provide medical treatment, a secure accommodation order under section 25 of the Children Act 1989 may be a preferred alternative to use of the MHA 1983 (see 1983 Code, paras 36.17 and 36.18). Regulation 5(1) of the Children (Secure Accommodation) Regulations 1991 (SI 1991/1505) provides that section 25 of the Children Act 1989 shall not apply to a child who is already detained under the MHA 1983.

24.5   COMMUNITY TREATMENT ORDERS

There is no lower age limit for the imposition of CTOs, although the 1983 Code notes (para 36.64) that the 'number of children and young people whose clinical and family circumstances make them suitable' for one is 'likely to be small'. Treatment provisions concerning children and young people subject to CTOs are considered in the context of CTOs generally in Chapter 20.

24.6   NEAREST RELATIVE OF A CHILD OR YOUNG PERSON

The normal rules (section 26 of the MHA 1983) will apply when identifying the nearest relative of a child or young person, subject to the following.

24.6.1   Local authority as nearest relative

Section 27 of the MHA 1983 provides that where a child or young person is in the care of a local authority by virtue of a care order within the meaning of the Children Act 1989, then that local authority 'shall be deemed to be the nearest relative of the patient in preference to any person except the patient's husband or wife or civil partner (if any)'.

24.6.2   Guardian or person named in residence order as nearest relative

Section 28 of the MHA 1983 provides that for any person who has not attained the age of 18 and who has had a guardian appointed under section 5 of the Children Act 1989 (not under section 7 of the MHA 1983), or is subject to a residence order under section 8 of the Children Act 1989, the guardian or the person named in the residence order shall 'to the exclusion of any other person, be deemed to be his nearest relative'.

Chapter 25

Mental Disorder and Criminal Law

25.1   INTRODUCTION

This chapter provides a summary overview of criminal law and procedure from the perspective of mentally disordered participants. In particular, it considers the challenges presented to the criminal process as a result of the involvement of those with mental disorder and the various ways in which the process is adapted to take account of their vulnerabilities and needs. It reviews all aspects of the criminal process from arrest through to sentence. While focussing in the main on the mentally disordered suspect or defendant, the chapter also considers matters affecting mentally disordered witnesses and victims of crime.

25.2   DETENTION IN A POLICE STATION

25.2.1   Diversion to hospital from the police station

Anyone who is detained in a police station following arrest and who is in need of treatment for a mental disorder should be considered for admission to hospital (1983 Code, para 33.2). Any such admission may then take place on a voluntary basis or under the MHA 1983. In the normal course of events, if a suspect requires immediate admission to hospital before a police investigation is complete, he will be bailed to return to the police station at a later date under section 37(2) of the PACE 1984.

25.2.2   Relevant provisions of the Police and Criminal Evidence Act 1984

While a mentally disordered suspect is at the police station, provisions concerning his treatment are contained in the PACE Code C. In summary:

- If an officer has any suspicion or is told in good faith that a person of any age may be mentally disordered, or otherwise mentally vulnerable, in the absence of clear evidence to dispel that suspicion, the person shall be treated as such (para 1.4).
- If a detainee is mentally disordered or otherwise mentally vulnerable, the custody officer must, as soon as practicable, inform the detainee's appropriate adult and ask the adult to come to the police station (para 3.15).
- The appropriate adult should be a relative, guardian or other person responsible for their care or custody, or someone experienced in dealing with mentally disordered or mentally vulnerable people but who is not a police officer or employed by the police (para 1.7).
- The custody officer must make sure that a detainee who appears to be suffering from a mental disorder receives appropriate clinical attention as soon as reasonably practicable (para 9.5).
- A caution should only be administered to a mentally disordered detainee in the presence of an appropriate adult (para 10.12).
- Before a detainee is interviewed, the custody officer should consult with a health care professional in order to assess whether the detainee is fit enough to be interviewed. This means 'determining and considering the risks to the detainee's physical and mental state if the interview took place and determining what safeguards are needed to allow the interview to take place' (para 12.3). In this respect, the custody officer and health care professional should have regard to PACE Code C, Annex G (Fitness to be interviewed), which provides, inter alia, that a detainee may be at risk in a police interview if it is considered that (para 2):

    (a)   conducting the interview could significantly harm the detainee's physical or mental state;

    (b)   anything the detainee says in the interview about their involvement or suspected involvement in the offence about which they are being interviewed might be considered unreliable in subsequent court proceedings because of their physical or mental state.

- Except in urgent cases, a mentally disordered detainee must not be interviewed, or asked to sign a written statement regarding his involvement in a criminal offence, in the absence of an appropriate adult (para 11.15).
- Because of the risk of unreliable evidence when interviewing mentally disordered detainees, it is important to obtain corroboration of any facts admitted wherever possible (Notes for Guidance, 11C).

25.3   DECISION TO PROSECUTE

As with any other suspect, the decision whether to prosecute a mentally disordered suspect will be taken by the Crown Prosecution Service (CPS). When making a decision in the case of a mentally disordered suspect, however, government guidance indicates that the CPS should have particular regard to the views of relevant mental health professionals and any other available information regarding the suspect's mental health.

Home Office Circular 12/95 (Mentally disordered offenders: inter-agency working) requires that, 'where offences have allegedly been committed by mentally disordered people, the question of public safety and any relevant information about the person's history are taken fully into account in deciding whether to charge', and CPS legal guidance, *Mentally Disordered Offenders* (www.cps.gov.uk/legal/l_to_o/mentally_disordered_offenders), suggests that:

> Where the police have been advised of the defendant's condition and prognosis by the Social Services, Probation Service, psychiatrists or other professionals, who may advocate a particular approach or disposal, the advising agency should be encouraged to set out their views in writing. Where this is not possible, the police should summarise any views expressed to them orally.

Where the suspect is already receiving treatment, the CPS legal guidance advises that the prosecutor should obtain:

- medical reports from the responsible clinician to explain the nature and degree of the disorder or disability, and any relationship between the disorder and the treatment and behaviour of the offender; and
- any other relevant information from hospital staff about the treatment and behaviour of the patient, including the treatment regime and any history of similar and recent behaviour.

Following consultation, any decision then taken by the CPS on whether to prosecute should be in accordance with the principles set out in *The Code for Crown Prosecutors* (7th edn, January 2013).

The decision involves a two-stage test:

- Is there sufficient evidence to provide a realistic prospect of conviction (the evidential test)?
- Is a prosecution required in the public interest (the public interest test)?

Evidential test

The evidential test calls for a consideration of whether the Crown will be able to prove all elements of the offence alleged. In the case of a mentally disordered suspect, this may require particular consideration of whether the suspect was capable of forming the *mens rea* required for the commission of the offence. As with other elements of the offence, the burden of proving the required *mens rea* falls on the Crown, which must establish it beyond reasonable doubt. A psychiatric opinion may, therefore, be called for to consider, for example, whether a mentally disordered suspect was capable of forming a dishonest intention to permanently deprive (theft) or forming an intention to cause grievous bodily harm (section 18 of the Offences Against the Person Act 1861).

The burden on the Crown to prove *mens rea* must be distinguished from the quite separate issue of insanity, which may be raised by the defendant as a common law defence to the offence alleged. Where insanity is raised as a defence, the burden of proving it falls on the defendant (see para 25.7).

The evidential test also calls for consideration of whether the Crown's evidence will be regarded by a court as reliable and admissible.

As far as reliability is concerned, reference has already been made (see para 25.2.2) to PACE Code C, Notes for Guidance, 11C, which highlights the importance of obtaining corroboration of any fact admitted by a mentally disordered suspect in interview. Absent any corroborative evidence, a prosecution based solely on the confession of a mentally disordered suspect may proceed, but there are bound to be concerns. Section 77(1) of the PACE 1984 requires a Crown Court judge to remind the jury of the 'special need for caution' before convicting a defendant where the case against the defendant depends wholly or substantially on a confession by him and the court is satisfied that he is mentally handicapped and that the confession was not made in the presence of an independent person. There is a similar requirement on magistrates to remind themselves of the special need for caution when faced with such evidence in summary trials (section 77(2)).

There may also be an issue as to the admissibility of any confession made by a mentally disordered suspect. Under section 76(2)(b) of the PACE 1984, a court may rule inadmissible any evidence of a confession where satisfied that the confession was or may have been obtained in consequence of anything said or done which was likely, in the circumstances existing at the time, to render the confession unreliable. Under section 78 of the PACE 1984, a court also has a general discretion to exclude evidence if satisfied having regard to all the circumstances, including the circumstances in which the evidence was obtained, that the admission of the evidence would have such an adverse effect on the fairness of the proceedings that the court ought not to admit it.

In *R v B* [2012] EWCA Crim 1799, the defendant was found unfit to plead in the light of expert evidence of a learning disability which prevented him from being able to instruct his legal team, understand the nature of the charge, understand the difference between a plea of guilty and not guilty, and understand the right to challenge a juror. At the subsequent trial on the facts, the defendant was found to have committed the sexual act alleged, a finding based largely on a confession made in interview. The Court of Appeal set aside this finding, holding that the evidence of the confession should have been ruled inadmissible. It was illogical to allow the confession to be admitted as reliable evidence of guilt when the experts suggested that the defendant's condition was the same at interview as it was when the finding of unfitness to plead was reached. How could it safely be concluded that someone who was unfit to plead would have understood the caution administered at the outset of the police interview? The fact that the defendant was represented at interview by an experienced solicitor and social worker, neither of whom suggested that he was unfit to be interviewed, made no difference.

Public interest test

Where there is sufficient evidence to prosecute, *The Code for Crown Prosecutors* (para 4.12) sets out a series of public interest factors which must then be considered before a decision on prosecution is finally made. These factors are:

- How serious is the offence committed?
- What is the level of culpability of the suspect?
- What are the circumstances of and the harm caused to the victim?
- Was the suspect under the age of 18 at the time of the offence?
- What is the impact on the community?
- Is prosecution a proportionate response?
- Do sources of information require protecting?

The weight to attach to each of the factors will vary from case to case, but in the cases of suspects with mental disorder, questions of culpability and proportionality may be particularly important. When considering culpability, for example, prosecutors should have regard to 'whether the suspect is, or was at the time of the offence, suffering from any significant mental or physical ill health' (*The Code for Crown Prosecutors*, para 4.12(b)). In some cases, reduced culpability as a result of mental ill health may mean that a prosecution is not required at all. As to proportionality, the fact that the suspect is already receiving the treatment that any court is likely to order by way of sentence is a relevant consideration, and, depending on other factors, little public interest may be served in prosecuting in such circumstances. *The Code for Crown Prosecutors* advises (para 7.1) that alternatives to prosecution (e.g. a police caution) should be considered where it is an appropriate response to the offender and/or the seriousness and consequences of the offending.

25.4   BAIL

Following charge, a mentally disordered defendant has the same entitlement to bail under the Bail Act 1976 as any other defendant. Section 4(1) creates a general presumption in favour of bail, subject to the exceptions set out in Schedule 1, para 2 of which provides that bail need not be granted if the court is satisfied that there are substantial grounds for believing that the defendant, if released on bail (whether subject to conditions or not) would:

(a)   fail to surrender to custody, or

(b)   commit an offence while on bail, or

(c)   interfere with witnesses or otherwise obstruct the course of justice, whether in relation to himself or any other person.

Schedule 1, para 3 to the Bail Act 1976 also allows a court to refuse bail where it is satisfied that the defendant should be kept in custody for his own protection. Section 3(6)(d) allows a court to impose a condition of bail requiring the defendant to make himself available for the purposes of enabling a report to be made to assist the court in dealing with him for the offence.

25.5   ASSESSMENT AND TREATMENT DURING CRIMINAL PROCEEDINGS

Once proceedings have commenced, the MHA 1983 provides a variety of ways by which a court may order that the defendant is removed to hospital for assessment or treatment.

25.5.1   Remand for report on mental condition – section 35 of the Mental Health Act 1983

Section 35 of the MHA 1983 allows magistrates or the Crown Court to remand a defendant to hospital for a report on his mental condition (see para 10.4.1).

25.5.2   Remand for treatment for mental disorder – section 36 of the Mental Health Act 1983

Section 36 of the MHA 1983 allows the Crown Court to remand a defendant awaiting trial to hospital for treatment (see para 10.4.2).

25.5.3   Interim hospital order – section 38 of the Mental Health Act 1983

Section 38 of the MHA 1983 allows magistrates and the Crown Court to make an interim hospital order in respect of a convicted defendant before deciding what sentence to finally impose (see para 10.4.3).

25.6   FITNESS TO PLEAD

25.6.1   Crown Court

The test for fitness to plead in the Crown Court remains the common law one set out in *R v Pritchard* (1836) 7 C and P 303. The question for the court is, therefore, whether the defendant is 'of sufficient intellect to comprehend the course of the proceedings and trial, so as to make a proper defence, to challenge a juror to whom he might wish to object and to comprehend the details of the evidence'.

Procedure concerning fitness to plead in the Crown Court is set out in section 4 of the Criminal Procedure (Insanity) Act 1964, as amended by the Criminal Procedure (Insanity and Unfitness to Plead) Act 1991, and by the Domestic Violence, Crime and Victims Act 2004 (DVCVA 2004). Whether the defendant is unfit to plead is for the judge to decide. The issue may be raised, at any stage before arraignment, by the defence, the prosecution or the judge. Although the issue should normally be dealt with as soon as it arises, the judge may postpone consideration until any time up to the opening of the defence case (section 4(2)), enabling the prospect of an acquittal before the issue needs to be decided at all (section 4(3)). When deciding on fitness to plead, the judge should consider evidence from two RMPs, at least one of whom should be approved under section 12 of the MHA 1983.

If a judge makes a finding that the defendant is unfit, the case is then referred to a jury, who must decide whether they are satisfied, beyond reasonable doubt, that the defendant did the act or made the omission charged (section 4A of the

Criminal Procedure (Insanity) Act 1964). Where there is evidence which raises a possible defence in law, for example that the act or omission was conducted in self-defence, the jury should not reach a finding that the defendant did the act unless also satisfied beyond reasonable doubt that the prosecution has disproved that defence (*R v Antoine* [2000] UKHL 20).

If a jury makes a finding that the defendant carried out the act or made the omission charged, the judge will sentence him in accordance with powers provided in section 5(2) of the Criminal Procedure (Insanity) Act 1964 (as amended by the Domestic Violence, Crime and Victims Act 2004). One of the following sentences must be imposed:

(a)   hospital order (with or without a restriction);
(b)   supervision order;
(c)   absolute discharge.

In circumstances where a hospital and restriction order is imposed following a finding of unfitness to plead, section 5A(4) of the Criminal Procedure (Insanity) Act 1964 (as inserted by section 24 of the Domestic Violence, Crime and Victims Act 2004) allows the SSJ to later remit that person for trial if he is satisfied 'after consultation with the RC that the person can properly be tried'.

25.6.2   Magistrates' court

In a magistrates' court, section 37(3) of the MHA 1983 provides that where the court would, on convicting a defendant, have the power to make a hospital order, then it may make the order without convicting the him if it is 'satisfied that [he] did the act or made the omission charged'. In other words, the court can embark on a fact-finding exercise and then proceed to make a hospital order without taking a plea or deciding on fitness to plead.

Section 37(3) of the MHA 1983 only applies to cases where the offence is punishable by imprisonment. What steps regarding fitness to plead the court should therefore take in respect of non-imprisonable offences is not clear, but the likelihood must be that the Crown will decide not to proceed with the case where there is a serious doubt about the defendant's fitness to plead.

25.7   INSANITY

25.7.1   Crown Court

The common law defence of insanity is available in Crown Court proceedings. Whether a defendant is insane for the purposes of any trial on indictment will be determined by an application of the M'Naghten Rules (*M'Naghten's Case*

[1843] All ER Rep 229), according to which insanity is established if it is shown that at the time of the act, the defendant was 'labouring under such a defect of reason, from disease of the mind, as not to know the nature and quality of the act he was doing; or if he did know it, that he did not know he was doing what was wrong'.

The procedure for dealing with the issue of insanity is governed by section 2 of the Trial of Lunatics Act 1883. It is not for the prosecution to accept a plea of not guilty by reason of insanity; the matter must go to a jury. The jury may then return the 'special verdict' if, following a fact-finding exercise, it is satisfied that the defendant did the act or made the omission, but was insane at the time. It is for the prosecution to prove, beyond reasonable doubt, that a defendant did the act or made the omission, and, if it raises the issue, for the defence to show, on the balance of probabilities, that he was insane.

If a defendant is found not guilty by reason of insanity then, as with defendants who are deemed unfit to plead, the judge will impose one of the three sentences available under section 5(2) of the Criminal Procedure (Insanity) Act 1964 (as amended by the Domestic Violence, Crime and Victims Act 2004): a hospital order (with or without restrictions), a supervision order or an absolute discharge.

25.7.2   Magistrates' court

In a magistrates' court, where the accused is so unwell that his sanity is in doubt, magistrates are able to use section 37(3) of the MHA 1983 to conduct a fact-finding exercise and proceed to impose a hospital order without taking a plea or ever needing to resolve the issue of sanity. In *R (on the application of Singh) v Stratford Magistrates' Court* [2007] EWHC 1582 (Admin), it was ruled that the common law defence of insanity is, nevertheless, available in magistrates' court proceedings, although the special verdict procedure under the Trial of Lunatics Act 1883 is not.

25.8   SPECIAL PROCEDURAL ARRANGEMENTS FOR DEFENDANTS WITH MENTAL DISORDER

25.8.1   Criminal Practice Directions 2013

Practice Direction 3G of the Criminal Practice Directions 2013 [2013] EWCA Crim 1631 applies to hearings which involve 'vulnerable defendants', defined to include defendants with a mental disorder or learning disability. The Practice Direction is drafted with rule 3.8(4) of the Criminal Procedure Rules 2013 (SI 2013/1554) in mind, which requires a court to take every reasonable step to facilitate the participation of the defendant at his trial. The Practice Direction, therefore, makes various recommendations about what steps ought to be taken. These include:

- Where the defendant is jointly charged, consideration should be given to directing that he should be tried separately.
- Consideration should be given to arranging for the defendant to visit the court room so that he can familiarise himself with it.
- Subject to security arrangements, any hearing should, if practicable, take place in a court room where the participants are all at the same level.
- Subject to security arrangements, the defendant should be allowed to sit with a family member or other supporting adult.
- The court should ensure that the court process is explained to the defendant at the outset in terms that he will understand, and should continue to ensure that the defendant understands what is happening.
- Any trial should be conducted according to a timetable which takes full account of the defendant's ability to concentrate.

25.8.2   Evidence via live link

Under section 33A of the Youth Justice and Criminal Evidence Act 1999 (as amended by section 47 of the Police and Justice Act 2006), a criminal court is able to direct that an adult defendant should give evidence via live link (absent from the court room, but able to participate via remote audio-visual technology) where satisfied that it is in the interests of justice to do so and that:

- the defendant suffers from a mental disorder (within the meaning of the MHA 1983) or otherwise has a significant impairment of intelligence and social function;
- he is for that reason unable to participate effectively in the proceedings as a witness giving oral evidence in court; and
- the use of a live link would enable him to participate more effectively in the proceedings as a witness (whether by improving the quality of his evidence or otherwise).

A court may make a similar order in respect of a defendant under the age of 18 where satisfied that it is in the interests of justice to do so and that:

- the defendant's ability to participate effectively in the proceedings as a witness giving oral evidence in court is compromised by his level of intellectual ability or social functioning; and
- the use of a live link would enable him to participate more effectively in the proceedings (whether by improving the quality of his evidence or otherwise).

25.9   SENTENCING

25.9.1   Custody

There is no reason in principle why a court should not sentence a mentally disordered offender to a term of imprisonment (*R v Drew* [2003] UKHL 25). Factors affecting whether a court will, in fact, impose a prison sentence, as opposed to a disposal under the MHA 1983, are considered in more detail at paras 10.2.3 and 11.4.

25.9.2   Sentences under the Mental Health Act 1983

The MHA 1983 provides a variety of sentencing options in respect of mentally disordered defendants, including: a hospital order under section 37, a guardianship order, also under section 37, a restriction order under section 41 and a restriction direction under section 45A. These sentences are considered in detail in Chapters 10, 11 and 13.

25.9.3   Community order

Section 177 of the Criminal Justice Act 2003 entitles a court to impose a community order on any adult convicted of an offence. The order may only be imposed, however, if the offence or combination of offences is serious enough to merit a community sentence (section 148). It is similar in form to what used to be known as a probation order and may be made subject to a variety of requirements, one of which is a 'mental health treatment requirement' (section 117(1)(h)).

Mental health treatment requirement

According to section 207(1) of the Criminal Justice Act 2003, a 'mental health treatment requirement' means that:

> (1)   ... the offender must submit, during a period or periods specified in the order, to treatment by or under the direction of a registered medical practitioner or a registered psychologist (or both, for different periods) with a view to the improvement of the offender's mental condition.

Types of treatment

According to section 207(2) of the Criminal Justice Act 2003, the following types of treatment may be specified in the order:

(a)   treatment as a resident patient in a care home within the meaning of the Care Standards Act 2000 (c. 14), an independent hospital or a hospital within the meaning of the Mental Health Act 1983 (c. 20), but not in hospital premises where high security psychiatric services within the meaning of that Act are provided;

(b)   treatment as a non-resident patient at such institution or place as may be specified in the order;

(c)   treatment by or under the direction of such registered medical practitioner or registered psychologist (or both) as may be so specified.

The order may not otherwise specify the nature of the treatment to be given.

Criteria

According to section 207(3) of the Criminal Justice Act 2003, the mental health treatment requirement may not be imposed unless:

(a)   the court is satisfied, on the evidence of a registered medical practitioner approved for the purposes of section 12 of the Mental Health Act 1983, that the mental condition of the offender—

    (i)   is such as requires and may be susceptible to treatment, but

    (ii)   is not such as to warrant the making of a hospital order or guardianship order within the meaning of that Act;

(b)   the court is also satisfied that arrangements have been or can be made for the treatment intended to be specified in the order (including arrangements for the reception of the offender where he is to be required to submit to treatment as a resident patient); and

(c)   the offender has expressed his willingness to comply with such a requirement

Breach of community order

Breach of a community order is dealt with under section 179 of and Schedule 8 to the Criminal Justice Act 2003. Where a defendant has failed without reasonable excuse to comply with the requirements of his community order, he may be given a warning or made subject to breach proceedings. If the failure to comply is the second one within a period of 12 months, there is no discretion to issue a warning and breach proceedings must be initiated. Breach proceedings will involve the defendant returning to the sentencing court who may deal with the breach (if proved) by making the order more onerous or by re-sentencing the defendant for the original offence(s).

25.10 MENTALLY DISORDERED PERSONS AS VICTIMS OF CRIME

There is a variety of legislation creating specific criminal offences in respect of the mistreatment of those with mental disorder and other vulnerable adults.

25.10.1 Offences under the Mental Health Act 1983

Forgery and False statements – section 126 of the Mental Health Act 1983

Section 126 of the MHA 1983 creates offences in respect of any forgery or false statement made in connection with an application for detention under Part II.

Under section 126(1) of the MHA 1983, it is an offence for any person to have in his custody or control, without lawful authority or excuse, any of the following documents knowing or believing it be false:

- any document purporting to be an application under Part II of the Act
- any document purporting to be a medical recommendation or report under the Act
- any document purporting to be any other document required or authorised to be made for any of the purposes of the Act.

Under section 126(2) of the MHA 1983, it is an offence for any person to have in his custody or control, without lawful authority or excuse, any document so closely resembling one of the documents to which section 126(1) applies as to be calculated to deceive.

Under section 126(4) of the MHA 1983, it is an offence for any person to:

(a)   wilfully [make] a false entry or statement in any application, recommendation, report, record or other document required or authorised to be made for any of the purposes of this Act; or

(b)   with intent to deceive, [make] use of any such entry or statement which he knows to be false.

Ill-treatment of patients – section 127 of the Mental Health Act 1983

Section 127 of the MHA 1983 creates offences of ill-treatment or wilful neglect of mentally disordered patients.

Under section 127(1) of the MHA 1983, it is an offence for any person who is an officer on the staff of or otherwise employed in, or who is one of the managers of, a hospital, independent hospital or care home:

> (a)   to ill-treat or wilfully to neglect a patient for the time being receiving treatment for mental disorder as an in-patient in that hospital or home; or
>
> (b)   to ill-treat or wilfully to neglect, on the premises of which the hospital or home forms part, a patient for the time being receiving such treatment there as an out-patient.

Under section 127(2) of the MHA 1983, it is an offence for any person to ill-treat or wilfully neglect a mentally disordered patient who is for the time being subject to his guardianship under the MHA 1983 or is otherwise in his custody or care.

Assisting patients to absent themselves without leave – section 128 of the Mental Health Act 1983

Section 128 of the MHA 1983 creates offences of inducing or assisting patients subject to the Act to absent themselves without leave, or harbouring them once they have absented themselves.

Under section 128(1) of the MHA 1983, it is an offence to induce or knowingly assist any of the following to go absent without leave:

- a person liable to detention within the meaning of Part II of the Act;
- a person subject to guardianship;
- a person subject to a CTO.

Under section 128(2) of the MHA 1983, it is an offence to induce or knowingly assist a person who is in legal custody under the Act (see section 137) to escape from such custody.

Under section 128(3) of the MHA 1983, it is an offence to knowingly harbour a patient who is AWOL or otherwise at large and liable to be retaken under the Act, or to give a patient assistance with intent to prevent, hinder or interfere with his being taken into custody, or returned to hospital or other place where he ought to be.

25.10.2   Offences under the Mental Capacity Act 2005

Ill-treatment or neglect – section 44 of the Mental Capacity Act 2005

Section 44 of the MCA 2005 creates the offence of ill-treating or wilfully neglecting P. The offence may be committed by:

- a person who has the care of P who lacks or who he reasonably believes lacks capacity;
- the donee of an LPA or enduring power of attorney created by P;
- a deputy appointed by the court for P

25.10.3 Offences under the Sexual Offences Act 2003

The Sexual Offences Act 2003 creates a number of offences in respect of sexual activity involving a person with a mental disorder. These can be summarised as follows.

Offences where the victim has a mental disorder which impedes choice

- Section 30 of the Sexual Offences Act 2003 – sexual activity with a person with a mental disorder impeding choice.
- Section 31 – causing or inciting a person with a mental disorder impeding choice to engage in sexual activity.
- Section 32 – engaging in sexual activity in the presence of a person with a mental disorder impeding choice.
- Section 33 – causing a person with a mental disorder impeding choice to watch a sexual act.

Offences where the victim has a mental disorder and is made subject to inducement, threat or deception

- Section 34 of the Sexual Offences Act 2003 – inducement, threat or deception to procure sexual activity with a person with a mental disorder.
- Section 35 – causing a person with a mental disorder to engage in or agree to engage in sexual activity by inducement, threat or deception.
- Section 36 – engaging in sexual activity in the presence, procured by inducement, threat or deception, of a person with a mental disorder.
- Section 37 – causing a person with a mental disorder to watch a sexual act by inducement, threat or deception.

Offences committed by care workers

- Section 38 of the Sexual Offences Act 2003 – care workers: sexual activity with a person with a mental disorder.
- Section 39 – care workers: causing or inciting a person with a mental disorder to engage in sexual activity.
- Section 40 – care workers: sexual activity in the presence of a person with a mental disorder.
- Section 41 – care workers: causing a person with a mental disorder to watch a sexual act.

25.11 VULNERABLE ADULTS AS WITNESSES

The Criminal Procedure Rules 2013 (SI 2013/1554) place on criminal courts various obligations which are relevant to the participation of mentally disordered witnesses:

- rule 3.2(1) requires courts to actively manage all cases, which should include the early identification of the needs of witnesses (rule 3.2(2)(b));
- rule 3.8(4)(a) requires a court, when preparing the case for trial, to take every reasonable step to encourage and to facilitate the attendance of witnesses;
- rule 3.10(c) (iv) allows a court, when managing a trial, to require parties to identify what arrangements are desirable to facilitate the giving of evidence by a witness.

When applying these rules in relation to mentally disordered or other vulnerable witnesses, the court should have in mind the 'special measures' that it may take under the Youth Justice and Criminal Evidence Act 1999 to facilitate the giving of their evidence. For special measures to be applied, a witness must first be eligible. Section 16(2) deals with eligibility on grounds of mental disorder or other incapacity. It provides that a witness in criminal proceedings becomes eligible for assistance if the quality of his evidence is likely to be diminished by virtue of the fact that he (section 16(2)(a)):

(i) suffers from mental disorder within the meaning of the Mental Health Act 1983, or

(ii) otherwise has a significant impairment of intelligence and social functioning;

Once eligibility is established, a court may then make a direction under section 19(2) of the Youth Justice and Criminal Evidence Act 1999 that a special measure or measures may be applied to the giving of the evidence by the witness, if satisfied that the measure is likely to improve the quality of evidence given by the witness. The special measures available are set out in sections 23–30:

- screening witness from accused (section 23);
- evidence by live link (section 24);
- evidence given in private (section 25);
- removal of wigs and gowns (section 26);
- video recorded evidence in chief (section 27);
- video recorded cross-examination or re-examination (section 28);
- examination of witness through intermediary (section 29);
- aids to communication (section 30).

25.12   DOMESTIC VIOLENCE, CRIME AND VICTIMS ACT 2004

The DVCVA 2004 establishes the right of the victim of a sexual or violent crime to be consulted or informed when the offender is about to be released into the community after his sentence is served. The Act applies equally to the victims of mentally disordered offenders as it does to the victims of any other type of offender, and specific provision is made for cases where the offender is in hospital following a disposal under the MHA 1983. The relevant sections of the DVCVA 2004 in this respect are sections 36–44B.

25.12.1   Cases to which the Domestic Violence, Crime and Victims Act 2004 applies

As the DVCVA 2004 was originally applied to cases involving mentally disordered offenders, the victim's right to be consulted or informed existed only in respect of violent or sexual offences where the offender was in hospital as a *restricted* patient. However, amendments introduced by the MHA 2007 meant that the right was extended to cases involving unrestricted patients. The cases where the right of the victim to be consulted or informed now, therefore, arises under the Act can be summarised as follows:

- Where the offender is convicted of a sexual or violent offence (or having been charged with such an offence, is found not guilty by reason of insanity or is found unfit to plead but to have committed the act or omission in question) and is given a hospital order under section 37, whether or not restricted (section 36(1)).
- Where the offender is convicted of a sexual or violent offence and is made subject to a hospital and limitation direction under section 45A of the MHA 1983, but only where the sentence involves a term of imprisonment of at least 12 months (section 39(1) of the DVCVA 2004). Where the patient receives a determinate term of imprisonment, the right will apply after the limitation direction comes to an end, that is after he becomes a notional hospital order patient (section 41A(1) of the DVCVA 2004).
- Where the offender is convicted of a sexual or violent offence, is given a sentence of imprisonment of at least 12 months, and is then transferred to hospital under section 47 of the MHA 1983, whether or not there is a restriction direction under section 49 (section 42(1) of the DVCVA 2004). If the transfer direction under section 47 is accompanied by a restriction direction under section 49, the right will apply after the restriction direction comes to an end (when any determinate prison sentence is deemed served), that is after the patient becomes a notional hospital order patient (section 44B(1) of the DVCVA 2004).

25.12.2   Duty on the local probation board to establish the victim's wishes

Assuming it is a case where the right arises, the relevant authorities must first establish whether the victim wishes to be consulted or informed when the offender's discharge into the community is imminent. The duty to establish the victim's wishes falls on the relevant local probation board, with sections 36(4), 39(2) and 42(2) of the DVCVA 2004 requiring the relevant local probation board to take all reasonable steps to establish:

- in restricted cases, whether the victim of the offence wishes to make representations about whether the offender should be subject to conditions on discharge and, if so, what those conditions should be;
- in unrestricted cases, whether the victim of the offence wishes to make representations as to what conditions the offender should be subject to in the event of his discharge from hospital under a CTO;
- in all cases, whether the victim of the offence wishes to receive information about any conditions imposed when the offender is discharged.

The relevant local probation board is the board for the area in which the offender is required to reside as a condition of his discharge, the board responsible for supervising the offender when required to do so following his release from prison or, in any other case, the board for the area in which the hospital or prison in which he was detained is situated (sections 37(8), 40(8) and 43(8) of the DVCVA 2004).

If the victim expresses a wish to either make representations or be kept informed, the steps outlined below must then be followed.

25.12.3   Right of the victim to make representations

Whether or not the patient is restricted, it should be remembered that the right of the victim is to make representations regarding conditions that should be imposed on discharge, not whether discharge should be taking place at all.

Restricted cases

In restricted cases when the victim wishes to make representations, the relevant local probation board must forward any such representations made to the SSJ or the MHT, as appropriate.

In order to ensure that a victim is able to make representations at the appropriate time, the SSJ must inform the relevant local probation board when he is considering removing a restriction order, discharging the patient or varying conditions of discharge, and the MHT must inform the probation board of any applications or references of the patient's case which may lead to discharge or variation of conditions. The probation board must pass this information on to a victim who has expressed a wish to make representations or who has already made representations (sections 37, 40 and 43 of the DVCVA 2004).

Unrestricted cases

In unrestricted cases where the local probation board is notified of the victim's wish to make representations, the board should notify the managers of the relevant hospital accordingly. Unlike in restricted cases, it is the hospital managers who then have responsibility for keeping the victim informed and for forwarding any representations of the victim to the relevant body.

In cases under sections 37 and 47 of the DVCVA 2004, the board 'must' notify hospital managers where the victim has expressed a wish to make representations (sections 36A(3) and 42A(3)), whereas in cases where the patient is unrestricted because a restriction order or a limitation or restriction direction has come to an end, the duty on the board is to take 'all reasonable steps' to notify hospital managers (sections 38B(3), 41A(3) and 44B(3)).

Hospital managers must be in a position to comply with their obligation to keep the victim informed. RCs must, therefore, advise managers if the patient is to be discharged, placed on a CTO or is to have a condition of a CTO varied. Similarly, MHTs must advise hospital managers when a patient makes an application or has his case referred to the MHT (see sections 37A, 38B, 41A, 43A and 44B of the DVCVA 2004).

25.12.4   Right of the victim to receive information

Restricted cases

In restricted cases when the victim has expressed a wish to receive information about conditions attached to the offender's discharge, the relevant local probation board is required to take all reasonable steps to pass on that information to him.

In order to ensure that the probation board is able to fulfil its responsibility to provide this information to the victim, the SSJ must inform the board if he is going to discharge the patient, whether there are to be any conditions of discharge and, if so, what they will be. He should also notify the board of any variation of conditions, any recall of the patient to hospital, or if the restriction order is to cease to have effect. Similarly, where there is an application or reference to an MHT, the tribunal must inform the probation board if the patient is to be discharged, of any proposed conditions of discharge, of any variation, or if the restriction order is to cease to have effect (see sections 38, 41 and 44 of the DVCVA 2004).

Unrestricted cases

In unrestricted cases when the victim has expressed a wish to receive information regarding conditions of discharge, the local probation board should notify the relevant hospital managers accordingly. The duty then falls on the hospital managers to provide the victim with the information required.

In order to ensure that hospital managers are able to provide the information required, there is a duty on RCs to keep hospital managers appropriately informed. RCs should ensure that the managers are informed when a patient is to be discharged, whether there is to be a CTO and, if so, what conditions will be attached, when there is a variation of the conditions attached to a CTO, when a CTO comes to an end and when detention for treatment will be allowed to expire without renewal of the section. The MHT must also inform the hospital managers if it directs the patient's discharge (see sections 38A, 38B, 41A, 44A and 44B of the DVCVA 2004).

25.13   MOTORING LAW

The Road Traffic Act 1988 (RTA 1988) and associated regulations contain provisions governing the issuing of driving licences to those with mental disorder.

25.13.1   Relevant and prospective disabilities

A *relevant disability* means any prescribed disability, or any other disability likely to cause the driving of a vehicle by a person in pursuance of a licence to be a source of danger to the public (section 92(2) of the RTA 1988). Severe mental disorder is a prescribed disability according to regulation 71(1) of the Motor Vehicles (Driving Licences) Regulations 1999 (SI 1999/2864), and is defined by regulation 71(4) to include 'mental illness, arrested or incomplete development of the mind, psychopathic disorder and severe impairment of intelligence or social functioning'.

A *prospective disability* is one which at the time of the application for the grant of a licence or, as the case may be, the material time for the purposes of the provision in which the expression is used, is not of such a kind that it is a relevant disability, but by virtue of the intermittent or progressive nature of the disability or otherwise, may become a relevant disability in course of time (section 92(2) of the RTA 1988).

25.13.2 Duty on driver to notify the Driver and Vehicle Licensing Agency of disability when applying for licence

Section 92(1) of the RTA 1988 requires any application for a driving licence to include a declaration by the applicant indicating whether he is suffering or has at any time suffered from a relevant or prospective disability.

25.13.3 Duty on the Secretary of State for Transport in respect of applications from people with relevant disability

A disability is not necessarily a bar to the issuing of a licence, however. Although section 92(3) of the RTA 1988 requires the Secretary of State for Transport (SST) to refuse to grant a licence to an applicant who has a relevant disability, this is subject to section 92(4). This provides that the SST must not refuse to grant a licence if the applicant has at any time passed a relevant test and it does not appear to the SST that the disability has arisen or become more acute since that time, or if the applicant satisfies such conditions as may be prescribed with a view to authorising the grant of a licence to a person in whose case the disability is appropriately controlled, or if the application is for a provisional licence.

25.13.4 Continuing duty of motorist to notify the Driver and Vehicle Licensing Agency of any disability

For as long as a licence is in place, however, there is a continuing duty on the licence holder to notify the Driver and Vehicle Licensing Agency (DVLA) if he becomes aware that he is suffering from a relevant or prospective disability that has not previously been disclosed to the DVLA, or if a previously disclosed one becomes acute. In either eventuality, section 94(1) of the RTA 1988 requires the licence holder to notify the DVLA of the nature and extent of the disability.

Section 94(2) of the RTA 1988 provides, however, that the licence holder need not notify the DVLA if:

(a) the disability is one from which he has not previously suffered, and
(b) he has reasonable grounds for believing that the duration of the disability will not extend beyond the period of three months beginning with the date on which he first becomes aware that he suffers from it.

A failure to notify in accordance with section 94(1) of the RTA 1988 is a criminal offence (section 94(3)), as is driving a motor vehicle after the point at which the licence holder ought to have notified the DVLA (section 94(3A)).

25.13.5 Power of the Secretary of State for Transport to revoke the licence of a person with relevant disabilities

When the SST is notified of a relevant disability, or that an existing disability has become more acute, he will consider exercising his power under section 93(1) of the RTA 1988 to revoke the person's licence. He may do so where satisfied that the licence holder has a relevant disability and that he would be required under section 92(3) to refuse an application for a licence made by the person at that time. A person who receives revocation in writing is required to deliver up his licence and counterpart (section 93(3)) and will be committing a criminal offence if he then drives (section 94A).

Revocation is not an inevitable conclusion of a relevant disability, however. Once notified of a relevant disability, the DVLA will make a decision on revocation by applying the national medical guidelines, which are contained in the DVLA booklet, *For medical practitioners: At a glance guide to the current medical standards of fitness to drive* (DVLA Drivers Medical Group, May 2014) (the Guide).

While the decision is being made, the patient retains the right to drive (section 88 of the RTA 1988), but doctors and health care professionals should draw the driver's attention to any advice regarding driving with the relevant disability in question contained within the Guide. In relation to 'acute psychotic disorders of any type', for example, the Guide states that driving 'must cease during the acute illness' (page 39).

25.13.6 Revocation and beyond

Revocation of the licence need only be temporary and a licence holder may apply for the re-instatement of his licence. The Guide contains advice on what the DVLA Drivers Medical Group would generally expect to see by way of recovery before any licence is returned. In relation to acute psychotic disorders, for example, the guidance states that where the licence is group one (cars, motor cycles, etc), re-licensing can be considered when the licence holder can satisfy the following conditions (page 39):

(a)   he has remained well and stable for at least 3 months
(b)   he is compliant with treatment
(c)   he is free from adverse effects of medication which would impair driving
(d)   he is subject to a favourable specialist report

25.13.7 Power of the Secretary of State for Transport to require information

Where the SST has reasonable grounds for believing that a person who is an applicant for a licence or a licence holder may be suffering from a relevant or prospective disability, the SST may, under section 94(5) of the RTA 1988:

(a)   require him to provide the Secretary of State, within such reasonable time as may be specified in the notice, with such an authorisation as is mentioned in subsection (6) below, or
(b)   require him, as soon as practicable, to arrange to submit himself for examination—

   (i)   by such registered medical practitioner or practitioners as may be nominated by the Secretary of State, or
   (ii)   with respect to a disability of a prescribed description, by such officer of the Secretary of State as may be so nominated,

   for the purpose of determining whether or not he suffers or has at any time suffered from a relevant or prospective disability, or
(c)   except where the application is for, or the licence held is, a provisional licence, require him to submit himself for such a test of competence to drive as the Secretary of State directs in the notice.

25.13.8 Appeal against revocation of licence

Section 100 of the RTA 1988 provides a driver with the right to appeal to a magistrates' court against a refusal to grant a licence or its revocation.

Appendix 1

Areas of Difference in Welsh Law and Procedure

Some significant areas where the Welsh law and procedure differs from the English are summarised as follows.

1.1   Code of Practice of the Mental Health Act 1983

Wales has its own MHA 1983 Code of Practice, which came into force on 3 November 2008. Although providing guidance on the same subject matter as the English one, and adopting broadly the same format, it is an entirely different document. One significant difference between the two, for example, is that, whereas the English Code is based on five guiding principles, the Welsh Code is based on nine; these, in turn, are based on four 'underpinning principles' (empowerment, equity, effectiveness, efficiency) derived from the Welsh Assembly Government mental health strategy, Adult Mental Health Services for Wales. Another difference is that the Welsh Code contains further guiding principles which apply specifically to the treatment and care of children and young people (Chapter 33), whereas the English Code does not.

1.2   Functions of the Secretary of State for Health

Various powers available to the SSH under the MHA 1983 have been transferred to the National Assembly for Wales, and are now exercisable by Welsh Ministers. These include the power under section 67 to refer the case of any unrestricted patient for a tribunal hearing, and the power under section 118 to prepare and revise the Welsh Code.

1.3   Mental health review tribunal for Wales

The independent judicial body which hears applications from, and references in respect of, patients subject to the MHA 1983 in Wales is the mental health review tribunal for Wales. Practice and procedure is determined by the Mental Health Review Tribunal for Wales Rules 2008 (SI 2008/2705), broadly similar in content to the English rules.

1.4   Mental health regulations

The Mental Health (Hospital, Guardianship and Treatment) (England) Regulations 2008 (SI 2008/1184) (see para 2.5) are of no application. Wales has its own set of regulations to accompany the MHA 1983 – the Mental Health (Hospital, Guardianship, Community Treatment and Consent to Treatment) (Wales) Regulations 2008 (SI 2008/2439) (W212). Wales, therefore, also has its own set of forms, prescribed by these regulations, for use by administrators, mental health professionals and clinicians in respect of admission to hospital, transfer, treatment, guardianship and CTOs.

1.5   Mental Health (Wales) Measure 2010

Unlike their English counterparts, those in Wales with mental health difficulties have a statutory entitlement to assessment and treatment, which comes from the Mental Health (Wales) Measure 2010 (2010 nawm 7).

Part 2 of the Measure places a duty on service providers to act in a coordinated manner to develop, provide and review a care and treatment plan for service users of all ages. It should be read in conjunction with the Mental Health (Care Co-ordination and Care and Treatment Planning) (Wales) Regulations 2011 (SI 2011/2942) (W318).

Part 3 of the Measure places a duty on local health boards (the equivalent in Wales of the CCG in England) and local authorities to assess whether former users of specialist care services may once again be in need of such services. It provides an entitlement to such an assessment without the need for a referral by a GP. It should be read in conjunction with the Mental Health (Assessment of Former Users of Secondary Mental Health Services) (Wales) Regulations 2011 (SI 2011/2500) (W272).

Part 4 of the Measure amends the MHA 1983 by inserting sections 130E–130L, dealing with the provision of independent mental health advocacy services. While broadly similar to the English system, the range of patients eligible for independent mental health advocacy services in Wales is wider and covers informal patients.

The Measure has its own Code of Practice, which came into force in June 2012.

1.6   Healthcare Inspectorate Wales

The health care regulator in Wales is the Healthcare Inspectorate Wales. It carries out the same functions as its English equivalent, the Care Quality Commission.

1.7   Deprivation of liberty safeguards

Wales has its own regulations to govern the DOLS application process:

- the Mental Capacity (Deprivation of Liberty: Appointment of Relevant Person's Representative) (Wales) Regulations 2009 (SI 2009/266) (W29); and
- the Mental Capacity (Deprivation of Liberty: Assessments, Standard Authorisations and Disputes about Residence) (Wales) Regulations 2009 (SI 2009/783) (W69).

The Welsh Assembly has also published its own guidance notes for managing authorities and supervisory bodies, which should be considered alongside the DOLS Code. The Assembly also produces its own standard forms and letters for use by managing authorities and supervisory bodies.

1.8   Approved mental health professionals

The regulations governing qualification as an AMHP in Wales for the purposes of the MHA 1983 are the Mental Health (Approval of Persons to be Approved Mental Health Professionals) (Wales) Regulations 2008 (SI 2008/2436) (W209).

1.9   Approved clinicians

The regulations governing qualification as an Approved Clinician in Wales for the purposes of the MHA 1983 are the Mental Health Act 1983 Approved Clinician (Wales) Directions 2008 (in force 3 November 2008).

1.10   Nurses

Rules governing which classes of nurse in Wales may exercise the holding power under section 5(4) of the MHA 1983 are set out the Mental Health (Nurses) (Wales) Order 2008 (SI 2008/2441) (W214).

Appendix 2

Glossary of Common Psychiatric Disorders

The following definitions of some commonly encountered mental disorders are taken from the World Health Organisation's *International Classification of Diseases*, Version 2010 (ICD-10). The references in brackets are the classification of the disorders, as per Chapter 5 of the ICD-10.

Anorexia nervosa (F50.0)

A disorder characterised by deliberate weight loss, induced and sustained by the patient. It occurs most commonly in adolescent girls and young women, but adolescent boys and young men may also be affected, as may children approaching puberty and older women up to the menopause. The disorder is associated with a specific psychopathology whereby a dread of fatness and flabbiness of body contour persists as an intrusive overvalued idea, and the patients impose a low weight threshold on themselves. There is usually under-nutrition of varying severity with secondary endocrine and metabolic changes and disturbances of bodily function. The symptoms include restricted dietary choice, excessive exercise, induced vomiting and purgation, and use of appetite suppressants and diuretics.

Autism (childhood) (F84.0)

A type of pervasive developmental disorder that is defined by:

(a) the presence of abnormal or impaired development that is manifest before the age of 3; and

(b) the characteristic type of abnormal functioning in all the three areas of psychopathology: reciprocal social interaction, communication, and restricted, stereotyped, repetitive behaviour.

In addition to these specific diagnostic features, a range of other non-specific problems are common, such as phobias, sleeping and eating disturbances, temper tantrums, and (self-directed) aggression.

Autism (atypical) (F84.1)

A type of pervasive developmental disorder that differs from childhood autism either in age of onset or in failing to fulfil all three sets of diagnostic criteria. This subcategory should be used when there is abnormal and impaired development that is present only after the age of 3, and a lack of sufficient demonstrable abnormalities in one or two of the three areas of psychopathology required for the diagnosis of autism (namely, reciprocal social interactions, communication, and restricted, stereotyped, repetitive behaviour) in spite of characteristic abnormalities in the other area(s). Atypical autism arises most often in profoundly retarded individuals and in individuals with a severe specific developmental disorder of receptive language.

Asperger syndrome (F84.5)

A disorder of uncertain nosological validity, characterised by the same type of qualitative abnormalities of reciprocal social interaction that typify autism, together with a restricted, stereotyped, repetitive repertoire of interests and activities. It differs from autism primarily in the fact that there is no general delay or retardation in language or in cognitive development. This disorder is often associated with marked clumsiness. There is a strong tendency for the abnormalities to persist into adolescence and adult life. Psychotic episodes occasionally occur in early adult life.

Bipolar affective disorder (F31)

A disorder characterised by two or more episodes in which the patient's mood and activity levels are significantly disturbed, this disturbance consisting on some occasions of an elevation of mood and increased energy and activity (hypomania or mania) and on others of a lowering of mood and decreased energy and activity (depression). Repeated episodes of hypomania or mania only are classified as bipolar.

Conduct disorders (F91)

Disorders characterised by a repetitive and persistent pattern of dissocial, aggressive, or defiant conduct. Such behaviour should amount to major violations of age-appropriate social expectations; it should, therefore, be more severe than ordinary childish mischief or adolescent rebelliousness and should imply an enduring pattern of behaviour (6 months or longer). Features of conduct disorder can also be symptomatic of other psychiatric conditions, in which case the underlying diagnosis should be preferred.

Examples of the behaviours on which the diagnosis is based include excessive levels of fighting or bullying, cruelty to other people or animals, severe destructiveness to property, fire-setting, stealing, repeated lying, truancy from school and running away from home, unusually frequent and severe temper tantrums, and disobedience. Any one of these behaviours, if marked, is sufficient for the diagnosis, but isolated dissocial acts are not.

Delusional disorder (F22.0)

A disorder characterised by the development either of a single delusion or of a set of related delusions that are usually persistent and sometimes lifelong. The content of the delusion or delusions is very variable. Clear and persistent auditory hallucinations (voices), schizophrenic symptoms such as delusions of control and marked blunting of affect, and definite evidence of brain disease are all incompatible with this diagnosis. However, the presence of occasional or transitory auditory hallucinations, particularly in elderly patients, does not rule out this diagnosis, provided that they are not typically schizophrenic and form only a small part of the overall clinical picture.

Dementia (F00–F03)

A syndrome due to disease of the brain, usually of a chronic or progressive nature, in which there is disturbance of multiple higher cortical functions, including memory, thinking, orientation, comprehension, calculation, learning capacity, language, and judgement. Consciousness is not clouded. The impairments of cognitive function are commonly accompanied, and occasionally preceded, by deterioration in emotional control, social behaviour, or motivation. This syndrome occurs in Alzheimer disease, in cerebrovascular disease, and in other conditions primarily or secondarily affecting the brain.

Depressive episode (F32)

In typical mild, moderate, or severe depressive episodes, the patient suffers from lowering of mood, reduction of energy, and decrease in activity. Capacity for enjoyment, interest, and concentration is reduced, and marked tiredness after even minimum effort is common. Sleep is usually disturbed and appetite diminished. Self-esteem and self-confidence are almost always reduced and, even in the mild form, some ideas of guilt or worthlessness are often present. The lowered mood varies little from day to day, is unresponsive to circumstances and may be accompanied by so-called 'somatic' symptoms, such as loss of interest and pleasurable feelings, waking in the morning several hours before the usual time, depression worst in the morning, marked psychomotor retardation, agitation, loss of appetite, weight loss, and loss of libido. Depending upon the number and severity of the symptoms, a depressive episode may be specified as mild, moderate or severe.

Generalised anxiety disorder (F41.1)

Anxiety that is generalised and persistent but not restricted to, or even strongly predominating in, any particular environmental circumstances (i.e. it is 'free-floating'). The dominant symptoms are variable but include complaints of persistent nervousness, trembling, muscular tensions, sweating, lightheadedness, palpitations, dizziness, and epigastric discomfort. Fears that the patient or a relative will shortly become ill or have an accident are often expressed.

Mental retardation (F70–F79) (otherwise known as intellectual or learning disability)

A condition of arrested or incomplete development of the mind, which is especially characterised by impairment of skills manifested during the developmental period, skills which contribute to the overall level of intelligence, i.e. cognitive, language, motor, and social abilities. Retardation can occur with or without any other mental or physical condition.

Degrees of mental retardation are conventionally estimated by standardised intelligence tests. These can be supplemented by scales assessing social adaptation in a given environment. These measures provide an approximate indication of the degree of mental retardation. The diagnosis will also depend on the overall assessment of intellectual functioning by a skilled diagnostician.

Intellectual abilities and social adaptation may change over time, and, however poor, may improve as a result of training and rehabilitation. Diagnosis should be based on the current levels of functioning.

Obsessive compulsive disorder (F42)

The essential feature is recurrent obsessional thoughts or compulsive acts. Obsessional thoughts are ideas, images, or impulses that enter the patient's mind again and again in a stereotyped form. They are almost invariably distressing and the patient often tries, unsuccessfully, to resist them. They are, however, recognised as his or her own thoughts, even though they are involuntary and often repugnant. Compulsive acts or rituals are stereotyped behaviours that are repeated again and again. They are not inherently enjoyable, nor do they result in the completion of inherently useful tasks. Their function is to prevent some objectively unlikely event, often involving harm to or caused by the patient, which he or she fears might otherwise occur. Usually, this behaviour is recognised by the patient as pointless or ineffectual and repeated attempts are made to resist. Anxiety is almost invariably present. If compulsive acts are resisted the anxiety gets worse.

Post-traumatic stress disorder (F43.1)

Arises as a delayed or protracted response to a stressful event or situation (of either brief or long duration) of an exceptionally threatening or catastrophic nature, which is likely to cause pervasive distress in almost anyone. Predisposing factors, such as personality traits (e.g. compulsive, asthenic) or previous history of neurotic illness, may lower the threshold for the development of the syndrome or aggravate its course, but they are neither necessary nor sufficient to explain its occurrence. Typical features include episodes of repeated reliving of the trauma in intrusive memories ('flashbacks'), dreams or nightmares, occurring against the persisting background of a sense of 'numbness' and emotional blunting, detachment from other people, unresponsiveness to surroundings, anhedonia, and avoidance of activities and situations reminiscent of the trauma. There is usually a state of autonomic hyperarousal with hypervigilance, an enhanced startle reaction, and insomnia. Anxiety and depression are commonly associated with the above symptoms and signs, and suicidal ideation is not infrequent. The onset follows the trauma with a latency period that may range from a few weeks to months. The course is fluctuating but recovery can be expected in the majority of cases. In a small proportion of cases the condition may follow a chronic course over many years, with eventual transition to an enduring personality change.

Schizoaffective disorders (F25)

Episodic disorders in which both affective and schizophrenic symptoms are prominent but which do not justify a diagnosis of either schizophrenia or depressive or manic episodes. Other conditions in which affective symptoms are superimposed on a pre-existing schizophrenic illness, or co-exist or alternate with persistent delusional disorders of other kinds, are classified under F20–F29. Mood-incongruent psychotic symptoms in affective disorders do not justify a diagnosis of schizoaffective disorder.

Specific personality disorders (F60)

These are severe disturbances in the personality and behavioural tendencies of the individual; not directly resulting from disease, damage, or other insult to the brain, or from another psychiatric disorder; usually involving several areas of the personality; nearly always associated with considerable personal distress and social disruption; and usually manifest since childhood or adolescence and continuing throughout adulthood.

Paranoid personality disorder (F60.0)

Personality disorder characterised by excessive sensitivity to setbacks; unforgiveness of insults; suspiciousness and a tendency to distort experience by misconstruing the neutral or friendly actions of others as hostile or contemptuous; recurrent suspicions, without justification, regarding the sexual fidelity of the spouse or sexual partner; and a combative and tenacious sense of personal rights. There may be excessive self-importance, and there is often excessive self-reference.

Schizoid personality disorder (F60.1)

Personality disorder characterised by withdrawal from affectional, social and other contacts with preference for fantasy, solitary activities, and introspection. There is a limited capacity to express feelings and to experience pleasure.

Dissocial personality disorder (F60.2)

Personality disorder characterised by disregard for social obligations, and callous unconcern for the feelings of others. There is gross disparity between behaviour and the prevailing social norms. Behaviour is not readily modifiable by adverse experience, including punishment. There is a low tolerance to frustration and a low threshold for discharge of aggression, including violence; there is a tendency to blame others, or to offer plausible rationalisations for the behaviour bringing the patient into conflict with society.

Emotionally unstable personality disorder (F60.3)

Personality disorder characterised by a definite tendency to act impulsively and without consideration of the consequences; the mood is unpredictable and capricious. There is a liability to outbursts of emotion and an incapacity to control the behavioural explosions. There is a tendency to quarrelsome behaviour and to conflicts with others, especially when impulsive acts are thwarted or censored. Two types may be distinguished: the impulsive type, characterised predominantly by emotional instability and lack of impulse control; and the borderline type, characterised in addition by disturbances in self-image, aims, and internal preferences, by chronic feelings of emptiness, by intense and unstable interpersonal relationships, and by a tendency to self-destructive behaviour, including suicide gestures and attempts.

Histrionic personality disorder (F60.4)

Personality disorder characterised by shallow and labile affectivity, self-dramatisation, theatricality, exaggerated expression of emotions, suggestibility, egocentricity, self-indulgence, lack of consideration for others, easily hurt feelings, and continuous seeking for appreciation, excitement and attention.

Anankastic personality disorder (F60.5)

Personality disorder characterised by feelings of doubt, perfectionism, excessive conscientiousness, checking and preoccupation with details, stubbornness, caution, and rigidity. There may be insistent and unwelcome thoughts or impulses that do not attain the severity of an obsessive-compulsive disorder.

Anxious [avoidant] personality disorder (F60.6)

Personality disorder characterised by feelings of tension and apprehension, insecurity and inferiority. There is a continuous yearning to be liked and accepted, a hypersensitivity to rejection and criticism with restricted personal attachments, and a tendency to avoid certain activities by habitual exaggeration of the potential dangers or risks in everyday situations.

Dependent personality disorder (F60.7)

Personality disorder characterised by pervasive passive reliance on other people to make one's major and minor life decisions, great fear of abandonment, feelings of helplessness and incompetence, passive compliance with the wishes of elders and others, and a weak response to the demands of daily life. Lack of vigour may show itself in the intellectual or emotional spheres; there is often a tendency to transfer responsibility to others.

Schizophrenia (F20)

The schizophrenic disorders are characterised in general by fundamental and characteristic distortions of thinking and perception, and affects that are inappropriate or blunted. Clear consciousness and intellectual capacity are usually maintained, although certain cognitive deficits may evolve in the course of time. The most important psychopathological phenomena include thought echo; thought insertion or withdrawal; thought broadcasting; delusional perception and delusions of control; influence or passivity; hallucinatory voices commenting or discussing the patient in the third person; thought disorders and negative symptoms.

Paranoid schizophrenia (F20.0)

Paranoid schizophrenia is dominated by relatively stable, often paranoid delusions, usually accompanied by hallucinations, particularly of the auditory variety, and perceptual disturbances. Disturbances of affect, volition and speech, and catatonic symptoms, are either absent or relatively inconspicuous.

Hebephrenic schizophrenia (F20.1)

A form of schizophrenia in which affective changes are prominent, delusions and hallucinations fleeting and fragmentary, behaviour irresponsible and unpredictable, and mannerisms common. The mood is shallow and inappropriate, thought is disorganised, and speech is incoherent. There is a tendency to social isolation. Usually, the prognosis is poor because of the rapid development of 'negative' symptoms, particularly flattening of affect and loss of volition. Hebephrenia should normally be diagnosed only in adolescents or young adults.

Catatonic schizophrenia (F20.2)

Catatonic schizophrenia is dominated by prominent psychomotor disturbances that may alternate between extremes such as hyperkinesis and stupor, or automatic obedience and negativism. Constrained attitudes and postures may be maintained for long periods. Episodes of violent excitement may be a striking feature of the condition. The catatonic phenomena may be combined with a dream-like (oneiroid) state with vivid scenic hallucinations.

Undifferentiated schizophrenia (F20.3)

Psychotic conditions meeting the general diagnostic criteria for schizophrenia but not conforming to any of the subtypes in F20.0–F20.2, or exhibiting the features of more than one of them without a clear predominance of a particular set of diagnostic characteristics.

Simple schizophrenia (F20.6)

A disorder in which there is an insidious but progressive development of oddities of conduct, inability to meet the demands of society, and decline in total performance. The characteristic negative features of residual schizophrenia (e.g. blunting of affect and loss of volition) develop without being preceded by any overt psychotic symptoms.

Appendix 3

Glossary of Common Psychiatric Terms

A selection of commonly used psychiatric terms, together with an attempt at a brief summary of their meanings, is set out below. The list is not in any sense definitive, it is based on a variety of clinical sources and is simply designed to give practitioners a basic understanding of terms that they will regularly encounter.

Affect	The external manifestation of a person's emotional state (contrast with mood – see below).
Circumstantial thinking	A digressive pattern of thinking, characterised in speech by a delay getting to the point and distraction by unnecessary information or detail. Different from tangential thinking (see below) in that the person will eventually get to the point.
Co-morbidity	The presence of a disorder or illness which exists alongside another disorder or illness.
Confabulation	The confusion of real with imagined memories.
Delusions	False but firmly held beliefs, out of step with reality, which cannot be altered by evidence to the contrary.
Depot	A special preparation of medication which is longer-acting and administered by deep, intra-muscular injection.
Dual diagnosis	Mental disorder complicated by co-existent substance or alcohol misuse.

Dysthymic	A low mood state.
Euthymic	A mood state which is neither abnormally high nor low.
Flight of ideas	Rapid flow of thoughts, involving lots of changes of topics and lots of unconnected ideas.
Grandiose	An exaggerated sense of one's importance, knowledge, achievements or worth.
Hallucinations	An imagined sensory perception.
Hypomania	A persistent elevated mood, similar to mania (see below), but, by definition, less marked. Not characterised by hallucinations or delusions.
Idea of reference	A mistaken belief that external innocuous events involve a reference to oneself. If the idea is firmly held and cannot be altered by evidence to the contrary, it will be a delusion of reference.
Knight's move thinking	A metaphor for a type of illogical thinking, also known as loosening of association (see below).
Labile	A mood which is uncontrolled and liable to rapid change.
Loosening of association	A lack of logical connection between thoughts and ideas.
Mania	A persistently elevated mood, which may be accompanied by over-activity, disinhibition, grandiosity, even delusions or hallucinations.
Mood	A person's own description of his emotional state.
Neologism	An invented word which only has meaning to the person using it, or, similarly, an invented meaning for an existing word.
Neuroleptic	A neuroleptic drug, more commonly known as an anti-psychotic drug, will usually be prescribed as

the main form of treatment for schizophrenia and other psychotic illnesses and disorders.

Paranoia

A type of psychosis which involves chronic, logical delusional systems, typically of grandeur or persecution.

Paraphrasia

The use of inappropriate or incorrect words or phrases during speech.

Passivity phenomena

A feeling that one is under the control of an external agent.

Pre-morbid

One's state or personality before the onset of an illness.

Pressured speech

Unrelenting, rapid, loud speech, difficult to interrupt.

Psychosis

A state of mind characterised by hallucinations, delusions or perceptual disturbances.

Tangential thinking

A digressive pattern of thinking characterised by a wandering from the topic of a conversation and a failure to get to the point.

Thought blocking

An abrupt block or break in the train of thought.

Thought broadcasting

The perception that one's thoughts are being shared with others.

Thought echo

The experience of one's thoughts being repeated inside one's head.

Appendix 4

Summary of Common Drugs Used to Treat Mental Disorder

A summary of some of the most common drugs used to treat psychotic disorder and episodes of mania or hypomania is set out below. The information is obtained from the *British National Formulary (BNF) 67* (March 2014), a joint publication of the British Medical Association and the Royal Pharmaceutical Society.

First-generation antipsychotic drugs

Tablet	Trade name
Chlorpromazine	Largactil
Flupentixol	Depixol
Haloperidol	Haldol
Pimozide	Ora
Sulpiride	Dolmatil
Trifluoperazine	Stelazine
Zuclopenthixol	Clopixol

Second-generation (atypical) antipsychotic drugs

Tablet	Trade name
Amisulpride	Solian
Aripiprazole	Abilify
Clozapine	Clozaril
Olanzapine	Zyprexa

Second-generation (atypical) antipsychotic drugs *(continued)*

Tablet	Trade name
Paliperidone	Invega
Quetiapine	Seroquel
Risperidone	Risperdal

Depot antipsychotics

Depot injection	Trade name
Flupenthixol decanoate	Depixol
Fluphenazine decanoate	Modecate
Haloperidol	Haldol decanoate
Paliperidone	Xeplion
Pipotiazine palmitate	Piportil
Risperidone	Risperdal Consta
Zuclopenthixol decanoate	Clopixol

Drugs used to treat mania and hypomania

Drug	Trade name
Asenapine	Sycrest
Carbamazepine	Tegretol
Sodium valproate	Epilim
Valproic acid	Depakote
Lithium carbonate	Camcolit
Lithium citrate	Priadel

Appendix 5

Summary of Admission Provisions – Part II of the Mental Health Act 1983

Section	Purpose	Grounds	Applicant	Duration	Renewable	Part IV	MHT
2	Detention for assessment	Mental disorder of nature/degree which warrants detention for assessment or assessment followed by treatment Ought to be so detained in the interests of health, safety or protection of others	AMHP or nearest relative	28 days	No	Yes	Yes
3	Detention for treatment	Mental disorder of nature/degree which makes hospital treatment appropriate Treatment necessary for health, safety or protection of others and cannot be provided unless detained Appropriate treatment available	AMHP or nearest relative	6 months	Yes	Yes	Yes
4	Detention for assessment	As for section 2 Of urgent necessity that patient is admitted Compliance with section 2 will involve undesirable delay	AMHP or nearest relative	72 hours	No	No	Yes
5(2)	Detention of in-patient to arrange MHA assessment	In-patient Application for admission to hospital under Part II ought to be made	RMP or approved clinician in charge of treatment	72 hours	No	No	No

Section	Purpose	Grounds	Applicant	Duration	Renewable	Part IV	MHT
5(4)	Detention to prevent in-patient from leaving	In-patient (for mental disorder) Mental disorder to such degree that necessary for health or safety or the protection of others that should be restrained from leaving Not practicable to secure immediate attendance of RMP or approved clinician for report under section 5(2)	Nurse (of prescribed class)	6 hours	No	No	No
7	Guardianship	Mental disorder of nature/degree which warrants reception into guardianship Necessary for welfare of patient or protection of others	AMHP or nearest relative	6 months	Yes	No	Yes
17A	Community treatment order	Mental disorder of nature or degree which makes treatment appropriate Necessary for health, safety or protection of others that receives such treatment Subject to liability to patient being liable to recall, treatment can be provided without detention in hospital RC needs to be able to exercise power of recall Appropriate treatment available	RC	6 months	Yes	No (Part 4A instead)	Yes

Appendix 6

Summary of Admission Provisions – Part III of the Mental Health Act 1983

Section	Purpose	Court	Grounds	Medical recommendation	Duration	Part IV	Eligibility to apply to MHT
35	Remand for report on mental condition	Magistrates' Crown	Reason to suspect mental disorder Impracticable for report on bail Arrangements to admit within 7 days	One RMP section 12	28 days at time to max of 12 weeks	No	No
36	Remand to hospital for treatment	Crown	Mental disorder of nature/degree which makes detention for treatment appropriate Appropriate treatment available	Two RMPs, one section 12	As above	Yes	No
37	Hospital order	Magistrates' Crown	Mental disorder of nature/degree which makes detention in hospital for treatment appropriate Appropriate treatment available Most suitable method of disposal	Two RMPs, one section 12	6 months (renewable)	Yes	Yes, second 6 months
37	Guardianship	Magistrates' Crown	16 years Mental disorder of nature/degree warrants reception into guardianship Most suitable method of disposal	Two RMPs, one section 12	6 months (renewable)	No	Yes

Section	Purpose	Court	Grounds	Medical recommendation	Duration	Part IV	Eligibility to apply to MHT
38	Interim hospital order	Magistrates' Crown	Mental disorder Hospital order may be appropriate Arrangements for admission within 28 days	Two RMPs, one section 12	Up to 12 weeks, renewable for 28 days at a time to max of 12 months	Yes	No
41	Restriction order	Crown only	Necessary for the protection of the public from serious harm	Two RMPs, one section 12	Indefinite	Yes	As section 37
45A	Hybrid hospital order/prison sentence	Crown only	Mental disorder of nature/degree which makes detention for treatment appropriate Appropriate treatment available	Two RMPs, one section 12	See para 13.7	Yes	Yes, second 6 months

Appendix 7

Use of the Mental Health Act 1983 in England 2008–13

The following figures show the number of individuals made subject to various provisions of the MHA 1983 in England in the years 2008–13. The figures are provided by the Health and Social Care Information Centre.

	2008/09	2009/10	2010/11	2011/12	2012/13
Part II of the MHA 1983					
Detention on admission					
Section 2	16,153	18,385	19,163	20,931	22,477
Section 3	9,601	9,545	8,174	7,701	7,776
Detention following admission					
Informal to section 2	3,788	3,391	3,347	3,398	3,974
Informal to section 3	5,003	4,658	4,199	4,114	3,895
Section 5(2) to section 2	2,539	2,666	2,973	3,264	3,601
Section 5(2) to section 3	2,623	2,443	2,309	2,437	2,361
Section 5(4) to section 2	106	41	72	63	57
Section 5(4) to section 3	55	37	40	22	41
Section 4 to section 2	476	408	401	344	280
Section 4 to section 3	111	68	56	38	40

	2008/09	*2009/10*	*2010/11*	*2011/12*	*2012/13*
CTOs					
CTO	2,134	4,107	3,834	4,220	4,647
Recall	207	1,217	1,601	2,082	2,272
Revocation	143	779	1,018	1,469	1,509
Discharge from	33	1,010	1,167	1,712	2,162
Part III of the MHA 1983					
Section 35	119	106	85	107	69
Section 36	19	30	16	16	16
Section 37	392	456	493	459	326
Section 37/41	565	547	508	522	435
Section 45A	3	5	1	8	3
Section 47	74	45	40	41	41
Section 47/49	433	458	430	427	404
Section 48	4	4	10	9	14
Section 48/49	341	360	403	398	371

Appendix 8

Table of Statutory Forms – England

The forms prescribed by the Mental Health (Hospital, Guardianship and Treatment) (England) Regulations 2008 (SI 2008/1184) and the Mental Health (Hospital, Guardianship and Treatment) (England) Regulations 2012 (SI 2012/1118) for use in England by mental health professionals when performing functions under the MHA 1983 are as follows.

Form	Purpose
A1	Section 2 – application by nearest relative for admission for assessment
A2	Section 2 – application by an approved mental health professional for admission for assessment
A3	Section 2 – joint medical recommendation for admission for assessment
A4	Section 2 – medical recommendation for admission for assessment
A5	Section 3 –application by nearest relative for admission for treatment
A6	Section 3 – application by an approved mental health professional for admission for treatment
A7	Section 3 – joint medical recommendation for admission for treatment
A8	Section 3 – medical recommendation for admission for treatment
A9	Section 4 – emergency application by nearest relative for admission for assessment
A10	Section 4 – emergency application by an approved mental health professional for admission for assessment
A11	Section 4 – medical recommendation for emergency admission for assessment
H1	Section 5(2) – report on hospital in-patient
H2	Section 5(4) – record of hospital in-patient

Form	Purpose
H3	Sections 2, 3 and 4 – record of detention in hospital
H4	Section 19 – authority for transfer from one hospital to another under different managers
H5	Section 20 – renewal of authority for detention
H6	Section 21B – authority for detention after absence without leave for more than 28 days
G1	Section 7 – guardianship application by nearest relative
G2	Section 7 – guardianship application by approved mental health professional
G3	Section 7 – joint medical recommendation for reception into guardianship
G4	Section 7 – medical recommendation for reception into guardianship
G5	Section 7 – record of acceptance of guardianship application
G6	Section 19 – authority for transfer from hospital to guardianship
G7	Section 19 – authority for transfer of a patient from the guardianship of one guardian to another
G8	Section 19 – authority to transfer from guardianship to hospital
G9	Section 20 – renewal of authority for guardianship
G10	Section 21B – authority for guardianship after absence without leave for more than 28 days
M1	Part 6 – date of reception of a patient in England
M2	Section 25 – report barring discharge by nearest relative
T1	Section 57 – certificate of consent to treatment and second opinion
T2	Section 58(3)(a) – certificate of consent to treatment
T3	Section 58(3)(b) – certificate of second opinion
T4	Section 58A(3) – certificate of consent to treatment (patients at least 18 years old)
T5	Section 58A(4) – certificate of consent to treatment and second opinion (patients under 18)
T6	Section 58A(5) – certificate of second opinion (patients who are not capable of understanding the nature, purpose and likely effects of the treatment)
CTO1	Section 17A – community treatment order

Form	Purpose
CTO2	Section 17B – variation of conditions of a community treatment order
CTO3	Section 17E – community treatment order: notice of recall to hospital
CTO4	Section 17E – community treatment order: record of patient's detention in hospital after recall
CTO5	Section 17F(4) – revocation of community treatment order
CTO6	Section 17F(2) – authority for transfer of recalled community patient to a hospital under different managers
CTO7	Section 20A – community treatment order: report extending the community treatment period
CTO8	Section 21B – authority for extension of community treatment period after absence without leave for more than 28 days
CTO9	Part 6 – community patients transferred to England
CT010	Section 19A – authority for assignment of responsibility for community patient to hospital under different managers
CTO11	Section 64C(4) – certificate of appropriateness of treatment to be given to community patient (Part 4A certificate)
CTO12	Section 64C(4A) – certificate that community patient has capacity to consent (or if under 16 is competent to consent) to treatment and has done so (Part 4A consent certificate)

Appendix 9

Table of Statutory Forms – Wales

The forms prescribed by the Mental Health (Hospital, Guardianship, Community Treatment and Consent to Treatment) (Wales) Regulations 2008 (SI 2008/2439) (W212) and the Mental Health (Hospital, Guardianship, Community Treatment and Consent to Treatment) (Wales) (Amendment) Regulations 2012 (SI 2012/1265) (W158) for use in Wales by mental health professionals when performing functions under the MHA 1983 are as follows.

Form	Purpose
HO1	Section 2 – application by nearest relative for admission for assessment
HO2	Section 2 – application by an approved mental health professional for admission for assessment
HO3	Section 2 – joint medical recommendation for admission for assessment
HO4	Section 2 – medical recommendation for admission for assessment
HO5	Section 3 – application by nearest relative for admission for treatment
HO6	Section 3 – application by an approved mental health professional for admission for treatment
HO7	Section 3 – joint medical recommendation for admission for treatment
HO8	Section 3 – medical recommendation for admission for treatment
HO9	Section 4 – emergency application by nearest relative for admission for assessment
HO10	Section 4 – emergency application by an approved mental health professional for admission for assessment
H011	Section 4 – medical recommendation for emergency admission for assessment
HO12	Section 5(2) – report on hospital in-patient

Form	Purpose
HO13	Section 5(4) – record of hospital in-patient
HO14	Sections 2, 3 and 4 – record of detention in hospital
HO15	Section 20 – renewal of authority for detention
HO16	Section 21B – authority for detention after absence without leave for more than 28 days
HO17	Section 23 – discharge by the responsible clinician or the hospital managers
GU1	Section 7 – guardianship application by nearest relative
GU2	Section 7 – guardianship application by an approved mental health professional
GU3	Section 7 – joint medical recommendation for reception into guardianship
GU4	Section 7 – medical recommendation for reception into guardianship
GU5	Section 7 – record of acceptance of guardianship application
GU6	Section 20 – renewal of authority for guardianship
GU7	Section 21B – authority for guardianship after absence without leave for more than 28 days
GU8	Section 23 – discharge by the responsible clinician or the responsible local social services authority
CP1	Section 17A – community treatment order
CP2	Section 17B – variation of conditions of a community treatment order
CP3	Section 20A – report extending the community treatment period
CP4	Section 21B – authority for community treatment after absence without leave for more than 28 days
CP5	Section 17E – notice of recall to hospital
CP6	Section 17E – record of patient's detention in hospital following recall
CP7	Section 17F – revocation of a community treatment order
CP8	Section 23 – discharge by the responsible clinician or the hospital managers
TC1	Section 19 – authority for transfer from one hospital to another under different managers
TC2	Section 19 – authority for transfer from hospital to guardianship
TC3	Section 19 – authority for transfer of a patient from the guardianship of one guardian to another

Form	Purpose
TC4	Section 19 – authority for transfer from guardianship to hospital
TC5	Section 19A – authority for assignment of responsibility for a community patient from one hospital to another under different managers
TC6	Section 17F(2) – authority for transfer of recalled community patient to a hospital under different managers
TC7	Part 6 – date of reception of a patient to hospital or into guardianship in Wales
TC8	Part 6 – transfer of patient subject to compulsion in the community
NR1	Section 25 – report barring discharge by nearest relative
CO1	Section 57 – certificate of consent to treatment and second opinion
CO2	Section 58(3)(a) – certificate of consent to treatment
CO3	Section 58(3)(b) – certificate of second opinion
CO4	Section 58A(3)(c) – certificate of consent to treatment (patients at least 18 years of age)
CO5	Section 58A(4)(c) – certificate of consent to treatment and second opinion (patients under 18 years of age)
CO6	Section 58A(5) – certificate of second opinion (patients who are not capable of understanding the nature, purpose and likely effects of the treatment)
CO7	Part 4A – certificate of appropriateness of treatment to be given to a community patient (Part 4A certificate)
CO8	Part 4A – certificate of consent to treatment for community patient (Approved Clinician Part 4A certificate)

Appendix 10

Checklist for Approved Mental Health Professionals – Applications under Section 2 of the Mental Health Act 1983

A summary of the key provisions with which the AMHP must comply when considering an application for admission to hospital under section 2 of the MHA 1983 is set out below. The summary also includes provisions with which the AMHP should comply as per guidance in the 1983 Code.

Assessment

- Has the AMHP interviewed the patient in a suitable manner (section 13(2))?
- Where the patient has expressed a wish for someone else to be present at the assessment, has the patient been assisted in efforts to secure that person's attendance (1983 Code, para 4.52)?
- Are there any particular communication difficulties which need addressing for the purposes of the assessment (e.g. signer, interpreter) (1983 Code, para 4.41)?
- Does the patient belong to a group which requires a particular expertise (e.g. child or young person, learning disability)? If so, does either the AMHP or one of the two RMPs (see below) have that expertise, or, failing that, has a profession with such expertise been consulted (1983 Code, para 4.38)?
- Where the patient is under the short-term influence of drugs or alcohol, is the AMHP able to wait until the effects have abated (1983 Code, para 4.55)?

Medical recommendations

- Is the application based on written recommendations from two RMPs (section 2(3))?
- Has each of the RMPs conducted a medical examination of the patient involving direct personal examination and consideration of all available clinical information (1983 Code, para 4.71)?
- Is one of the RMPs approved under section 12 (section 12(2))?
- If practicable, does one of the RMPs have previous acquaintance with the patient (section 12(2))?
- Where the two RMPS have seen the patient separately, have they seen the patient within 5 days of each other (section 12(1))?
- Has the AMHP seen the patient with at least one of the two RMPs (1983 Code, para 4.44)?
- Has the AMHP discussed the patient's case with each of the RMPs (1983 Code, para 4.45)?
- Does each RMP recommend that the patient is suffering from mental disorder of a nature or degree which warrants his detention in hospital for assessment (or for assessment followed by medical treatment) for at least a limited period, and that he ought to be so detained in the interests of his own health or safety or with a view to the protection of others (section 2(2))?
- Does each RMP give reasons for the opinions stated in their recommendations (1983 Code, para 4.76)?
- Is the AMHP satisfied that the provision of neither medical recommendation creates a conflict of interest for the purposes of section 12A (section 12(3))?

Consultations

- Taking account of the patient's wishes and right to privacy, has the AMHP taken such steps as are practicable to inform the nearest relative (before or within reasonable time of the application) that the application is to be or has been made (section 11(3))?
- Taking account of the patient's wishes and right to privacy, are there any other family members or carers who should be consulted (1983 Code, para 4.66)?
- Where the patient has appointed an attorney under an LPA, or the Court of Protection has appointed a deputy, has the AMHP consulted the attorney or deputy (1983 Code, para 4.70)?

Decision-making

- Is the AMHP satisfied, having interviewed the patient, that detention in a hospital is in all the circumstances of the case the most appropriate way of providing the care and medical treatment of which the patient stands in need (section 13(2))?
- Is the AMHP of the opinion having regard to any wishes expressed by relatives of the patient or any other relevant circumstances, that it is necessary or proper for the application to be made (section 13(1A)(b))?
- Before concluding that admission to hospital is required, has the AMHP considered alternative means of providing care and treatment required without a hospital admission (1983 Code, para 4.4)?
- Before concluding that admission to hospital as a detained patient is necessary, has the AMHP considered the possibility of informal admission to hospital (1983 Code, para 4.9)?
- Where the patient lacks capacity and is not objecting to hospital admission, can he be admitted and treated under the MCA 2005 (possibly applying DOLS) (1983 Code, paras 4.14 and 4.15)?

Making the application

- Have the RMPs or, where local protocol requires it, the AMHP taken the necessary steps to secure a hospital bed (1983 Code, para 4.75)?
- Does the application name a specific hospital (section 6(1))?
- Is the AMHP satisfied that there is no conflict of interest for purposes of section 12A which prevents him from making the application (section 11(1A))?
- Is the application made within 14 days of the AMHP last having seen the patient (section 11(5))?
- Are the medical recommendations signed on or before the date of the application by the AMHP (section 12(1))?
- Has the AMHP ensured that appropriate arrangements are in place for the immediate care of the patient's children or other dependants (1983 Code, para 4.88)?
- Has the AMHP made arrangements for the care of any pets of the patient, and to secure the patient's home and property (1983 Code, para 4.89)?
- Is the patient taken to hospital within 14 days of the patient last being examined by an RMP for purposes of giving a medical recommendation (section 6(1)(a))?
- Has the AMHP prepared an outline report to be provided to the hospital at the time the patient is admitted (1983 Code, para 4.94)?
- Where the patient is a restricted patient, has the AMHP notified the MOJ (1983 Code, para 4.97)?

Appendix 11

Checklist for Approved Mental Health Professionals – Applications under Section 3 of the Mental Health Act 1983

A summary of the key provisions with which the AMHP must comply when considering an application for admission to hospital under section 3 of the MHA 1983 is set out below. The summary also includes provisions with which the AMHP should comply as per guidance in the 1983 Code. Many of the requirements are identical to those in respect of section 2 applications (see Appendix 10), the major differences being in relation to the legal criteria that need to be satisfied and the role of the nearest relative.

Assessment

- Has the AMHP interviewed the patient in a suitable manner (section 13(2))?
- Where the patient has expressed a wish for someone else to be present at the assessment, has the patient been assisted in efforts to secure that person's attendance (1983 Code, para 4.52)?
- Are there any particular communication difficulties which need addressing for the purposes of the assessment (e.g. signer, interpreter) (1983 Code, para 4.41)?
- Does the patient belong to a group which requires a particular expertise (e.g. child or young person, learning disability)? If so, does either the AMHP or one of the two RMPS (see below) have that expertise, or, failing that, has a profession with such expertise been consulted (1983 Code, para 4.38)?
- Where the patient is under the short-term influence of drugs or alcohol, is the AMHP able to wait until the effects have abated (1983 Code, para 4.55)?

Medical recommendations

- Is the application based on written recommendations from two RMPs (section 3(3))?
- Has each of the RMPs conducted a medical examination of the patient involving direct personal examination and consideration of all available clinical information (1983 Code, para 4.71)?
- Is one of the RMPs approved under section 12 (section 12(2))?
- If practicable, does one of the RMPs have previous acquaintance with the patient (section 12(2))?
- Where the two RMPS have seen the patient separately, have they seen the patient within 5 days of each other (section 12(1))?
- Has the AMHP seen the patient with at least one of the two RMPs (1983 Code, para 4.44)?
- Has the AMHP discussed the patient's case with each of the RMPs (1983 Code, para 4.45)?
- Does each RMP recommend that the patient is suffering from mental disorder of a nature or degree which makes it appropriate for him to receive medical treatment in hospital, that it is necessary for the health or safety of the patient or for the protection of others that he should receive such treatment, and that it cannot be provided unless he is detained under section 3 (section 3(2))?
- Where the mental disorder is a learning disability, does each RMP also recommend that the disability is associated with abnormally aggressive or seriously irresponsible conduct (section 1(2A))?
- Does each RMP recommend that appropriate treatment is available for the patient (section 3(2))?
- Does each RMP identify the specific hospital(s) in which appropriate treatment will be available (1983 Code, para 4.77)?
- Does each RMP give reasons for the opinions stated in their recommendation (1983 Code, para 4.76)?
- Is the AMHP satisfied that the provision of neither medical recommendation creates a conflict of interest for the purposes of section 12A (section 12(3))?

Consultations

- Taking account of the patient's wishes and right to privacy, has the AMHP consulted the nearest relative? If not, can the AMHP confirm that such a consultation would not be reasonably practicable or would cause unreasonable delay (section 11(4))?
- Where the nearest relative has been consulted, can the AMHP confirm that the nearest relative has not objected to the application (section 11(4))?

- Taking account of the patient's wishes and right to privacy, are there any other family members or carers who should be consulted (1983 Code, para 4.66)?
- Where the patient has appointed an attorney under an LPA, or the Court of Protection has appointed a deputy, has the AMHP consulted the attorney or deputy (1983 Code, para 4.70)?

Decision-making

- Is the AMHP satisfied, having interviewed the patient, that detention in a hospital is in all the circumstances of the case the most appropriate way of providing the care and medical treatment of which the patient stands in need (section 13(2))?
- Is the AMHP of the opinion, having regard to any wishes expressed by relatives of the patient or any other relevant circumstances, that it is necessary or proper for the application to be made (section 13(1A)(b))?
- Before concluding that admission to hospital is required, has the AMHP considered alternative means of providing the care and treatment required without a hospital admission (1983 Code, para 4.4)?
- Before concluding that admission to hospital as a detained patient is necessary, has the AMHP considered the possibility of informal admission to hospital (1983 Code, para 4.9)?
- Where the patient lacks capacity and is not objecting to hospital admission, can he be admitted and treated under the MCA 2005 (possibly applying DOLS) (1983 Code, paras 4.14 and 4.15)?

Making the application

- Have the RMPs or, where local protocol requires it, the AMHP taken the necessary steps to secure a hospital bed (1983 Code, para 4.75)?
- Does the application name a specific hospital (section 6(1))?
- Is the AMHP satisfied that there is no conflict of interest for purposes of section 12A which prevents him from making the application (section 11(1A))?
- Is the application made within 14 days of the AMHP last having seen the patient (section 11(5))?
- Are the medical recommendations signed on or before the date of the application by the AMHP (section 12(1))?
- Has the AMHP ensured that appropriate arrangements are in place for the immediate care of the patient's children or other dependants (1983 Code, para 4.88)?

- Has the AMHP made arrangements for the care of any pets of the patient, and to secure the patient's home and property (1983 Code, para 4.89)?
- Is the patient taken to hospital within 14 days of the patient last being examined by an RMP for purposes of giving a medical recommendation (section 6(1)(a))?
- Has the AMHP prepared an outline report to be provided to the hospital at the time the patient is admitted (1983 Code, para 4.94)?
- Where the patient is a restricted patient, has the AMHP notified the MOJ (1983 Code, para 4.97)?

Appendix 12

Proposed Changes to Existing Law and Guidance

Introduction

This Appendix summarises two significant developments in mental health law due in 2015. Firstly, proposed changes to the 1983 Code, and, secondly, the implementation of the Care Act 2014.

Code of Practice of the Mental Health Act 1983

In July 2014, the Department of Health produced the draft of a new 1983 Code (Draft Code), due for publication in April 2015. According to the Draft Code, the core of the existing 1983 Code will remain the same, but will have a number of significant updates and additions.

Factors creating the need for such updates and additions were identified in the Department of Health consultation document published on 7 July 2014 (*Stronger Code: Better Care, consultation on the proposed changes to the Code of Practice: Mental Health Act 1983*). These include:

- changes in general health and social care practice brought about in response to public inquiries, such as that conducted by Robert Francis QC into Mid Staffordshire NHS Foundation Trust (www.midstaffspublicinquiry.com/report);
- changes in practice and procedure arising from the Winterbourne View Hospital scandal (www.gov.uk/government/publications/winterbourne-view-hospital-department-of-health-review-and-response);
- the Care Act 2014 (see below);
- concerns regarding the treatment of detained patients highlighted by annual Care Quality Commission reports;
- various other changes to law, policy and procedure that have occurred since the last 1983 Code was published in 2008.

It remains to be seen what the final version of the new 1983 Code will look like (consultations on the proposed changes having taken place in 2014), but the most significant aspects of the Draft Code are as follows.

Guiding principles

Chapter 1 of the Draft Code contains five new guiding principles for using the MHA 1983. These are:

- least restrictive option and maximising independence;
- empowerment and participation;
- respect and dignity;
- purpose and effectiveness;
- efficiency and equity.

Equality and human rights

The Draft Code contains a new chapter (Chapter 3) dealing with equality and human rights as a discrete topic.

Protecting patients' rights and autonomy

Chapters 4–12 of the Draft Code are grouped together in a section entitled 'Protecting patients' rights and autonomy'. Of note within this section are the following points:

- The importance of the role played by carers is emphasised at various stages, but in Chapter 4 (Information for patients, nearest relatives, carers and others) at paras 4.40–4.43 in particular.
- Where a patient is deemed to lack the capacity to decide whether to appoint an IMHA, an IMHA should be introduced to the patient so that the IMHA can explain what help he can offer (Chapter 6, Independent Mental Health Advocates, para 6.13).
- The wording of the 1983 Code is strengthened and clarified to address concerns that insufficient attention is paid to a patient's right to meet or communicate in private with family, friends and carers (Chapter 8, Privacy, Safety and Dignity, paras 8.2–8.7 in particular).
- Also in Chapter 8, hospital managers are provided with new guidance on the need to avoid blanket restrictions (applying across a ward or a hospital) in relation to, for example, a locked-door policy (paras 8.37–8.48).

Assessment, treatment and admission to hospital

Chapters 13–18 of the Draft Code are grouped together in a section entitled 'Assessment, treatment and admission to hospital'. Of note within this section are the following points:

- Chapter 13 deals with mental capacity and deprivation of liberty, a subject which is now deemed to require its own chapter within the Draft Code, reflecting the increasing importance of the DOLS provisions under Schedule A1 to the Mental Capacity Act 2005 and the need for guidance on the interface between those provisions and the MHA 1983.
- Chapter 14 deals with applications for detention in hospital under the MHA 1983. The responsibility of a CCG to commission mental health services which meet the needs of its areas is emphasised. Significantly, however, it is now specified that this should include 'arrangements for the reception of patients in cases of special urgency or the provision of appropriate accommodation for patients under the age of 18' (para 14.71). This builds on the new 'least restrictive option and maximising independence' principle, which identifies the need for detention in hospital to 'be delivered as close to the patient's home or family as reasonably possible' (para 1.2).
- Chapter 16 deals with police powers and places of safety. It covers the same subject matter as Chapter 10 in the 1983 Code, but provides yet more emphasis on the need to avoid a police station as a place of safety for the purposes of sections 135 and 136 of the MHA 1983. Now, therefore, it is proposed that 'wherever practicable, detention in a police station under section 136 should not need to exceed a maximum period of 24 hours' (para 16.39).

Additional considerations for specific patients

Chapters 19–22 of the Draft Code are grouped together in a section entitled 'Additional considerations for specific patients'. This section looks at how the MHA 1983 should be applied to certain categories of patients: children and young people, people with learning disabilities or autistic spectrum disorders, people with personality disorders, and patients concerned with criminal proceedings.

Children and young people

Chapter 19 updates and clarifies guidance on the treatment and care of children and young people. The main changes from the current guidance in this area (Chapter 36 in the 1983 Code) are as follows:

- Greater clarity is provided in respect of various existing aspects of the guidance, for example assessment of competence or capacity (paras 19.23–19.24) and the 'zone of parental control' (paras 19.37–19.41).
- More cross-referencing is provided between the contents of Chapter 19 and other parts of the Draft Code.
- There is a restructuring of the order of the chapter.
- New areas for guidance are included, for example children and young people in the youth justice system, and use of sections 135 and 136 of the MHA 1983 for the under-18s.

People with learning disabilities or autistic spectrum disorders

Chapter 20 of the Draft Code updates guidance on the treatment and care of people with learning disabilities or autistic spectrum disorder (currently found in Chapter 34 of the 1983 Code), and now includes guidance on the application of the MCA 2005 and the Equality Act 2010 to these types of cases.

People with personality disorders

Chapter 21 of the Draft Code provides a minor update of the guidance on the treatment and care of people with personality disorder. Such guidance is currently found in Chapter 35 of the 1983 Code.

Patients concerned with criminal proceedings

Chapter 22 of the Draft Code updates guidance on the treatment and care of patients concerned with criminal proceedings. Such guidance is currently found in Chapter 33 of the 1983 Code. The Draft Code provides a much more comprehensive summary of the provisions in the MHA 1983 concerning restricted patients.

Care, support and treatment in hospital

Chapters 23–26 of the Draft Code are grouped together in a section entitled 'Care, support and treatment in hospital'. This section contains guidance on the appropriate treatment test (Chapter 23), medical treatment under the MHA 1983 (Chapter 24), treatments subject to special rules and procedures (Chapter 25), and safe and therapeutic responses to disturbed behaviour (Chapter 26). Of particular note is the attempt in Chapter 26 to provide much clearer guidance on when and how restrictive interventions (physical restraint, medication, rapid-tranquilisation, mechanical restraint and seclusion) may be used.

Leaving hospital

Chapters 27–34 of the Draft Code are grouped together in a section entitled 'Leaving hospital'. This section covers leave under section 17 (Chapter 27), absence without leave (Chapter 28), community treatment orders (Chapter 29), guardianship (Chapter 30), a comparison of statutory frameworks for after-care (Chapter 31), and renewal, extension and discharge (Chapter 32). Chapter 33 provides updated guidance on after-care to take account of the Care Act 2014 (see below), while Chapter 34 is a new addition and provides guidance on the care programme approach.

Professional responsibilities

Chapters 35–40 of the Draft Code are grouped together in a section entitled 'Professional responsibilities'. Of note is Chapter 37, which deals with the functions of hospital managers. It includes updated guidance on the transfer of detained patients between hospitals. Where transfer of a patient to a high security hospital is contemplated, then, unless the circumstances are urgent or it is for some other significant reason inadvisable, the patient and/or his representative should be given the opportunity to make written representations to the admissions panel of the receiving hospital (para 37.21). Also of note is Chapter 40, an entirely new chapter entitled 'Support for victims', summarising the statutory rights of victims to information about mentally disordered offenders.

Care Act 2014

Aside from the Draft Code, the other main area of change due in 2015 is the implementation of the Care Act 2014. The Act was given Royal Assent on 14 May 2014, and is said to represent the most fundamental reform of adult social care for the last 60 years. One of the Act's main aims is to make social care law simpler and more coherent. It therefore replaces a multiplicity of earlier legislation with a single law, at the heart of which is a set of core legal duties and powers in relation to adult social care. The Act has implications for mental health law, and two of the main areas of change in this regard are considered below. As with most of the Act, these changes are due for implementation in April 2015.

After-care under section 117 of the Mental Health Act 1983

The Care Act 2014 amends certain parts of section 117 of the MHA 1983 with regard to the provision of after-care.

Most notably perhaps, section 75(5) inserts a new section 117(6), which, for the first time, provides a statutory definition of the term 'after-care'. After-care services will now be defined as:

> services which will have both of the following purposes:
> (a)   meeting a need arising from or related to the person's mental disorder; and
> (b)   reducing the risk of a deterioration of the person's mental condition (and, accordingly, reducing the risk of the person requiring admission to a hospital again for treatment for mental disorder).

Section 75(3) amends section 117(3) of the MHA 1983 in an effort to provide greater clarity on which CCG or LSSA will have responsibility for providing after-care services (see para 19.6). According to the amendment, if a person is 'ordinarily resident' in England or Wales immediately before being detained, the relevant CCG or LSSA will be the one for the area in which he was so 'ordinarily resident'. The standard government guidance on defining ordinary residence will apply (see para 19.6).

Significantly, section 75(4) also inserts new sections 117(4) and (5) into the MHA 1983, which create new powers for the Secretary of State for Health to resolve disputes between local authorities as to responsibility for providing after-care.

Section 75(6) creates a new section 117A of the MHA 1983 which will enable the Secretary of State for Health to require local authorities to enable a person who qualifies for accommodation under section 117 to live in accommodation of his choice providing he is prepared to pay a top-up fee.

Assessment of social care needs

The current statutory entitlement to an assessment of social care needs (including those arising from mental health problems) is created by section 47 of the NHSCCA 1990 (see 19.11.2). The NHSCCA 1990 is to be repealed, however, and a similar entitlement to an assessment of care needs will be created instead by section 9 of the Care Act 2014.

According to section 9(1) of the Care Act 2014, a local authority will be under a duty to carry out a 'needs assessment' where it appears that an adult 'may have needs for care and support'. In such cases, the local authority must assess whether the adult does have needs for care and support and, if so, what those needs are.

As with the current law, the local authority will be under no obligation to meet assessed needs unless they are deemed eligible (section 13(1)). Eligibility will be determined according to criteria set out in regulations (section 13(7)). These criteria will replace the current FACS criteria (see 19.11.2).

Index

References are to page numbers